EUNICE 2005: NETWORKS AND APPLICATIONS TOWARDS A UBIQUITOUSLY CONNECTED WORLD

IFIP – The International Federation for Information Processing

IFIP was founded in 1960 under the auspices of UNESCO, following the First World Computer Congress held in Paris the previous year. An umbrella organization for societies working in information processing, IFIP's aim is two-fold: to support information processing within its member countries and to encourage technology transfer to developing nations. As its mission statement clearly states,

> IFIP's mission is to be the leading, truly international, apolitical organization which encourages and assists in the development, exploitation and application of information technology for the benefit of all people.

IFIP is a non-profitmaking organization, run almost solely by 2500 volunteers. It operates through a number of technical committees, which organize events and publications. IFIP's events range from an international congress to local seminars, but the most important are:

• The IFIP World Computer Congress, held every second year;
• Open conferences;
• Working conferences.

The flagship event is the IFIP World Computer Congress, at which both invited and contributed papers are presented. Contributed papers are rigorously refereed and the rejection rate is high.

As with the Congress, participation in the open conferences is open to all and papers may be invited or submitted. Again, submitted papers are stringently refereed.

The working conferences are structured differently. They are usually run by a working group and attendance is small and by invitation only. Their purpose is to create an atmosphere conducive to innovation and development. Refereeing is less rigorous and papers are subjected to extensive group discussion.

Publications arising from IFIP events vary. The papers presented at the IFIP World Computer Congress and at open conferences are published as conference proceedings, while the results of the working conferences are often published as collections of selected and edited papers.

Any national society whose primary activity is in information may apply to become a full member of IFIP, although full membership is restricted to one society per country. Full members are entitled to vote at the annual General Assembly, National societies preferring a less committed involvement may apply for associate or corresponding membership. Associate members enjoy the same benefits as full members, but without voting rights. Corresponding members are not represented in IFIP bodies. Affiliated membership is open to non-national societies, and individual and honorary membership schemes are also offered.

EUNICE 2005: NETWORKS AND APPLICATIONS TOWARDS A UBIQUITOUSLY CONNECTED WORLD

IFIP International Workshop on Networked Applications, Colmenarejo, Madrid/Spain, 6-8 July, 2005.

Edited by

Carlos Delgado Kloos
Universidad Carlos III de Madrid, Spain

Andrés Marín
Universidad Carlos III de Madrid, Spain

David Larrabeiti
Universidad Carlos III de Madrid, Spain

 Springer

EUNICE 2005: Networks and Applications Towards a Ubiquitously Connected World
Edited by Carlos Delgado Kloos, Andrés Marín, and David Larrabeiti

p. cm. (IFIP International Federation for Information Processing, a Springer Series in Computer Science)

ISSN: 1571-5736 / 1861-2288 (Internet)
ISBN-10: 1-4899-8617-0
ISBN-13: 978-1-4899-8617-7
Printed on acid-free paper

9 8 7 6 5 4 3 2 1
springeronline.com

Dedication

to Pedro J. Lizcano Martín

Contents

Contributing Authors

Preface

EUNICE is a network of Universities throughout Europe. The EUNICE network has been created to foster the mobility of students, faculty members and research scientists working in the field of information and communication technologies and to promote educational and research cooperation between its member institutions. The prime means for implementing these goals is the annual Summer School organized by the member institutions.

From its conception, the EUNICE Summer Schools were designed as unique events where the joint participation of PhD students and supervisors working in the field of information and communication technologies (ICT) is the key to create an event that goes far beyond a conventional international workshop. Furthermore, the Summer School is an open forum for the cooperation of the European member institutions and any other organisation interested European academic/research centre at all levels. This cooperation is paramount to successfully construct and participate in the European Higher Education Area, and especially, to achieve easy and effective exchange of research activities.

This year, the eleventh edition of the EUNICE Summer School took place in Colmenarejo (Madrid/Spain) from 6 to 8 July 2005, organized by the Department of Telematics Engineering of the Universidad Carlos III de Madrid. It was devoted to the theme of *Networked Applications*. Participants have shared their vision on advanced engineering features such as ubiquitous computing, full mobility and real-time multimedia, into real services, applications, protocols and networks. Communication engineering and telematics research efforts are making sci-fi scenarios a reality in our lives.

The Technical Program Committee assigned three qualified reviewers to each of the 54 papers submitted. The quality of the submissions was high, as expected in a conference of professional researchers. The outcome of the peer review process was that 35 full papers and 10 short papers were selected.

Besides paper sessions, the Summer School offered three excellent invited talks: *SIP: a Standardization Update*, by Gonzalo Camarillo, head of the Advanced Signalling Research Laboratory of Ericsson in Helsinki; *Intra-domain Traffic Engineering - Principles, Algorithms and Toolbox*, by Guy Leduc, head of the Research Unit in Networking in the University of Liège; and *Interoperable Middleware for Ambient Intelligence Systems*, by Valerie Issarny, head of the ARLES INRIA research project-team at INRIA-Rocquencourt.

This book constitutes a post-proceedings volume for the Summer School. Out of the accepted papers the authors of the 21 best-qualified in the review process were given the opportunity to revise their paper once more on the basis of the feedback received at the Summer School. In this way, this volume constitutes an excellent snapshot of the State of the Art in the research field of Telematics, watched from the perspective and activity of young researchers in Europe.

We wish to thank the members of the Technical Programme Committee for their excellent job in the review process. The full list is the following:

- Carlos Delgado Kloos, Universidad Carlos III de Madrid, Spain (Conference chair)
- David Larrabeiti, Universidad Carlos III de Madrid, Spain (Programme Committee co-chair)
- Andrés Marín, Universidad Carlos III de Madrid, Spain (Programme Committee co-chair)
- Finn Arve Aagesen, University of Trondheim, Norway
- Sebastian Abeck, Universität Karlsruhe, Germany
- Arturo Azcorra, Universidad Carlos III de Madrid, Spain
- József Bíró, Budapest University of Technology and Economics, Hungary
- Rolv Braek, University of Trondheim, Norway
- Tomás de Miguel, Technical University of Madrid, Spain

- Irek Defee, Tampere University of Technology, Finland
- Jörg Eberspächer, Technical University of Munich, Germany
- Serge Fdida, U. Paris Pierre et Marie Curie, France
- Olivier Festor, Université Henri Poincaré - Nancy, France
- Edit Halász, Budapest University of Technology and Economics, Hungary
- Jarmo Harju, Tampere University of Technology, Finland
- Tamas Henk, Budapest University of Technology and Economics, Hungary
- Sandor Imre, Budapest University of Technology and Economics, Hungary
- Yvon Kermarrec, ENST Bretagne, France
- Yevgeni Koucheryavy, Tampere University of Technology, Finland
- Paul Kühn, University of Stuttgart, Germany
- Frank Li, University of Oslo, Norway
- Pedro Lizcano, Telefonica I+D, Spain
- Pekka Loula, Tampere University of Technology, Finland
- Jean-Philippe Martin-Flatin, CERN, Switzerland
- Maurizio Munafo, Politecnico di Torino, Italy
- Joao Orvalho, University of Coimbra, Portugal
- Zdzislaw Papir, AGH University of Science and Technology, Poland
- Aiko Pras, University of Twente, The Netherlands
- Andras Racz, Ericsson Research, Hungary
- Sebastià Sallent, Polytechnic University of Catalonia, Spain
- Jorge Sá Silva, University of Coimbra, Portugal
- Dimitrios Serpanos, University of Patras, Greece
- Mikhail Smirnov, Fraunhofer FOKUS, Germany
- Ioannis Stavrakakis, U. of Athens, Greece
- Burkhard Stiller, University of Zurich and ETH Zurich, Switzerland
- Samir Tohme, Université de Versailles St Quentin, France
- Marten van Sinderen, University of Twente, The Netherlands
- Giorgio Ventre, University of Naples, Italy
- Gennady Yanovsky, St. Petersburg State University of Telecommunications, Russia

The financial support given by Spanish Ministry of Education and Science and by the Department of Telematics Engineering of the Universidad Carlos III de Madrid is also gratefully acknowledged. The co-sponsors of EUNICE 2005 were the IST E-NEXT Network of Excellence, the IST UBISEC project, IFIP WG6.6, WG6.4, and WG6.9, and the Universidad Carlos III de Madrid. Special thanks to all of them for their support, especially with invited lecturers and students grants.

We also want to highlight the outperforming efforts of the Organising Committee. Without their support, the editing of the proceedings, and the local arrangements for the Summer School would not have been possible. Their commitment to this event has shown us that producing scientific work and planning social activities can be carried out by the same team. Their names are:

- Celeste Campo, Universidad Carlos III de Madrid, Spain (Organizing Committee co-chair)
- Ricardo Romeral, Universidad Carlos III de Madrid, Spain (Organizing Committee co-chair)
- Iria Estévez-Ayres, Universidad Carlos III de Madrid, Spain
- Manuel Urueña, Universidad Carlos III de Madrid, Spain

Finally, our warmest thanks go to professors Dr. Jarmo Harju and Dr. Edit Halász, organisers of the two previous editions, for their helpful advice to keep the quality and philosophy of EUNICE.

Many thanks go also to Springer staff for the preparation of this book, in particular, to Amy Brais and Jennifer Evans.

This volume is dedicated to *Pedro J. Lizcano Martín*, a good friend and excellent professional, director for the Research Center of Telefónica I+D in Barcelona (Spain), and for some time also professor at the Universidad Carlos III de Madrid, who recently passed away. He served in the Programme Committee of the Summer School. May his intellectual brightness and energy be an example for all of us.

Carlos Delgado Kloos, Andrés Marín, David Larrabeiti
Universidad Carlos III de Madrid
Colmenarejo, August 2005

PART ONE

NETWORK DESIGN AND PERFORMANCE

DESIGN AND EVALUATION OF A BURST ASSEMBLY UNIT FOR OPTICAL BURST SWITCHING ON A NETWORK PROCESSOR

Jochen Kögel, Simon Hauger, Sascha Junghans, Martin Köhn,
Marc C. Necker, and Sylvain Stanchina
University of Stuttgart
Institute of Communication Networks and Computer Engineering (IKR)
Pfaffenwaldring 47, 70569 Stuttgart, Germany
{koegel, hauger, junghans, koehn, necker, stanchina}@ikr.uni-stuttgart.de

Abstract   Optical Burst Switching (OBS) has been proposed in the late 1990s as a novel photonic network architecture directed towards efficient transport of IP traffic. OBS aims at cost-efficient and dynamic provisioning of sub-wavelength granularity by optimally combining electronics and optics. In order to reduce the number of switching decisions in OBS core nodes, traffic is aggregated and assembled to bursts by the Burst Assembly Unit in an OBS ingress edge node. This Burst Assembly Unit is responsible for buffering incoming packets in queues and sending them as bursts as soon as a minimum burst length is reached and/or a timer expires. Typically, dozens of different queues must be able to handle high volumes of traffic.

This paper presents the design and implementation of a Burst Assembly Unit for a Network Processor. In an evaluation of the realized implementation we point out the ability to handle traffic at line speed while having fine grained timers for all queues.

Keywords: Optical Burst Switching, Traffic Aggregation, Network Processor, System Design

1.   Introduction

Optical Burst Switching has been introduced as a new switching paradigm for transport networks in order to compensate the two main drawbacks of todays network architectures [Qiao, 1999]. First, today's optical transmission technology is only used for point-to-point links between network nodes, while switching and routing is done in the electrical domain. Thus, all data has be converted optical-to-electrical (O/E) and electrical-to-optical (E/O) in every node. With optical switching, data would always remain in the optical domain and thus O/E and E/O conversion would only be necessary on the edge. Second, transport networks either rely on the packet or on the circuit switching principle. In packet switched networks, statistical multiplexing gain can be realized leading to a high efficiency, but at the cost of a high processing overhead and the need for buffering. In circuit switched networks, in a core node only simple operations are required to forward the incoming data stream to the responsible output port without large buffers, but it cannot capitalize on any statistical multiplexing. In OBS, packets are collected in the edge nodes and assembled according to a certain strategy [Dolzer, 2002] into bursts with a size usually between 10 kilobit and some 100 kilobits [Gauger, 2003]. These bursts are sent through the core network to the egress node remaining always in the optical domain. Here, the bursts are disassembled and the packets are forwarded towards their destination. With this, still statistical multiplexing can be used to increase the efficiency of the network, while the processing overhead is essentially reduced in relation to packet switched networks. Furthermore, O/E and E/O conversion is necessary only at the edge of the network.

In an OBS edge node, the task of the Burst Assembly Unit (BAU) is to classify incoming packets, buffer them in the corresponding queues, assemble the bursts, and finally schedule and transmit them. A BAU could be implemented on several types of hardware: ASICs, FPGAs, Network Processors (NP) or even General Purpose Processors (GPP). In contrast to a GPP, an NP is equipped with fast media interfaces and optimized for parallel and pipelined processing as it is typical for network applications. Compared to hardwired solutions, network nodes using NPs can be adapted to new requirements by simply changing the program. Most NPs are designed for classical IP processing applications consisting mainly of packet classification, forwarding, queueing and scheduling. Further, the manufacturers provide software frameworks optimized for applications based on IP and Ethernet. Nevertheless, in a BAU several new aspects like creating new packets or multi stage queueing become important. These new tasks are a challenge to the NP's flexibility.

This paper presents the design of a BAU for an Intel IXP2400 Network Processor. We will show how the BAU has been realized by a Burst Assembly Module (BAM) that has been integrated in the manufacturer's software framework.

The remainder of this paper is structured as follows: Section 2 introduces OBS and Burst Assembly, Section 3 describes the Network Processor used. In Section 4, the design of the BAM is presented, which is integrated in the BAU in Section 5. The results of the performance evaluation are presented in Section 6. The last section concludes the paper.

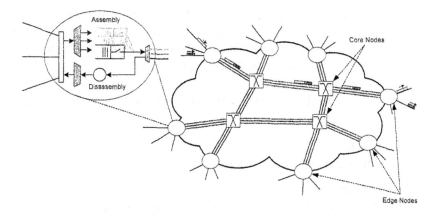

Figure 1. OBS Network

2. Optical Burst Switching

Current network architectures use fibers with several wavelengths for point-to-point links between nodes. On each node, data has to go through O/E conversion for switching and through E/O conversion thereafter. In OBS, data remains in the optical domain throughout the network.

Figure 1 shows an OBS-network. It consists of edge nodes, core nodes and fiber bundles connecting the nodes. The edge nodes aggregate traffic to bursts, which are then sent through the core to the egress node. Arriving at the egress node, the Disassembly Unit extracts the packets from the burst and forwards them to their destination.

A closer look on the Burst Assembly Unit in Fig. 2 reveals its functional blocks. First, received packets are forwarded according to egress node and

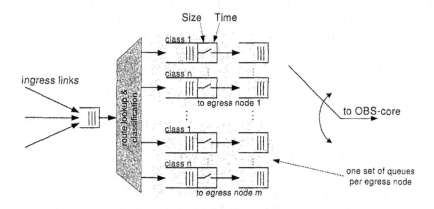

Figure 2. Burst Assembly Unit for n traffic classes and m egress nodes

traffic class to one of n queues of the m sets of queues. Once finalization is triggered, all packets of a queue are assembled to a burst and forwarded to the next queue. On finalization, a header is generated containing information on the positions of the packets within the burst, needed for disassembly on the egress. After finalization, the burst is queued in another queue before it is scheduled for transmission to the OBS core. Finalization can be triggered based on the following criteria:

- **Size-based**
  Once the queue length reaches a minimum size.

- **Time-based**
  A predefined time after the first packet has been enqueued.

- **Combined**
  Reaching the minimum size or timeout trigger finalization.

In the time-based case, the maximum delay of a packet due to queueing is determined by the timeout set. Furthermore, for providing several levels of Quality of Service (QoS) for different traffic classes, the size/timeout values can be set accordingly and appropriate scheduling can be employed [Vokkarane, 2002].

Due to properties of the OBS network, the maximum burst size might be limited. If this is the case, finalization has also to be triggered in cases where a burst would become too large by enqueueing another packet, since neither size-based nor time-based strategies assure a maximum burst size.

3.   Network Processors

3.1   Overview

Processing tasks in network nodes can be classified in data path and control path tasks: While the majority of packets has to be forwarded through the node on the data path, some packets are addressed to the network node itself for network control and routing. For the data path, Network Processors integrate several Special Purpose Processors (SPP) optimized for forwarding large amounts of data. For control path processing and management tasks, a General Purpose Processor (GPP) is often included.

The architectures of the SPPs are optimized for the characteristics of the data path: Operations like table lookup or queueing are supported by special units and several SPPs do processing tasks either as a functional pipeline, in parallel, or in a combination of both. In network nodes, packets have to be read and written at high speed, while only the header, a small part of this data, is processed. Therefore, and because the header has to be processed only once, there is no temporal or spacial locality of this data and thus, caching of data is not useful. However, the processor should not waste processing time while waiting for memory operations. Since no cache can hide this memory latency, other methods, like hardware-supported multithreading, are employed.

The common processing approach in network nodes is to first do packet processing (e.g. forwarding), followed by a queueing stage. Afterwards, the scheduler decides when a packet should be transmitted. Following this pattern, some NPs reflect this principle in their hardware design: A cluster of SPPs for packet processing and a dedicated "Queue Manager" (QM) for queueing. Often, these two components are implemented in separate chips with different hardware requirements: While the QM needs a high amount of memory for packet buffers, the SPPs require low latency memory for tables and a small amount of packet buffer memory only.

Different from this common principle, for Burst Assembly two stages of queueing are needed: First, the packets have to be queued until a burst is finalized and second, the burst is queued until it will be scheduled. Obviously, an NP that does not need an external QM component is better suited for this kind of application than a two-chip solution. For the implementation of the BAU, an NP of Intel's IXP2XXX series has been chosen, since these processors do not adhere to the division of NP and QM.

3.2 The IXP2400

There are five different NPs in Intel's IXP2XXX series. All of them comprise of the same type of SPPs (called microengines) for data path processing. The different models of the IXP2XXX series differ in the number of micro-engines employed, as well as in memory size and clock frequency of micro-engines. For our implementation, an IXP2400 has been chosen, which contains eight microengines and consists of the basic blocks that are shown in Fig. 3.

Microengines are simple 32-Bit RISC processors that allow hardware mul-tithreading by supporting fast context switches between the eight register sets. In addition to the registers that are intended for per-packet data, local mem-ory within each microengine can be used to keep state information accessible for all threads. All microengines have access to the media interface, the ex-ternal memory and to a fast on-chip memory. While the external memory is intended for packet buffers and lookup tables, the on-chip memory is used for inter-microengine communication. Additional hardware support for ring buffers (FIFO queues) allows for atomic concurrent access to this shared on-chip memory. Since all microengines can access the same units in the same way, the tasks of the packet-processing pipeline can be mapped onto the mi-croengines in either way, parallel or pipelined.

A software framework [Intel, 2003] is provided by the manufacturer, which contains building blocks for common processing tasks and defines data struc-

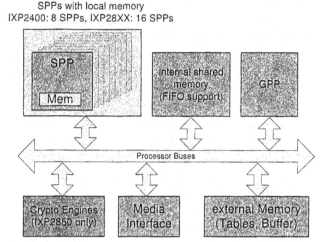

SPPs with local memory
IXP2400: 8 SPPs, IXP28XX: 16 SPPs

Figure 3.   Simplified architecture of the IXP2XXX

tures as well as interfaces. This framework enables designing reusable and flexible software blocks for all models of the NP series.

3.3   Mapping of functions to microengines

The software framework defines one possibility of mapping processing functions to microengines. In the following we will introduce the framework briefly, since building blocks of it have been reused for the BAU.

Figure 4 shows from top to bottom the basic tasks of a packet processing node, the decomposition of the tasks in basic functions, and the mapping to microengines as defined by the software framework. This functional pipeline works as follows: The RX and TX blocks transfer packet data from the media interface to DRAM and vice versa. For passing the packet from block to block, only a pointer to the packet (packet handle) is used. This handle is passed together with other information between microengines by the use of FIFOs residing in the shared on-chip memory.

The packet processing stage incorporates all processing on a packet and its headers, like decapsulation, encapsulation, validation, forwarding and classification. Since this stage needs the most of both, processing power and memory access, it runs in parallel on several microengines. The queue and scheduler blocks each run on separate microengines and are interconnected by FIFOs for transferring control messages, not packet handles. Once a packet is scheduled, its handle is forwarded to the TX stage, which can run in parallel on two microengines for performance reasons.

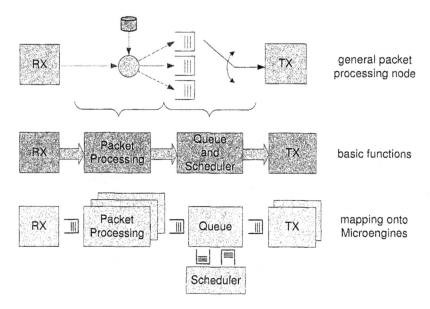

Figure 4. Mapping of functions to microengines as defined by the software framework

4. Design of the Burst Assembly Module

For queueing of packets and assembling bursts, a software module has been implemented that is designed for running on a single microengine using the eight hardware-supported threads. Other functional blocks, necessary for a complete BAU have been realized by the reuse of existing building blocks. The BAM can be integrated in the functional pipeline defined by the software framework (section 3.3), as it will be shown in Section 5.

4.1 Basic tasks

As shown in Fig. 5, the BAM receives packets from the input FIFO and sends bursts by writing to the output FIFO. In addition, it is capable of prepending headers to bursts.

For storing packets, the software framework defines a buffer structure of a fixed size. In the case of large packets, several buffers can be concatenated by means of pointers resulting in a linked list. Converting this multi-buffer packet back to a contiguous packet is done at the end of the pipeline by the TX-block, which reads all buffers of such a list and sends the data to the media interface.

The BAM uses this support for linked lists to build chains of packets. These chains are used for both, queueing of packets, as well as for sending the burst to downstream blocks, which will handle the linked list as if it was a single

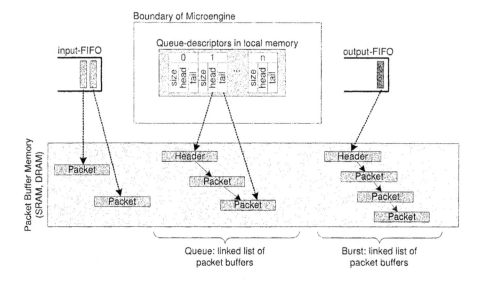

Figure 5.   Queueing and assembly using linked lists of packet buffers

multi-buffer packet. The chains are managed by queue descriptors (see Fig. 5), which keep a pointer to the head and tail of the queue as well as its size.

For enqueueing packets, a data structure from the input FIFO is read, which contains the packet handle and information on the packet size and queue number. The queue number is determined by upstream blocks and based on its value, a queue descriptor is selected and the packet is enqueued to the tail of the corresponding queue. Before the first packet is added to a queue, a buffer for the header is allocated and enqueued, which provides enough memory space for a complete burst header.

Finalizing a burst is accomplished by writing a data structure to the output FIFO and resetting the queue, which is done by setting its size to zero, and enqueueing a new header buffer. The data structure written to the output FIFO contains the handle of the first packet and the queue number. This handle contains sufficient information for downstream blocks to have access to the complete burst, while the queue number is needed since the next stage is a queueing stage that uses the same queue numbering as the BAM. Triggering the finalization of a burst for the size-based case is simply done by checking the size of the queue, while for time-based assembly, a timer mechanism is employed, which will be explained in section 4.2.

The burst header contains one field for the number of packets, one for the size of the header and one for the size of every packet. Obviously, the size of the header is not fixed and is only known when the burst is finalized.

For performance reasons, the header is written in chunks of eight bytes. Since each header field has a size of 16 bits, four packet size fields have to be buffered within the microengine before they are written to the buffer. When the burst is finalized, the remaining buffered size fields are written.

4.2 Timers

As seen above, timers are necessary for time-based assembly for every queue. A timer is started when the first packet for a new burst is received and disarmed when the burst is sent. When a timer expires, the corresponding burst is finalized.

Although there are eight hardware timers per microengine, they are not used since they cannot be disarmed and it is rather difficult to map about dozens of timers to eight hardware timers efficiently. Therefore, a timer mechanism based on polling of a timestamp register has been realized.

This timer mechanism saves the target times, at which the timer expires, in local memory and checks them periodically. For the target times, a contiguous block of memory is reserved, with each timer occupying a 32-bit word. For efficiency reasons, processing the timers is distributed among all threads with each thread handling up to eight timers. Thus, with eight threads, up to 64 timers can be processed. This implementation is very fast, because eight contiguous memory words can be accessed very efficiently with this hardware and thus needs less processing time than an implementation with longer lists or calendars. For keeping the program simple, each thread processes the same number of timers. Hence, the number of timers is always a multiple of eight, which may result in spare timers that remain always disarmed.

A system time, which is provided by a 32-bit timestamp register in each microengine, is used for this timer scheme. The system clock increments this timestamp every 16 processor cycles, which is obviously too fine-grained for our needs. Therefore, the desired granularity is achieved by executing a right shift operation on this timestamp value, thus the granularity can be adjusted easily. For reducing jitter, the internal granularity for saving target times in memory is four times finer than the timer's granularity.

When designing a timer, which relies on an advancing system time, overflows of this value have also to be considered. This can be accomplished in several ways, which all introduce additional checks and expensive branch instructions. This design circumvents overflow handling by only checking for equality of system time and target time instead of doing a less-or-equal check for determining exceeded timers. However, in this case, it has to be guaranteed that all timers can be processed fast enough before the time advances. This condition has to be checked for a desired timer granularity and if it does not hold, a coarser granularity has to be chosen.

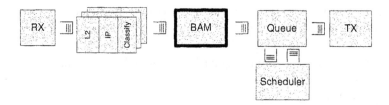

Figure 6.   Integration of the BAM into the BAU

5.   Integration and Test

For a complete BAU, the BAM has been integrated in the functional pipeline between packet processing stage and queue (Fig. 6). This functional pipeline reflects the BAU introduced in Fig. 2. All other blocks can be realized by the use of existing building blocks with minor changes.

The BAU has been realized on a Radisys ENP-2611 Network Processor Board, which is equipped with an IXP2400, three optical Gigabit Ethernet ports, and various other supporting components (e.g. memory for packet buffers and tables). The Ethernet ports are connected to the media interface of the IXP2400.

Using this hardware, it is possible to test the BAU as part of a network scenario, where IP packets are received and bursts are sent over Ethernet. Thus, in contrast to future OBS applications, the burst size is limited for this implementation to 9000 bytes (Ethernet jumbo frames).

As shown in Fig. 7, the test setup consists of the NP board and two computers, working as source and destination node. On the destination node, a disassembly program extracts packets from the received bursts and forwards them to the local network stack. In order to acknowledge test packets received, a feedback link is set up directly between the two test nodes. On the destina-

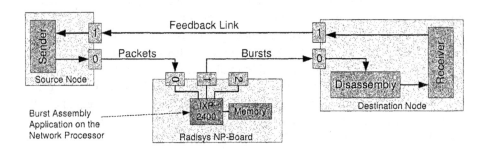

Figure 7.   Setup for testing

tion node, a receiver software for responding to test packets is running, which can be an ICMP stack for simple tests.

Using this setup, the functionality of the BAU could be validated and a throughput of 500 MBit/s was achieved, using [Iperf] as measurement tool. A higher bandwidth could not be achieved due to limitations of the computers used as source and destination. However, as the next section will show, the BAM is capable of handling traffic rates that are higher than the interface speed. Thus, it is impossible to measure the BAM's maximum throughput using the test setup described.

6.   Evaluation of the BAM

In this section, the scalability and performance of the BAM is evaluated. Other pipeline stages and their impact on the performance are not considered.

6.1   Scalability

In the following, the scalability limited by the amount of microengine-internal memory will be discussed. The memory requirement per queue depends on the desired assembly strategy and on whether a header should be prepended to the burst or not: In equation (1) M, the amount of local memory needed, is determined by the number of queues (n_q), the size of the queue descriptor (s_{qdesc}) and the memory needed for one timer (s_{timer}), which is always 4 bytes. For size-based assembly without header generation, s_{qdesc} is 16 bytes, while it is 32 bytes for all other cases.

$$M = n_q \cdot s_{qdesc} + \left\lceil \frac{n_q}{8} \right\rceil \cdot s_{timer} \qquad (1)$$

Since the microengines of the IXP2400 have 2560 bytes of local memory each, 64 queues can be handled if all features are used. This number would be enough for a wide area network (WAN) of the size of Germany for example. Such a network might have about 30 edge nodes and for service differentiation, two traffic classes could be employed, which would result in about 60 queues per BAU. For more queues, external memory had to be employed resulting in more complex and slower design.

6.2   Performance Estimation

In this section, we will show how the BAM has been evaluated by calculations based on the worst case cycle count. The results are presented for different configurations of the BAM.

In order to calculate the number of packets that can be processed per second, the proceeding is as follows: First, the number of cycles needed for the various tasks of burst assembly has to be counted and second, it has to be calculated how many of these tasks can be processed within a given period of time, resulting in the number of packets processed.

Calculating the throughput based on cycle count is possible due to the properties of the microengine's architecture: The microengines are based on a RISC architecture with a single execution path. Therefore, one instruction is processed in one clock cycle. Additionally, the integrated instruction memory is fast enough to read the next instruction within one clock cycle, hence there is no latency for reading program data.

The microengines are programmed in an assembly language using the instructions that will be executed on the processor. Thus, by counting the instructions in the program code, it is possible to give the number of cycles needed for the execution of the program. However, the time needed for I/O instructions depends on the load of the processor buses used by all processor units. Due to the hardware-supported multithreading, threads waiting for I/O instructions can swap out, leaving the processor to threads that are ready to run, thus keeping the processor at full load. For this performance evaluation it is assumed that I/O operations always terminate fast enough for keeping the processor busy at all times.

The results of the these calculations are shown in Fig. 8 for different configurations of the BAM. The performance is given in packets per seconds for different timer granularities, which result from multiplications of the clock period by a power of two and are given as rounded values in the chart. The results for 27.3 μs and 13.7 μs granularity drop to zero as soon as the timer condition (see 4.2) cannot be fulfilled any more, since giving the performance for configurations at which proper operation of the timer mechanism cannot be guaranteed does not make sense.

As shown, performance decreases approximately linear for an increasing number of queues, since every additional queue needs additional processing time for a timer and for finalization. However, the curves are not straight due to effects like processing deactivated timers and writing parts of the header for every fourth packet.

In order to give an impression of the performance that can be achieved by the BAM, the maximum packet rate that can occur in the NP using our hardware is shown as a horizontal line in the chart. With the three Gigabit Ethernet ports, a maximum packet rate of 4.5 Million packets per second is possible considering the smallest Ethernet frame size. As shown in the chart, the BAM can handle 64 queues with a timer granularity of 54.6 μs per timer at this rate.

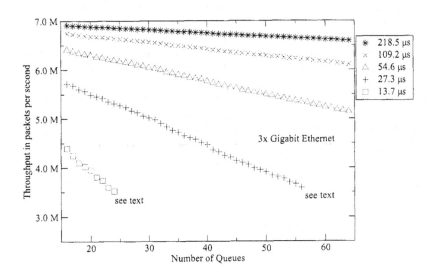

Figure 8. Calculated throughput of the BAM for different timer granularities

7. Conclusion

In this work, a Burst Assembly Unit on a Network Processor has been implemented and evaluated. It was shown that a Network Processor is suitable for such an implementation although the characteristics differ from typical network applications. Both assembly strategies – time-based and size-based – have been realized. For this, an efficient timer mechanism has been found that is able to provide Burst Assembly at line speed.

In a detailed performance evaluation, a method to calculate the maximum packet rate for a certain setup has been developed. With this, the throughput for a number of relevant scenarios has been calculated. It was shown that the Burst Assembly Module can handle up to 6.8 Million packets per second.

As a next step, the task of Burst Disassembly, which is currently implemented on a PC for testing purposes, has to be implemented as a software module for the NP. This module then could be integrated in the NP that also runs the BAU, in order to provide complete edge node functionality on an NP.

References

Dolzer, K.: Assured Horizon - A New Combined Framework for Burst Assembly and Reservation in Optical Burst Switched Networks, Proceedings of the European Conference on Networks and Optical Communications (NOC 2002), Darmstadt, 2002.

Gauger, C. M.: Trends in Optical Burst Switching. Proceedings of SPIE ITCOM 2003, Orlando, 2003.

Intel Corporation: Intel Internet Exchange Architecture Portability Framework Developer's Manual, 2003

Iperf bandwidth measurement tool: http://dast.nlanr.net/Projects/Iperf

Qiao, C., and M. Yoo: Optical Burst Switching - A New Paradigm for an Optical Internet, Journal of High Speed Networks, Special Issue on Optical Networks, Vol. 8, No. 1, pp.69-84, 1999.

Vokkarane, V.M. ,K. Haridoss, and J. P. Jue: Threshold-Based Burst Assembly Policies for QoS Support in Optical Burst-Switched Networks. Proceedings, SPIE Optical Networking and Communication Conference (OptiComm) 2002, Boston, MA, pp.125-136, 2002.

ANALYZING PACKET INTERARRIVAL TIMES DISTRIBUTION TO DETECT NETWORK BOTTLENECKS

Pál Varga
Department of Telecommunications and Media Informatics,
Budapest University of Technology and Economics (BME-TMIT)
Address: Magyar tudósok körútja 2., Budapest, Hungary, H-1117.
Phone: +36-1-463-3424.

pvarga@tmit.bme.hu

Abstract   This paper analyzes the properties of packet interarrival time (PIT) distribution functions of network segments including bottlenecks. In order to show the correlation between bottleneck behavior and packet interarrival time distribution, the alteration of probability distribution function (PDF) is observed through simulations including tighter and tighter bottleneck connections. The process of network bottleneck detection by passive monitoring requires effective metrics for distinguishing seriously congested links from normal or underutilized connections. The paper evaluates the third and fourth central moments (skewness and kurtosis, respectively) of PIT distribution as possible metrics for bottleneck detection. Simulation results as well as real measurement data analysis showed that PIT kurtosis can be a powerful measure of bottleneck behavior.

Keywords: passive monitoring, bottleneck detection, kurtosis

1.   Introduction

Passive monitoring-based bottleneck detection requires a complex collecting, pre-processing and evaluation system. Although the collection and pre-processing of the large amount of data are demanding tasks by themselves, it is also challenging to find appropriate measures for evaluating whether a link is bottleneck or not. This paper introduces a novel metric, which seems to be powerful enough to distinguish traffic carried over a network bottleneck from "traffic flowing with its own pace".

There are various measures suggested by [Varga et al., 2003] and [Moldován et al., 2004], each derived from transport-level flow analysis. These studies investigate several metrics (loss-rate, speed-averages, variance of flow-level throughput, delay-factor) to be used in bottleneck detection by passive monitoring, and found that they work with different accuracy under different conditions. The two most promising ones are the "X-measure" [Moldován et al., 2004] (like peakedness [Molnár and Miklós, 1998], it is a *coefficient of variation*-type metric applied for the throughput) and the delay factor calculated from the inter-arrival times of flows (based on the M/G/R – PS model) [Riedl et al., 2000; Varga et al., 2003]. Nevertheless, a recent study [Varga et al., 2004] evaluating these metrics on live traffic showed that they are not yet accurate enough and need further fine-tuning.

Packet pair method [Keshav, 1991; Kang et al., 2004] is widely used for bottleneck bandwidth estimation. This technique includes, however, intrusion of active probe traffic to the network before analyzing the results [Carter and Crovella, 1996]. The current paper focuses on non-intrusive bottleneck detection methods only. The entropy-based clustering method (introduced in [Katabi and Blake, 2002]) seems to be powerful to find connections sharing a bottleneck; the referred paper, however, misses to provide a range for packet interarrival time entropy that suggests bottleneck behavior.

The current paper introduces a novel metric to be used in bottleneck detection. It is based on the analysis of the probability distribution function (PDF) of packet interarrival times, which exhibit different shapes (with some common patterns) as seen during studying network bottlenecks using transport-level flow interarrival time distributions.

2.   Packet Interarrival Times Distribution

There is a good visual interpretation of packet interarrival times PDF patterns in [Katabi and Blake, 2002]. The authors describe PDFs computed in scenarios with no experienced queuing, significant queuing and queued traffic influenced by cross-traffic. Spikes and "spike-trains" in the PDF are found to suggest bottlenecks – or at least significant queuing in the analyzed path.

Nevertheless, there is an important difference in naming conventions used in [Katabi and Blake, 2002] and in this paper. The referred study considered connections as "bottlenecks" where the packets experienced "significant queuing". This is a very loose definition, even though it is hard to give a firm description of network bottleneck (other definitions would be connected with loss, throughput limits, high utilization, significant delay [Varga et al., 2003]).

The current paper considers a link as "bottleneck" where packets experience continuous, severe queuing and even being dropped due to the finite queue-lengths. Let us take an other viewpoint: consider a user utilizing similar networked services on server a and on server b (the servers offer similar processing performance). The user can reach server a on route A, whereas he/she gets serviced by server b on route B. In case this user is satisfied with the network performance towards server a, but he/she can notice performance problems towards server b, then route B contains bottleneck link(s) – at least more of them, than scenario A does.

Obviously this is not a precise definition of a bottleneck either. Finding an appropriate metric to distinguish bottleneck links from well-dimensioned ones could help clarifying the issues of having different definitions for the same underlying problem (which is ultimately reflected in user satisfaction of using networked services).

2.1   Higher Order Statistical Properties

The first and second central moment (mean and variance) of statistical distributions are widely used for briefly characterizing a distribution. Higher order statistical properties [Kenney and Keeping, 1951], as the third central moment (skewness) and the fourth central moment (kurtosis) are more rarely used in the engineering practice (although their applicability is wide-scale).

Skewness characterizes the degree of symmetry – or rather, the asymmetry – of a distribution around its mean. Positive skewness indicates a distribution with a probability-peak on the lower values and an extending tail towards the higher values. On the contrary, negative skewness indicates a distribution having a probability-peak on the higher values and an asymmetric tail extending towards the lower values.

Equation 1 shows the definition of skewness.

$$\gamma_1 = \frac{E[(\xi - E(\xi))^3]}{\sigma^3}, \tag{1}$$

where $E()$ stands for expectation, ξ is the statistical variable (hence $E(\xi)$ is the mean of ξ) and σ is the standard deviation. For measured data with finite number of measured entities, estimated skewness can be calculated as

$$\gamma_1 = \frac{n}{(n - 1)(n - 2)} \sum_{i=1}^{n} \left(\frac{x_i - x_{mean}}{s^*} \right)^3, \tag{2}$$

where n is the number of entities, x_i is the value of the actual item, x_{mean} is the mean of the measured values of x and s^* is the standard deviation.

Kurtosis characterizes the relative peakedness or flatness of a distribution compared to the normal distribution. The distribution is leptokurtic (or more peaked than the standard normal distribution) if the kurtosis excess (see Equation 3) is positive. Negative kurtosis excess indicates a platykurtic (or relatively flat) distribution. The term "kurtosis" was first used in [Pearson, 1905].

Equation 3 shows the definition of "kurtosis excess", which is widely used in the practice of mathematical statistics. The outcome of this type of kurtosis is normalized for easier comparison with the normal distribution. "Kurtosis proper" is by definition the fourth central moment, and it misses the normalizing element of -3.

$$\gamma_2 = \frac{E[(\xi - E(\xi))^4]}{\sigma^4} - 3. \tag{3}$$

The statistical estimate of kurtosis with finite number of measured entities comes from the formula

$$\gamma_2 = \frac{n(n-1)}{(n-1)(n-2)(n-3)} \sum_{i=1}^{n} \left(\frac{x_i - x_{mean}}{s^*} \right)^4 - \\ -3\frac{(n-1)^2}{(n-2)(n-3)}. \tag{4}$$

The next chapter introduces the features of PDFs derived from packet interarrival times of computer networks. We shall see that deriving skewness and kurtosis helps distinguishing bottleneck scenarios from un-congested measurement setup.

2.2   Packet Interarrival Times PDF of Links with No Congestion

The probability distribution function (PDF) of packet interarrival times (PIT) should be extremely flat in a non-queued aggregated network-link. This is because several links with various capacities can carry packets to the observed aggregated link. Independent sources generating traffic in such topology causes absolutely random interrarrival times.

In case a node aggregates numerous links with various capacities (and no queuing), the PIT PDF at that node appears to be flat, as shown in Figure 1.a (showing probability and PIT (in microseconds) on the axes).

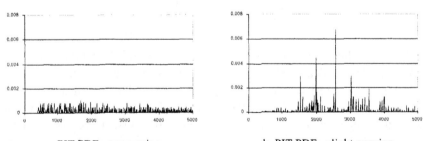

a. PIT PDF - no queuing   b. PIT PDF - slight queuing

Figure 1.   Packet interarrival times PDF on an aggregated link with no queuing (left) and on an aggregated link, with eventual queuing (right)

Once the link gets more busy, the relevant network node must queue some packets, and place them on the line right after the previous packet (back-to-back). The more of this queuing is applied, the less "flat" the PDF becomes: spikes starting to appear at the interarrival times where queued packets has followed each other back-to-back. Figure 1.b depicts a scenario where several lower capacity links – having different peak rates – connect to an aggregation node. The packets have experienced some – not severe – queuing before arriving to the aggregated link. Skewness of such PIT distributions are close to zero, or negative, whereas their kurtosis is negative, emphasizing that these PDFs are relatively flat.

2.3   Effects of the Bottleneck Behavior on Interarrival Times Distribution

Theoretically what one should expect during the observation of a link getting congested is the following. As the observed link starts showing bottleneck behavior, most of the eventual spikes of the PDF gets less noticeable and the spike around the lowest possible interarrival times starts dominating the PDF. Under severe congestion this spike fully dominates the PDF, as packets arrive back-to-back during the whole measurement period. Both skewness and kurtosis exhibit more positive values. The more dominant the spike around the lower PIT values gets, the more skewed the PDF becomes. Similarly, as kurtosis is, as the definition suggests the "peakedness" or "spikeness" of the distribution [Darlington, 1970], PIT kurtosis assumes higher values as the spike dominates the PDF. Since eventual queuing already makes the PDF skewed, one can expect that kurtosis should be more robust metric of bottleneck behavior than skewness. The following sections provide simulation results and analysis of real-life experiments to detail and support the above theory.

3.   Bottleneck Detection: PIT PDF, Skewness and Kurtosis

3.1   Simulation Environment

The network topology used during the simulation is shown by Figure 2. OP-NET was chosen as a simulation tool, as previous work on bottleneck detection has proven its applicability [Varga et al., 2003]. During each simulation period, traffic was generated to traverse the network for 15 minute long measurements.

From the simulation's point of view the traffic sources were the ISP's (aggregation nodes of Internet Service Providers) The characteristics of the traffic matches service types such as e-mail, ftp, http and database-access. There is also some asymmetry in the link capacities, since one of the ISP's is connected to the backbone through a bottleneck link ($link\_2$ between routers R2 and R5 in Figure 2).

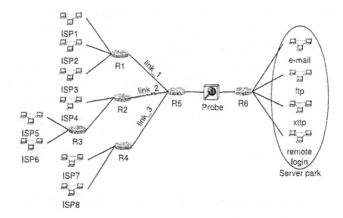

Figure 2.   Network topology used during the simulations

The applied data collection and evaluation steps are as follows.

- the Probe captures traffic on an aggregated link (between R5 and R6 in Figure 2),

- traffic flowing from the same directions are distinguished by IP-address ranges belonging to the source ISP's of a given direction,

- after separating the captured traffic by directions, the PIT-characteristics of each direction is analyzed.

To evaluate kurtosis and skewness as possible metrics for bottleneck detection, the bottleneck in our simulation environment has been set tighter in several steps. This way one can evaluate how much difference in utilization and also in available bandwidth (ABW) would result in a loose or tight bottleneck. The bottleneck was created in the simulation topology by defining $link\_2$ having relatively low bandwidth, whereas $link\_1$ and $link\_3$ were equal, higher capacity connections.

The bottleneck was set tighter and tighter by increasing the maximum ABW of $link\_1$ and $link\_3$ (up to 1000 Mbps) and simultaneously decreasing the capacity of $link\_2$ (down to 300 Mbps). The tightest bottleneck was set to be able to handle merely 30% of the traffic of the other links (loaded by the same amount of traffic). In the following this scenario will be referred to as "1000/300", suggesting the "higher/lower"-bandwidth values applied for "$link\_1, 3/link\_2$".

3.2   Common patterns of PIT PDFs

In order to validate the theory about PIT PDF structures (see Section 2.3) an exhaustive study was carried out using different source traffic characteristics, topologies and utilizations (the latter has ranged from scenario 675/625 to scenario 1000/300). Typical results for the two extreme scenarios are plotted in Figures 3.a-f.

The somewhat normal condition can be described as "packets experience queuing, but no loss" (scenario 700/600). The other extreme is a real bottleneck condition (scenario 1000/300).

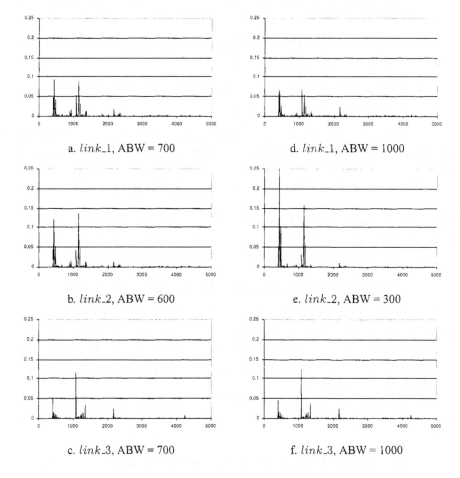

a. *link_1*, ABW = 700

d. *link_1*, ABW = 1000

b. *link_2*, ABW = 600

e. *link_2*, ABW = 300

c. *link_3*, ABW = 700

f. *link_3*, ABW = 1000

Figure 3.   Packet interarrival time PDFs in simulation scenarios 700/600 (left) and 1000/300 (right)

Comparing the resulting PDFs, there are numerous observations that can be made:

- the PDF keeps its general shape (number and place of the spikes) in a given link, as long as the same type of traffic flows through it,

- great spikes appearing in the PDF do not necessarily hide bottleneck condition,

- if the highest spike is not positioned at the lower PIT values, the packets are not following each other back-to-back (hence there is no severe congestion, see Figures 3.c,f),

- the PDF looses some of its peakedness if the available bandwidth increases (compare Figures 3.a and d),

- as expected, the PDF gets extremely peaked and skewed under bottleneck conditions (see Figure 3.e),

- as expected, the spike at the lower PIT values are dominant under bottleneck conditions (see Figure 3.e).

Unfortunately, drawing conclusions from the comparison of plotted diagrams is not a feasible network maintenance practice. Even in a medium-sized network the high number of network connections makes such comparisons impossible. A more decent metric is needed that is able to distinguish PDFs of congested connections from other cases without significant queuing. As anticipated, skewness and kurtosis of PITs should be able to suggest whether a severe bottleneck exists or not. The following section evaluates the usability of these higher order statistical properties in bottleneck detection.

3.3   Performance Evaluation Based on Simulations

The statistical properties skewness and kurtosis of PITs were calculated using Equation 2 and Equation 3 respectively. During the simulations the same network topology (see Figure 2.) were loaded by similar source traffic. The only major difference between the simulation scenarios is the ABW assigned to links 1, 2 and 3 in Figure 2.

Table 1. provides skewness values of the three links for the different bottleneck scenarios. The following observations can be made by evaluating the results:

- as expected, skewness of a bottleneck link is positive,

- the tighter the bottleneck is, the more positive skewness is observed,

- skewness assumes positive values also for links with eventual queuing, hence it is difficult to distinguish these from severely congested links,

- connections with less traffic and almost no queuing can be characterized with negative or close to zero skewness value.

Table 1. PIT skewness values in simulated environment

Name	675/625	700/600	800/500	900/400	1000/300
link_1	0.75527	0.80733	0.66632	0.57561	0.41202
link_2	0.95506	1.05409	1.10767	1.48124	1.65051
link_3	-0.09488	-0.09007	-0.11049	-0.04702	-0.03974

To conclude, skewness of PITs noticeably acquires positive values in bottle-neck scenarios, although it may do so for links with eventual queuing.

Table 2. summarizes PIT kurtosis values observed in different simulation scenarios. There are merely two positive values appearing among the results, both observed on the bottleneck link in serious bottleneck scenarios (900/400 and 1000/300). It is also noticeable that the PIT distribution gets more platykurtic (flat) as ABW increases (*link_1*) and changes its platykurtic character into leptokurtic (peaked) as ABW decreases as far as causing bottle-neck behavior (*link_2*). There is a less practical, but interesting feature of PIT kurtosis, namely, that it does not assume noticeably lower (more negative) values if the capacity of an underutilized link increases (*link_3*). To summarize,

Table 2. PIT kurtosis values in simulated environment

Name	675/625	700/600	800/500	900/400	1000/300
link_1	-0.96502	-0.87263	-1.04085	-1.23243	-1.45336
link_2	-0.59994	-0.35450	-0.28027	0.71819	1.31911
link_3	-1.62645	-1.63841	-1.63470	-1.63417	-1.61983

PIT kurtosis seems to be an appropriate metric for detecting bottlenecks. This is further validated in the following section.

3.4   Using PIT Kurtosis to Detect Bottlenecks in Real, Operational Networks

In order to validate metrics for passive bottleneck detection, a series of measurements have been taken place at sites of a major Hungarian network operator. During the measurements a passive network monitoring tool (Network Associates' Sniffer and Snifferbook Ultra) have been used, capturing continuous data traversed on Gigabit Ethernet interfaces. The measurements covered normal and busy hour conditions, connections to the operator's Internet Data Center and to routers/switches at the edge of the core network.

The measurements captured traffic during severe bottleneck conditions also. The topology of the network segment that contained a bottleneck link during the measurements can be studied in Figure 4. Traffic is flowing from the Digital Subscriber Line Access Multiplexers (DSLAM) towards the core network (and back), going through internal ATM (STM-1) links. The network monitoring tool has been connected to the aggregated link, and captured all packet headers of the measurement period. As part of the data-processing, packet-headers were sorted by direction (ATM sub-network). The moments of packet interarrival time distribution was calculated for each direction. Most of the measurements have been carried out under normal network conditions. During one of the monitoring sessions, an ATM link loading the OpR_1 - $OpSW$ segment got overloaded. (this fact has been indicated by other network analysis tools also).

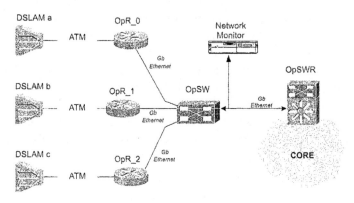

Figure 4.   Measurement topology at the operator's site

Skewness analysis resulted positive values for all cases. The bottleneck link provided higher PIT skewness value comparing to the others, but still the difference was not significant, leaving skewness to be unable to detect bottleneck by itself.

The results of PIT kurtosis calculations are demonstrated in Table 3. These kurtosis values clearly meet the expectations set up in Section 3.3. Traffic measured under normal network conditions (underutilized links) provide negative values; although OpR_1 - $OpSW$ shows kurtosis close to zero, suggesting some uncertainty. During the congestion on this route (remember that not the monitored link, but an ATM link, being two hops behind the monitoring unit has been congested), kurtosis reached the positive domain, suggesting severe bottleneck condition. In this period noticeable packet loss and over 90% link utilization was observed also (using monitoring tools covering the targeted, lower capacity links).

The PIT PDFs calculated for the three connected links under normal and high traffic conditions are shown in Figure 5.a-c and Figure 5.d-f respectively. After analyzing these PDFs based on the assumptions of Section 3.2, the following observations can be made. Figures 5.a, c and d suggest healthy traffic

Table 3.   PIT kurtosis values of measurements at the operator's site

Link name	normal conditions	OpR_1 overloaded
OpR_0 - $OpSW$	-0.46420	-0.45571
OpR_1 - $OpSW$	-0.06267	1.15119
OpR_2 - $OpSW$	-0.11180	-0.13289

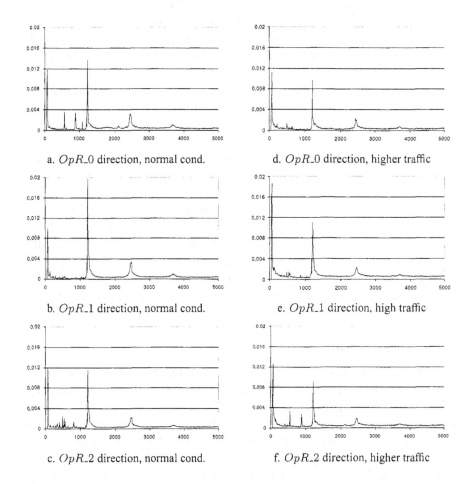

a. OpR_0 direction, normal cond.

d. OpR_0 direction, higher traffic

b. OpR_1 direction, normal cond.

e. OpR_1 direction, high traffic

c. OpR_2 direction, normal cond.

f. OpR_2 direction, higher traffic

Figure 5.   Packet interarrival time PDFs calculated based on real network data

flow, with a normal amount of queuing considering the high aggregation level. Figure 5.b includes a noticeable spike, however it is found at the higher PIT values, which means there were no severe congestion. The visual comparison of Figures 5.e and f does not reveal any major difference, as in both figures the PDF spikes at the lowest possible PITs, although the spike is significantly higher at the real bottleneck case (Figure 5.e).

In fact, kurtosis – as a metric for bottleneck behavior – has clearly distinguished these situations as well. It provided the positive result of 1.15119 for the bottleneck case visualized by Figure 5.e as opposed to the otherwise normal traffic condition shown in Figure 5.f, where kurtosis was calculated to be -0.13289 (see Table 3).

During the various simulations and measurements it was noticed that PIT kurtosis calculated on the full PIT distribution depends slightly on link capacity. When two links have the same utilization (in percentage), the link having the higher capacity appear to have higher kurtosis. The reason behind this observation is not clearly identified yet. The consequences of this behavior, however, can lead far. In an extreme scenario the kurtosis of a *higher capacity, less utilized* connection can be higher than the kurtosis of a *lower capacity, more utilized* link. This would weaken the accuracy of PIT kurtosis as a bottleneck metric.

To overcome the above obstacle, a correction of PIT kurtosis should be considered for bottleneck detection. This correction should be linked to the analyzed data volume somehow.

Current analysis shows that PIT kurtosis scales well and provides more accurate, less capacity-dependent results when the it is calculated on a subset of the PIT-distribution. Leaving the 10 percent tail out of the analysis and calculating kurtosis up to the 90 percentile point of the PIT-distribution has provided satisfactory results on the available data sets. Future work should verify this observation, and clarify the issue of the slight capacity-dependency of PIT kurtosis.

4.   Conclusions

Bottleneck detection based on passive measurements can be supported by analyzing Packet interarrival time (PIT) distribution. The more packets experience queuing at a network node, the more of them leave the node back-to-back. Under normal conditions the PIT probability distribution function (PDF) is relatively "flat": spikes due to typical packet lengths and minimal following times are visible, but appear to be small. As queuing turns into severe congestion, the spike around the lowest possible PIT value gets dominant. This fact is indicated by the fourth central moment – kurtosis – also: it gets more positive. Beside this, the third central moment, skewness gets more and more positive, also. Kurtosis of distributions more flat than normal distribution have negative kurtosis, whereas peaked distributions charaterize themselves with positive kurtosis. Applying this to packet interarrival times distributions, positive kurtosis suggests serious bottleneck behavior, while negative kurtosis is a property of underutilized links. Values being very close to zero is hard to evaluate, but probably hide serious queuing in the path.

Both skewness and kurtosis appeared to acquire higher values as the available bandwidth of a link decreased in the OPNET-based simulation environment. While both measures performed well as relative metrics, only *kurtosis* is powerful enough to distinguish bottleneck links from underutilized connections. Current studies show that kurtosis is slightly dependent on capacity, hence the metric should be refined for more accure bottleneck detection: kurtosis should be calculated up to the 90 percentile of the PIT distribution.

Analysis of real measurement data has also been carried out, supporting that PIT kurtosis can be a powerful metric of detecting bottlenecks. The usability of PIT skewness and kurtosis in network performance analysis is for further study. The idea of PIT skewness and kurtosis to be used for bottleneck detection has been first submitted as an article for EUNICE 2005. The generalized idea and the more detailed methodology of bottleneck detection based on passive measurement at an aggregated link has then appeared later, at [Varga and Kún, 2005].

References

Carter, Robert L. and Crovella, M. E. (1996). Measuring bottleneck link speed in packet-switched networks. *Performance Evaluation*, 27-28:297–318.

Darlington, R.B. (1970). Is kurtosis really peakedness? *American Statistician*, 24(19-22).

Kang, S., Liu, X., Dai, M., and Loguinov, D. (2004). Packet-pair bandwidth estimation: Stochastic analysis of a single congested node. In *Proceedings of IEEE ICNP 2004*.

Katabi, D. and Blake, C. (2002). Inferring congestion sharing and path characteristics from packet interarrival times. Technical report, MIT-LCS-TR-828, MIT.

Kenney, J. F. and Keeping, E. S. (1951). *Mathematics of Statistics*, volume 2. Princeton, NJ: Van Nostrand, 2nd edition.

Keshav, S. (1991). A control-theoretic approach to flow control. In *Proceedings of SIGCOMM*.

Moldován, I., Dang, T. Dinh, Bíró, J., Satoh, D., and Ishibashi, K. (2004). Bottleneck links detection method based on passive monitoring. In *Iasted CIIT 2004*.

Molnár, S. and Miklós, Gy. (1998). Peakedness characterization in teletraffic. In *IFIP TC6, WG6.3 conference PICS'98*.

Pearson, K. (1905). Das fehlergesetz und seine verallgemeinerungen durch fechner und pearson. *Biometrika*, 169–212.

Riedl, A., Perske, M., Bauschert, T., and Probst, A. (2000). Dimensioning of ip access networks with elastic traffic. In *First Polish-German Teletraffic Symposium (PGTS 2000)*.

Varga, P. and Kún, G. (2005). Utilizing higher order statistics of packet interarrival times for bottleneck detection. In *Proceedings of IFIP/IEEE E2EMon*.

Varga, P., Kún, G., Fodor, P., Bíró, J., Satoh, D., and Ishibashi, K. (2003). An advanced technique on bottleneck detection. In *IFIP WG6.3 workshop, EUNICE 2003*.

Varga, P., Moldován, I., Dang, T. Dinh, Simon, Cs., Kún, G., and Tatai, P. (2004). Developing a passive measurement-based methodology for detecting network bottlenecks in ip networks. Technical report, Study for Hungarian Telecom, in Hungarian.

TUNABLE LEAST SERVED FIRST

A New Scheduling Algorithm with Tunable Fairness

Pablo Serrano, David Larrabeiti, and Ángel León
Universidad Carlos III de Madrid
Departamento de Ingeniería Telemática
Av. Universidad 30, E-28911 Leganés, Madrid, Spain
{pablo,dlarra,aleon}@it.uc3m.es

Abstract   At high transmission speeds, complexity of implementation for fair queuing disciplines can impose a bottleneck to the overall system performance. Available scheduling algorithms set a fixed trade off between fairness and complexity, fairer systems involving more operations per packet and vice versa. In this paper first a new fair queuing scheme is proposed, with almost the same fairness and complexity propierties achieved so far by most used algorithms. Later on a tunable parameter is introduced, which allows the modification of the above mentioned trade off between fairness and complexity depending on working conditions and thus enlarging the field of application of the scheduler.

Keywords: Fair scheduling, tunable fairness.

Introduction

In past years, round-robin-like disciplines were the most established schemes of scheduling. This was mainly because only one class of traffic (computer data) was supported, with no quality of service (QoS) guarantees, and because packet transmission time was large compared to round trip time (and thus reactive congestion control could be used to control traffic sources). The emergence of high-speed data networks has changed these conditions, leading researchers to investigate on new directions for traffic control. First-in-first-out (FIFO) queuing disciplines have been proved to be no good nor to provide QoS guarantees nor fairness in the event of congestion. Three are the main properties required for a queuing discipline ([Bensaou et al., 2001]):

- Simplicity: the processing overhead must be orders of magnitude smaller than the average packet transmission time.

- Robustness (isolation): well-behaved traffic flows cannot be hurt by mis-behaving flows.

- Fairness: all bandwidth should be given to active traffic flows proportional to their weight.

Some examples of unfair queuing disciplines are: FIFO, where a session can increase its share of service by just presenting more demand, or Round robin (RR) ([Hahne, 1986]), where a flow with higher mean packet size will obtain more bandwidth at the expense of another flow with equal packet injection rate, but less sized packets.

Most Fair Queuing (FQ) algorithms aim to approach the fairness provided by the generalized processor sharing (GPS) algorithm [Parekh and Gallager, 1993]. GPS, also called fluid fair queuing (FFQ), is a theoretical algorithm based on the assumption that traffic is infinitesimally divisible, and hence can be served by infinitesimally small quanta (leading to the ideal situation where bits from different packet flows are transmitted concurrently). But in real switched networks packets are not divisible, and a flow seizes all channel during the transmission time (so no other flow is given service), which prevents the implementation of an absolute fairness system ([Golestani, 1994]).

Zhang's *virtual clock* scheme [Zhang, 1990] can be considered pioneering, due to the introduction of a metric (a virtual clock), an effective tool for both formulating fairness and representing the progress of work in the queuing system. But virtual clock-based algorithms (WFQ [Demers et al., 1990], W2FQ [Bennett and Zhang, 1996]) involves considerable computational complexity. Most of the recent research in reducing the processing requirement of the scheduler has concentrated on modifying the basic WFQ paradigm. One exception is the DRR [Shreedhar and Varghese, 1995] algorithm and its variants, which achieve lower complexity at the expense of lower fairness. In [Chaskar and Madhow, 2003] modifications to the weighted round-robin approach are discussed, with performance characteristics similar to those of W2FQ but with lower complexity of implementation (for fixed packet sizes).

This paper proposes and analyses a new paradigm of fair squeduling, Least Served First (LSF), and extends it with a parameter which tunes the trade off between complexity per packet and fairness (T-LSF). LSF serves at any instant the flow which has received less service since it arrived to the scheduler, while T-LSF deals with *groups* of flows that have received *similar* service. This tunable fairness (and complexity) enlarges the field of application of a scheduler: instead of imposing the design criterium a priori (based on the expected number of flows, line speeds, ...), it is possible to tune a parameter a posteriori based on *real* working conditions. On maximum fairness configuration it possesses similar characteristics than those of SCFQ [Golestani, 1994].

The remainder of the paper is organized as follows. Section 1 deals with the network model, giving definitions about fairness and the algorithm. Section 2 presents the basic version of LSF, without tunable fairness/complexity, and analyses its performance. On Section 2.4 we present T-LSF, with the tunable parameter N that reduces (increases) complexity (unfairness). Finally, on Section 3 we draw our conclusions and point out future lines of research.

1. Preliminaries

The network node we consider is modeled as a multiplexer fed by a superposition of M traffic flows, sharing a link of capacity C. Each flow i, $i = 1, \ldots, M$ is associated a counter W_i and a bandwidth share r_i, with $\sum_{i=1}^{M} r_i = C$. A flow i is said to be backlogged at time t if a packet from flow i is being served or it is waiting to be served at that time. A flow i is backlogged during (t_1, t_2) if it is backlogged during all the interval. $B(t_1, t_2)$ is the set of sessions which are backlogged during the entire interval (t_1, t_2). According to a *sorted* flow list (based on the values of the W_i), the LSF algorithm selects the next packet to be transmitted and updates the value of the counters. $S_i(t_1, t_2)$ is the amount of traffic served during (t_1, t_2) to flow i, while $W_i(t_1, t_2)$ is the difference of the values for the counter W_i (i.e. $W_i(t_1, t_2) = W_i(t_2) - W_i(t_2)$). Throughout the paper, and until explicitly claimed, t_n is the time when a packet n has finished its transmission.

The notion of fairness in this paper is defined according to the criterium of proportional rate sharing: if a traffic flow i is not active, its bandwidth share r_i should be allocated to the other active flows in a fashion proportional to their share. Under the fluid flow assumption, a scheduling algorithm is said to be fair if and only if

$$\forall\, t_1, t_2\; \forall i, j : i, j \in B(t_1, t_2), \left| \frac{S_i(t_1, t_2)}{r_i} - \frac{S_j(t_1, t_2)}{r_j} \right| = 0$$

$S_i(t_1, t_2)/r_i$ is defined as the *normalized service received* by flow i. In a non-fluid network model, where traffic flows are served by a non negligible quantum of variable size, the aim is to give a bound for the above substraction:

$$\left| \frac{S_i(t_1, t_2)}{r_i} - \frac{S_j(t_1, t_2)}{r_j} \right| \leq FI$$

FI is defined as the *fairness index* (also called *proportional fairness index* [Chaskar and Madhow, 2003] or *relative fairness* [Zhou and Sethu, 2002]) of the scheduling discipline. The smaller the FI, the fairer the scheduling algorithm. On the other hand, the *absolute fairness* is defined as the difference on normalized service received between a flow served by the queuing discipline under study, and the same flow in a GPS environment. Although this is a better measurement of the performance of the algorithm, in situations with a high number of flows both fairness values remain close to each other ([Zhou and Sethu, 2002]), and thus we are able to keep focus on FI.

The main features of most common available scheduling algorithms are summarized on Table 1, and compared to LSF and T-LSF, i, j being any two

Table 1.   Fairness Bounds and Computational Complexity per Packet

Algorithm	Fairness Bound	Complexity
SCFQ	$L_i^{MAX}/r_i + L_j^{MAX}/r_j$	$O(log(M))$
W2FQ	$L_i^{MAX}/r_i + L_j^{MAX}/r_j$	$O(log(n))$
DRR	$L_i^{MAX} + L_i^{MAX}/r_i + L_j^{MAX}/r_j$	$O(1)$
LSF	$2 \cdot max\{L_i^{MAX}/r_i\}$	$O(log(M))$
T-LSF	$2 \cdot max\{L_i^{MAX}/r_i\} \cdot \ 1 + \frac{1}{N-1}$	$O(log(N))$

flows, M the number of flows and n the number of packets in the system, and N the configurable parameter for T-LSF, $N \in \{2, 3, \ldots, M\}$ (although usually $N << M$).

2.   Least Served First

2.1   General LSF Algorithm

Consider a system with M flows. A flow i, $i \in \{1, \ldots, M\}$ is associated a bandwidth share r_i and a counter W_i. This counter is used to store an estimation of the normalized service received by flow i. In order to maximize fairness, the algorithm aims to minimize the maximum difference in service received by any two flows: the flow with minimum W_i is always the next flow to be served.

LSF Algorithm

- Initialization.
$$W_i := 0, \ i = 1, \ldots, M$$

- Operation.

    1 Transmit the head-of-line (HOL) packet of flow j with minimum W_i and size $L_{HOL(j)}$, i.e.
    $$j := arg \ min^1\{W_i\}$$

    2 Once departed packet from flow j update W_j,
    $$W_j := W_j + L_{HOL(j)}/r_j$$

    3 Goto (1).

- Flow arrival. When a flow k is backlogged, it is initialized to the maximum of $\{W_i\}$,
$$W_k := max\{W_i\}$$

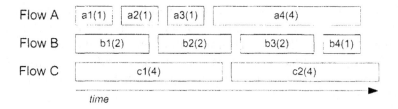

Figure 1. Example with three flows

Table 2. Example for LSF

Packet Served		a1	b1	c1	a2	a3	b2	a4
W_A	0	1	1	1	2	3	3	7
W_B	0	0	2	2	2	2	4	4
W_C	0	0	0	4	4	4	4	4

In order to illustrate the behaviour of LSF with an example, suppose a system with three flows, each of them backlogged with packets of different sizes. This situation is represented on Fig. 1 (each packet is given an identifier, with its size in parenthesis). All flows start with $W_i = 0$, and $r_i = r_j = 1, \forall i, j$. The scheduler algorithm will serve packets as shown on Table 2[2]. Due to the behaviour of the algorithm, the maximum difference between any two normalized service counters ($|W_i - W_j|$) at any packet departure is equal to the maximum packet length in the system, which is the base for the analysis of the fairness of LSF.

2.2 Fairness Analysis

In this section we show that LSF achieves a fairness bound close to the one obtained in [Demers et al., 1990; Bennett and Zhang, 1996; Golestani, 1994]. This is stated on the following Theorem, proved through a sequence of four lemmas.

THEOREM 1 (FAIRNESS INDEX OF LSF) *For any two flows* $i, j \in B(t_1, t_2)$ *and* $p \in \{1, \dots, M\}$

$$\left| \frac{S_i(t_1, t_2)}{r_i} - \frac{S_j(t_1, t_2)}{r_j} \right| \leq 2 \cdot max_p \left(\frac{L_p^{MAX}}{r_p} \right)$$

For ease of notation, we are going to define the quantity K_p as:

$$K_p = max_p \left(\frac{L_p^{MAX}}{r_p} \right), p \in \{1, \dots, M\}$$

In order to demonstrate the Theorem, we will first bound the difference between W_i and W_j (at two different t_n) for any two flows i and j (by Lemma 2, Lemma 3 and Corollary 4). Then we will extend it for the normalized service received, S_i/r_i (via Corollary 5). At last, we will allow the comparaison between any two time instants -not only departure times- via Lemma 6, concluding the proof.

LEMMA 2 *For any two flows* $i, j \in B(t_n, t_m)$, *if* $W_i(t_n) = W_j(t_n)$ *then*

$$|W_i(t_n, t_m) - W_j(t_n, t_m)| \leq K_p$$

Proof: *Because* $W_i(t_n) = W_j(t_n)$, *we have* $|W_i(t_n, t_m) - W_j(t_n, t_m)| = |(W_i(t_m) - W_j(t_m)) - (W_i(t_n) - W_j(t_n))| = |W_i(t_m) - W_j(t_m)|$. *With* $p \in \{1, \ldots, M\}$ *this difference is bounded by:*

$$|W_i(t_m) - W_j(t_m)| \leq \left| max\{W_p\}_{t_m} - min\{W_p\}_{t_m} \right|$$

With $max\{W_p\}_{t_m}$ $(min\{W_p\}_{t_m})$ *being the maximum (minimum) of all active counters at* t_m. *Because* $m \geq n$, *and by writing* $m = n + k$, *we can proceed by induction on* k:

- $k = 1$:
  $|max\{W_i\}_{t_{n+1}} - min\{W_i\}_{t_{n+1}}| \leq K_p$
  The demonstration is trivial: $W_i(t_n) = W_j(t_n)$, *and in* t_{n+1} *only one packet has departed, thus the difference in* t_{n+1} *is bounded by the maximum of all possible increments (which is* K_p).

- $k \Rightarrow k + 1$:
  for ease of notation (and without loss of generality), we can assume $n = 0$, *so* $t_{n+k+1} = t_{k+1}$. *Then we have* $|max\{W_i\}(t_k) - min\{W_i\}(t_k)| \leq K_p$, *and we are going to prove it for* $k + 1$. *We need to consider all possible cases:*

  - $min\{W_i\}(t_k) = min\{W_i\}(t_{k+1})$ *and* $max\{W_i\}(t_{k+1}) \geq max\{W_i\}(t_k)$
    This only happens if $max\{W_i\}(t_k) = min\{W_i\}(t_k)$, *an thus we are in the case* $k = 1$.
  - $max\{W_i\}(t_{k+1}) = max\{W_i\}(t_k)$ *and* $min\{W_i\}(t_{k+1}) \geq min\{W_i\}(t_{k+1})^3$.
    In this case, $|max\{W_i\}(t_{k+1}) - min\{W_i\}(t_{k+1})| = |max\{W_i\}(t_k) - min\{W_i\}(t_{k+1})| \leq |max\{W_i\}(t_k) - min\{W_i\}(t_k)| \leq K_p$.
  - $max\{W_i\}(t_{k+1}) \geq max\{W_i\}(t_k)$ *and* $min\{W_i\}(t_{k+1}) \geq min\{W_i\}(t_k)$
    The only possible case is $max\{W_i\}(t_{k+1}) = min\{W_i\}(t_k) + \frac{L_k}{r_k}$, L_k *being the size of the packet transmitted at* t_k *and* r_k *the flow associated with it. Then* $|max\{W_i\}(t_{k+1}) - min\{W_i\}(t_{k+1})| \leq |max\{W_i\}(t_{k+1}) - min\{W_i\}(t_k)| = |min\{W_i\}(t_k) + \frac{L_k}{r_k} - min\{W_i\}(t_k)| \leq K_p$

LEMMA 3 *For any two flows* $i, j \in B(t_n, t_m)$, *if* $|W_i(t_n) - W_j(t_n)| \leq K_p$ *the following inequality holds:*

$$|W_i(t_n, t_m) - W_j(t_n, t_m)| \leq 2 \cdot K_p$$

Proof: $|W_i(t_n, t_m) - W_j(t_n, t_m)| = |(W_i(t_m) - W_j(t_m)) - (W_i(t_n) - W_j(t_n))|$. *Because* $|A - B| \leq |A| + |B|$, *we can bound* $|W_i(t_n, t_m) - W_j(t_n, t_m)| \leq |(W_i(t_m) - W_j(t_m))| + |(W_i(t_n) - W_j(t_n))|$. *The first term is bounded by* K_p *by Lemma 2, and the second term bounded by hypothesis.*

COROLLARY 4 *For any two flows* $i, j \in B(t_n, t_m)$,

$$|W_i(t_n, t_m) - W_j(t_n, t_m)| \leq 2 \cdot K_p$$

Proof: *On* t_n, *there are two possibilities for the relation between* W_i *and* W_j: *either* $W_i(t_n) = W_j(t_n)$, *or* $W_i(t_n) \neq W_j(t_n)$. *The first case is bounded via Lemma 2 by* K_p. *The second case is bounded via Lemma 3: in LSF any flow* i *who begins backlogged its counter* W_i *is imposed to initialize from the maximum of active counters. By Lemma 2, the maximum difference between any two active counters is* K_p, *which is the hypothesis of Lemma 3.*

COROLLARY 5 *For any two flows* $i, j \in B(t_n, t_m)$,

$$\left| \frac{S_i(t_n, t_m)}{r_i} - \frac{S_j(t_n, t_m)}{r_j} \right| \leq 2 \cdot K_p$$

Proof: *First we are going to define the predicate* $isMin$

$$isMin(W_l, \{W_p\}) \begin{cases} 1, & l = arg\ min\{W_p\} \\ 0, & l \neq arg\ min\{W_p\} \end{cases}$$

Then we can $W_i(t_m)$ *as*

$$W_i(t_m) = W_i(t_n) + \sum_{k=1}^{m} (isMin(W_i, \{W_p\}) \times \frac{L_i^k}{r_i}$$

When the predicate $isMin$ *equals 1 is when packet* i *is the next to be served; thus we have*

$$W_i(t_m) - W_i(t_n) = \sum_{k=1}^{m} (isMin(W_i, \{W_p\}) \times \frac{L_i^k}{r_i} \triangleq \frac{S_i(t_n, t_m)}{r_i}$$

And then the bound of Corollary 4 on $|W_i(t_n, t_m) - W_j(t_n, t_m)|$ *applies directly to* $|S_i(t_n, t_m)/r_i - S_j(t_n, t_m)/r_j|$

LEMMA 6 *For any two flows* $i, j \in B(t_1, t_2)$ (t_1, t_2 *being any two instants of time, and not just packet departure instants), the following inequality holds:*

$$\left| \frac{S_i(t_1, t_2)}{r_i} - \frac{S_j(t_1, t_2)}{r_j} \right| \leq 2 \cdot K_p$$

Proof: *For a continuous t_k, we define t_{k+} as the instant when the next packet leaves the system after t_k, and t_{k-} when the previous packet has left the system. Thus we have either $i, j \in B(t_{1-}, t_{2+})$ or $i, j \notin B(t_{1-}, t_{2+})$.*

1 *$i, j \in B(t_{1-}, t_{2+})$. Because the difference is bounded for discretized t_n, it is bounded for the intervals (t_{1-}, t_{2+}), (t_{1-}, t_{2-}), (t_{1+}, t_{2+}) and (t_{1+}, t_{2-}). Depending on whether i of j transmit, and on relative values of S_i and S_j, it is easy to bound the difference between them (using the* pinching *or* sandwich *theorem [de Burgos, 1995]). The detailed demonstration for this case is given on the Appendix.*

2 *$i, j \notin B(t_{1-}, t_{2+})$. We have to consider t_1 and t_2 nearness.*

- *t_2. If i (j) $\notin B(t_2, t_{2+})$, then no packet from i (j) left the system at t_{2+} and thus $S_{i(j)}(t_1, t_2) = S_{i(j)}(t_1, t_{2-})$.*
- *t_1. If both $i, j \notin B(t_{1-}, t_1)$, none of them receives service at t_1 and $S_{i,j}(t_1, t_2) = S_{i,j}(t_{1-}, t_2)$.*
  If flow i was receiving service on t_1, flow j will behave as any other flow k, $k \in B(t_{1-}, t_2)$, which received service just before t_{1-}, and whose difference on service is bounded. If no other flow k is available, flow j will initialize with $W_j(t_1) = W_i(t_{1-})$ and we could extend $S_j(t_1, t_2)$ to $S_j(t_{1-}, t_2)$ without any obstacles.

2.3 Complexity

The initializing/flow arrival phase does not involve any significant number of operations. Packet departure, on the other hand, besides a fixed number of operations (a multiplication and an addition) requires the management of a sorted list. This list does not need to be sorted at each packet departure, because only the served flow may change its placement. Thus the required complexity for LSF is $O(log(M))$, M being the number of flows at the system. All possible improvements discussed in [Bensaou et al., 2001] (independence of counters, flow insertion while a packet is served) are also applicable.

2.4 Tunable LSF

Tunable LSF Algorithm For N batches,

- Initialization. Initialize counters and insert all flows into the first batch,

$$W_i := 0, \ batch_1 \leftarrow i, i = 1, \ldots, M$$

- Operation.

  1 Serve a flow j on the first batch (with any scheduling discipline, e.g. round robin)

Table 3. Example for T-LSF, N=2, PQ

Packet Served		a1	a2	a3	a4	b1	b2	c1	*shift*
W_A	0	1	2	3	7	7	7	7	3
W_B	0	0	0	0	0	2	4	4	0
W_C	0	0	0	0	0	0	0	4	0

2 Once departed packet from flow j, proceed to update W_j,

$$W_j = W_j + L_j/r_j$$

3 Assign j to a batch k, $k = 1 \ldots N$,

$$(k-1) \cdot \frac{K_p}{N-1} \leq W_i < k \cdot \frac{K_p}{N-1} \Rightarrow batch_k \leftarrow i$$

4 Goto (1) until $batch_1$ becomes empty ($i \notin batch_1, \forall i, i = 1, .., M$).

5 Proceed to *normalize* the $\{W_i\}$,

$$W_i := W_i - \frac{K_p}{N-1}, i = 1, \ldots, M$$

6 Reassign flows to batches (shift from $batch_n$ to $batch_{n-1}$, $n = 1, \ldots, N$)

7 Goto (1)

- Flow arrival. When a new flow k arrives to the system, its counter is initialized to the maximum value of W_i, and it is placed on $batch_N$.

$$W_k := max \{W_i\} , \ batch_N \leftarrow k$$

An example of T-LSF operation with the situation of Fig. 1 with $N = 2$ it is shown on Table 3. A "priority queuing" discipline is considered inside the batches. When a counter W_i exceeds the maximum packet size ($K_p = 4$) the flow is moved to the second batch (packets $a4$, $b2$ and $c1$ for each flow). After first batch is emptied (departure of $c1$), all counters are shifted K_p. For this case, the maximum difference between any two counters is less than twice K_p.

2.5 Fairness Analysis of T-LSF

LSF bounds the maximum difference between any two counters W_i and W_j by K_p. From this quantity is obtained the fairness index FI, twice this value. Tunable LSF bounds that difference by twice the value. Following the same steps of Section 2.2, the fairness index (which is a function of N, the number of batches) is

$$FI(N) = 2 \cdot K_p \cdot \left(1 + \frac{1}{N-1}\right)$$

2.6   Complexity

Complexity of LSF is related to the number of elements of a list. By modifying this number, more unfairness is allowed in order to decrease computational burden. This way, in situations where $M \gg 1$ and computational burden imposes an appreciable bottleneck, choosing a $N \ll M$ will decrement the complexity at the expense of losing fairness. It should be noted that with $M = N$, T-LSF performs *worse* than LSF, because the comparisons are made with thresholds that need not to coincide with the counter values $\{W_i\}$.

3.   Conclusions and Future Work

In this paper we proposed a new family of fair scheduling algorithms, with the main newness of a tunable trade-off between fairness and complexity. No fixed size nor any other additional hypothesis is assumed. For the most complex case the fairness is close to the one obtained by similar complexity algorithms. The flexibility of our algorithm allows the establishment of a trade off between complexity and fairness once real working conditions are known. We believe this is a new path of research in fair queuing. On future work we will continue analyzing the features of T-LSF, providing bounds for delay. We will also provide a full comparison between it and the other algorithms, both by theoretical analysis and simulation.

Acknowledgments

This work has been partly supported by the European Union under the e-Photon/ONe Project (FP6-001933) and by the Spanish Research Action CI-CYT CAPITAL (MEC, TEC2004-05622-C04-03/TCM). We also thank the reviewers of this paper for their valuable comments.

Appendix: Proof of Part (1) of Lemma 6

Taking into account that $i, j \in B(t_{1-}, t_{2+})$, and the difference is bounded for any pair of *discretized* t_k. We consider all possible cases (for ease of notation, we omit the $r_{i,j}$ in the demonstration):

- Neither i nor j transmitted at t_{1-} or t_{2-}. So $S_{i,j}(t_1, t_2) = S_{i,j}(t_{1-}, t_{2+})$ which is bounded by Lemma 6.

- Only flow i transmits at t_{1-} but not at t_{2-}. Then $S_i(t_{1+}, t_2) < S_i(t_1, t_2) < S_i(t_{1-}, t_2)$. Because $S_j(t_{1+}, t_2) = S_j(t_1, t_2) = S_j(t_{1-}, t_2)$, we have $|S_i(t_{1-}, t_2) - S_j(t_1, t_2)| \leq$

K_p and $|S_i(t_{1+}, t_2) - S_j(t_1, t_2)| \leq K_p$, thus we conclude $|S_i(t_1, t_2) - S_j(t_1, t_2)| \leq K_p$.

- Only flow i transmits at t_{2-} but not at t_1. The demonstration is analogous to the previous case.

- Flow i transmits at both t_{1-} and t_{2-}. The demonstration is again analogous, starting with $S_i(t_{1+}, t_{2-}) < S_i(t_1, t_2) < S_i(t_{1-}, t_{2+})$.

- Flow i transmits at t_{1-} and flow j transmits t_{2-}. We consider two cases:

  - Suppose $S_i(t_1, t_2) > S_j(t_1, t_2)$. Then $S_i(t_1, t_2) - S_j(t_1, t_2) < S_i(t_1, t_{2-}) - S_j(t_1, t_{2-}) < S_i(t_{1-}, t_{2-}) - S_j(t_{1-}, t_{2-}) < K_p$.
  - If $S_j(t_1, t_2) > S_i(t_1, t_2)$. Then $S_j(t_1, t_2) - S_i(t_1, t_2)$
    $< S_j(t_{1+}, t_2) - S_i(t_{1+}, t_2) < S_j(t_{1+}, t_{2+}) - S_i(t_{1+}, t_{2+}) < K_p$.

Notes

1. throughout the paper and in order to ease the analysis, we assume a minimum function with a proper tie-breaker
2. in case of ties, the priority is $A > B > C$
3. $min\{W_i\}(t_{k+1}) < min\{W_i\}(t_k)$ is not possible

References

Bennett, J. C. R. and Zhang, H. (1996). Wf2q: Worst-case fair weighted fair queueing. In *In Proc. IEEE INFOCOM 96, San Francisco, CA, Mar. 1996*.

Bensaou, B., Tsang, D.H.K., and Chan, King Tung (2001). Credit-based fair queueing (cbfq): a simple service-scheduling algorithm for packet-switched networks. In *IEEE/ACM Trans. Netw., Volume: 9, Issue: 5, Oct. 2001 Pages:591 - 604*.

Chaskar, Hemant M. and Madhow, Upamanyu (2003). Fair scheduling with tunable latency: a round-robin approach. *IEEE/ACM Trans. Netw.*, 11(4):592–601.

de Burgos, Juan (1995). *Calculo infinitesimal de una variable*. McGraw-Hill, Madrid.

Demers, A., Keshav, S., and Shenker, S. (1990). Analysis and simulation of a fair queueing algorithm. In *Journal of Internetworking Research and Experience, pages 3-26, October 1990. Also in Proceedings of ACM SIGCOMM89, pp 3-12*.

Golestani, S. (1994). A self-clocked fair queueing scheme for broadband applications. In *Proceedings of IEEE INFOCOM 94, pages 636-646, Toronto, CA, June 1994*.

Hahne, E. (1986). Round robin scheduling for fair flow control. In *Ph.D. thesis, Dept. Elect. Eng. And Comput. Sci., M.I.T., Dec. 1986*.

Parekh, Abhay K. and Gallager, Robert G. (1993). A generalized processor sharing approach to flow control in integrated services networks: the single-node case. *IEEE/ACM Trans. Netw.*, 1(3):344–357.

Shreedhar, M. and Varghese, George (1995). Efficient fair queueing using deficit round robin. In *Proceedings of the conference on Applications, technologies, architectures, and protocols for computer communication*, pages 231–242. ACM Press.

Zhang, L. (1990). Virtual clock: a new traffic control algorithm for packet switching networks. In *Proceedings of the ACM symposium on Communications architectures & protocols*, pages 19–29. ACM Press.

Zhou, Y. and Sethu, H. (2002). On the relationship between absolute and relative fairness bounds. In *IEEE Comm. Letters, vol. 6, no. 1, pp. 37–39, Jan. 2002*.

PART TWO

ROUTING

DYNAMIC ROUTING IN QOS-AWARE TRAFFIC ENGINEERED NETWORKS

Stefano Avallone,[1] Fernando Kuipers,[2] Giorgio Ventre,[1] and Piet Van Mieghem[2]

[1] *COMICS Lab*
Dipartimento di Informatica e Sistemistica
Università di Napoli Federico II
Via Claudio 21, 80125 Napoli, Italy
{stavallo, giorgio}@unina.it

[2] *Network Architectures and Services*
Faculty of Electrical Engineering, Mathematics and Computer Science
Delft University of Technology
P.O. Box 5031, 2600 GA Delft, The Netherlands
{F.A.Kuipers, P.VanMieghem}@ewi.tudelft.nl

Abstract   We propose a proper length function for an existing QoS routing algorithm (SAMCRA) that attempts to optimize network utilization while still offering QoS guarantees. This paper presents a comparison between several proposed algorithms via simulation studies. The simulations show that SAMCRA with a proper length performs similarly or even better than the best among the other algorithms and it has a fast running time.

Keywords: QoS routing, Traffic Engineering, network dynamics

1.   Introduction

The Internet research community is making a great effort in order to define efficient network management and control functions. The driving forces behind this effort are new applications with specific performance requirements. For instance, real-time applications need delay and jitter guarantees, while a financial transaction must have low or virtually no packet loss. By offering service differentiation combined with the maximization of throughput, ISPs can increase their revenues. The challenge is therefore to define a routing algorithm which meets the users' requirements and which optimizes network resources.

Many algorithms [Kuipers et al., 2002] have been proposed to find the shortest path subject to multiple constraints. This problem, called MCOP (Multi-

Constrained Optimal Path), is NP-complete. Therefore, although there exist exact algorithms such as SAMCRA [Van Mieghem and Kuipers, 2004], mainly heuristics have been proposed for this problem. Such algorithms usually do not address the maximization of the throughput and the number of admitted calls. Instead, optimizing these parameters is the goal of another class of algorithms, denoted as traffic engineering algorithms. While focused on the behaviour in a dynamic scenario, most of them do not take into account additive QoS constraints and only consider bandwidth.

In this paper we present a routing scheme that aims at maximizing throughput (or minimizing blocking), while satisfying the users' QoS requirements. It is our goal to combine these two objectives as efficiently as possible. We propose to use SAMCRA [Van Mieghem and Kuipers, 2004] with a special path length definition that guarantees the QoS constraints and accounts for the traffic engineering objectives. For clarity, we name this variant SAMCRA-B.

The performance of SAMCRA-B and several other algorithms is evaluated through simulations. All the considered algorithms do not make use of any a-priori knowledge about either predicted traffic or future demands. In the literature, such algorithms are denoted as online. We assume the knowledge of quasi-static information such as the network topology and the set of ingress-egress nodes of the network. The only dynamic information is the residual bandwidth (i.e. the portion of the link capacity not yet reserved) of each link in the network.

This paper is structured as follows. In Section 2 we give a formal definition of the considered routing problem. Some solutions for routing bandwidth-guaranteed paths are discussed in Section 3. Section 4 overviews SAMCRA and the choice of a proper length function. The performance studies are shown in Section 5. Section 6 concludes our work.

2.   Problem Statement

The network is modelled as a graph $G(N, E)$, where N is the set of nodes and E is the set of links. With a slight abuse of notation we will also denote by N and E, respectively, the number of nodes and the number of links. Each link $l \in E$ is assigned an $(m + 1)$-dimensional QoS link weight vector $\vec{w}(l) = [w_0(l), w_1(l), \ldots w_m(l)]$, where $w_0(l)$ is the available bandwidth on link l and the other components are the values of m additive QoS measures. Additionally, the capacity of a link l is denoted by $C(l)$.

A flow request is defined by a triple $(s, d, \vec{Q})$, where s is the source node, d is the destination node and $\vec{Q} = [Q_0, Q_1, \ldots Q_m]$ is a vector representing its QoS requirements. Specifically, Q_0 is the requested bandwidth while the other components are constraints on the values of the additive QoS measures along the path. Even though minimum (maximum) QoS constraints can be easily treated by omitting all links which do not satisfy the requirement, we explicitly consider available bandwidth due to its central role played in resource optimization strategies. Multiplicative QoS measures are disregarded because, if we assume independent measures over the links, we can transform them into additive QoS measures by taking the logarithm [Van Mieghem and Kuipers, 2004].

When a flow request arrives, the routing algorithm searches for a feasible path P that obeys:

$$\begin{cases} w_0(P) \overset{def}{=} \min_{l \in P} w_0(l) \geq Q_0 \\ w_i(P) \overset{def}{=} \sum_{l \in P} w_i(l) \leq Q_i, \quad \forall i = 1, \ldots m \end{cases}$$

In case no feasible path is found, the request is rejected. In presence of multiple feasible paths, the algorithm chooses the one which is thought to optimize network utilization. Typically, a path length function is defined and the feasible path with the smallest length is selected.

2.1   Discussion on QoS link weights

This subsection discusses the setting of QoS link weights $(\vec{w}(l))$ in a dynamic scenario. The guideline is the fulfillment of the QoS requirements of the flows. It is safe to state that the link weight associated with the available bandwidth should be as close as possible to the current bandwidth availability. As far as additive link weights, a path P returned by an exact algorithm is such that $\sum_{l \in P} w_i(l) \leq Q_i$, $i = 1, \ldots m$. But, the QoS requirements of a flow are satisfied if the *perceived* QoS is within the constraints, i.e. $\sum_{l \in P} q_i(l) \leq Q_i$, $i = 1, \ldots m$, where $q_i(l)$ is the value of the i-th QoS measure experienced crossing link l.

Assume to set the additive QoS link weights $(w_i(l))$ equal to the current experienced values (i.e. $q_i(l)$). Hence $\sum_{l \in P} q_i(l) = \sum_{l \in P} w_i(l) \leq Q_i$ and the QoS constraints are met. But, as a consequence of routing new flows on links of P, the actual QoS values $q_i(l)$ deteriorate and therefore the QoS granted to already admitted flows may not be preserved. Instead, we assume that the QoS link weights are constant and independent of the current link status $(q_i(l))$. Their value is an upper bound to the actual QoS value, in the sense that if the allocated bandwidth is less than the link capacity, then the QoS values experienced by packets crossing the link do not exceed the QoS weights. This assures that $\sum_{l \in P} q_i(l) \leq \sum_{l \in P} w_i(l) \leq Q_i, i = 1, ..., m$, i.e. the additive QoS constraints will be satisfied even after new flows are routed.

3.   Existing Traffic Engineering Algorithms

Among the earliest proposed algorithms, widest-shortest path [Guerin et al., 1997] (labeled as \WSP(MinHop)"throughout this paper) selects the path with the minimum hop count among all paths having sufficient residual bandwidth. If there are several such paths, the one with the maximum residual bandwidth is selected.

Most recently proposed algorithms are inspired by the work of Kar, Kodialam and Lakshman [Kar et al., 2000]. They presented an online routing algorithm (MIRA) based on the concept of minimum interference. The amount of interference on a particular source-destination pair (s, d) due to routing a flow between some other source-destination pair is defined as the decrease in the maxflow between s and d. The maxflow [Ahuja et al., 1993] value is an upper bound on the total amount of bandwidth that can be routed between two edge nodes. The minimum interference path between a particular source-destination pair is the path which maximizes the minimum maxflow between all other source-destination pairs. The idea is that a new request must follow a path that does not \interfere excessively" with a route that may be critical to satisfy a future demand. The problem of finding the minimum interference path is proved to be NP-hard. Therefore, Kar et al. [Kar et al., 2000] proposed to determine appropriate link costs, prune links with insufficient available bandwidth and compute the shortest path in the pruned topology.

Wang et al. [Wang et al., 2002] proposed a different definition for link costs in MIRA. We denote this variant of MIRA as "NewMIRA". The performance evaluation in [Wang et al., 2002] shows that, in a dynamic scenario, NewMIRA outperforms MIRA.

Banerjee and Sidhu [Banerjee and Sidhu, 2002] proposed two algorithms: TE-B, which takes into account only a bandwidth requirement, and TE-DB, which considers also a delay constraint. The authors introduced three objectives for traffic engineering: (a) reducing the blocking of flows, (b) minimizing network cost and (c) distributing network load. This formulation has three objective functions (plus the delay constraint in the case of TE-DB) and is proved to be NP-complete [Banerjee and Sidhu, 2002]. Banerjee and Sidhu presented another formulation in which objective functions (a) and (b) are transformed into constraints. Both TE-B and TE-DB use TAMCRA [De Neve and Van Mieghem, 2000], the predecessor of SAMCRA [Van Mieghem and Kuipers, 2004], to find a set of k paths satisfying the set of constraints and then select the one with the shortest length according to (c).

Iliadis and Bauer [Iliadis and Bauer, 2002] introduced a new class of routing algorithms, called SMIRA (simple minimum-interference routing algorithms). These algorithms evaluate the interference on a source-destination pair by means of a k-shortest-path-like computation instead of a maxflow computation. The set of k paths between a source-destina-tion pair (s, d) is determined by first computing the widest-shortest path [Guerin et al., 1997] between s and d. Then, all the links along this path with a residual bandwidth equal to the bottleneck bandwidth of the path are pruned. The second path is the widest-shortest path in the pruned topology. This procedure is repeated until either k paths are found or no more paths are available. The cost of links belonging to the set of k paths is increased proportionally to the weight of the path and the ratio of bottleneck bandwidth to residual bandwidth. Iliadis and Bauer [Iliadis and Bauer, 2002] proposed two algorithms, MI-BLA and MI-PA. The simulations in [Iliadis and Bauer, 2002] show that MI-PA outperforms MI-BLA.

4. SAMCRA

To guarantee QoS constraints and optimize network resource usage, we decided to use SAMCRA [Van Mieghem and Kuipers, 2004] with a new path length function and to study its behaviour in a dynamic scenario. First, we briefly review the basic concepts on which SAMCRA relies. The length of a path P proposed in [Van Mieghem and Kuipers, 2004] is a non-linear function of the m additive QoS measures it considers:

$$L(P) = \max_{1 \leq i \leq m} \frac{w_i(P)}{Q_i} \tag{1}$$

so that path P satisfies the constraints when $L(P) \leq 1$. An important corollary of a non-linear path length is that the subsections of shortest paths in multiple dimensions are not necessarily shortest paths. This necessitates a k-shortest path approach, which is essentially Dijkstra's algorithm that does not stop when the destination is reached, but continues until the destination has been reached k times. Not all sub-paths are stored, but an efficient distinction based on non-dominance is made: a (sub)-path P_1 is dominated by a (sub)-path P_2 if $w_i(P_2) \leq w_i(P_1)$ for $i = 1, ..., m$, with an inequality for at least one link weight component i. SAMCRA only considers non-dominated (sub)-paths.

We refer for more details on the above concepts, possible improvements and an implementation of the algorithm to [Van Mieghem and Kuipers, 2004]. Here, we explain the above concepts through a simple example. Like Dijkstra's algorithm, SAMCRA starts from the source node and explores the neighboring nodes while moving toward the destination node. Unlike Dijkstra, SAMCRA may have to store more than only the shortest sub-path for each visited node. To explain this point, consider the simple network of Figure 1. The vector $\vec{w}(l) = [w_0(l), \ldots w_3(l)]$ of QoS link weights is shown around each link. SAMCRA does not consider the available bandwidth constraint, but it suffices to prune from the network graph all the links with insufficient available bandwidth and run the algorithm on the reduced graph. Suppose SAMCRA has to route a flow from A to G subject to the QoS constraint vector $Q = [5, 14, 11, 22]$. Three sub-paths are available from the source node A to the intermediate node E. The lengths of those sub-paths are:

$$L(P_{ABE}) = \max \quad \frac{4+3}{14}, \frac{1+7}{11}, \frac{7+1}{22} = 0.73$$

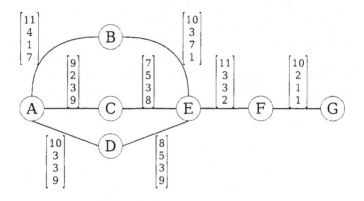

Figure 1. Simple network to illustrate SAMCRA's principles

$$L(P_{ACE}) = \max \left\{ \frac{2+5}{14}, \frac{3+3}{11}, \frac{9+8}{22} \right\} = 0.77$$

$$L(P_{ADE}) = \max \left\{ \frac{3+5}{14}, \frac{3+3}{11}, \frac{9+9}{22} \right\} = 0.82 .$$

The lengths of their corresponding paths from A to G are:

$$L(P_{ABEFG}) = \max \left\{ \frac{12}{14}, \frac{12}{11}, \frac{11}{22} \right\} = 1.09$$

$$L(P_{ACEFG}) = \max \left\{ \frac{12}{14}, \frac{10}{11}, \frac{20}{22} \right\} = 0.91$$

$$L(P_{ADEFG}) = \max \left\{ \frac{13}{14}, \frac{10}{11}, \frac{21}{22} \right\} = 0.95 .$$

P_{ABE}, is the shortest sub-path, but it leads to a non-feasible path, since $L(P_{ABEFG}) > 1$. If the algorithm stores just the shortest sub-path in the intermediate nodes, it erroneously concludes that a feasible path does not exist (the two other paths are feasible). In order to reduce complexity (while still returning the exact solution), SAMCRA does not store all the sub-paths but discards the dominated ones. In the example, sub-path P_{ADE} is dominated by P_{ACE} since $w_i(P_{ACE}) \leq w_i(P_{ADE})$ for $i = 1, 2, 3$. Given (1) as path length function and non-negative QoS link weights, sub-path P_{ADE} can be safely discarded.

As discussed in [Van Mieghem and Kuipers, 2004] SAMCRA can be used with any path length function, but the definition (1) is a function of the QoS link weights $(w_i(l), i = 1, \ldots m)$ and of the QoS constraints $(Q_i, i = 1, \ldots m)$. As discussed in Section 2.1, static QoS link weights should be considered. Thus, if link weights are load-independent, the path length function (1) does not take into account network utilization. We expect that a better dynamic behavior can be achieved by letting the path length be a function of dynamic information such as the available bandwidth. We assume:

$$L(P) = \sum_{l \in P} c(l) \tag{2}$$

where $c(l)$ is a link cost that depends on dynamic information related to link l. For clarity we name this variant SAMCRA-B. It selects the shortest path according to (2) among those satisfying the QoS constraints. Using such a path length function requires to add one more parameter to the dominance check. SAMCRA-B can discard a sub-path P_1 when there exists a sub-path P_2 such that $w_i(P_2) \leq w_i(P_1)$ for $i = 1, \ldots m$ and $L(P_2) \leq L(P_1)$. To clarify why, consider again the example shown in Figure 1 and compute the lengths (according to (2)) of the three sub-paths from A to E and the corresponding paths from A to G using, for instance, $c(l) = \frac{1}{w_0(l)}$, i.e. the cost of a link is the reciprocal of the available bandwidth:

$$L(P_{ABE}) = \frac{1}{11} + \frac{1}{10} = 0.19$$

$$L(P_{ACE}) = \frac{1}{9} + \frac{1}{7} = 0.25$$

$$L(P_{ADE}) = \frac{1}{10} + \frac{1}{8} = 0.23$$

The lengths of their corresponding paths from A to G are:

$$L(P_{ABEFG}) = \frac{1}{11} + \frac{1}{10} + \frac{1}{11} + \frac{1}{10} = 0.38$$

$$L(P_{ACEFG}) = \frac{1}{9} + \frac{1}{7} + \frac{1}{11} + \frac{1}{10} = 0.44$$

$$L(P_{ADEFG}) = \frac{1}{10} + \frac{1}{8} + \frac{1}{11} + \frac{1}{10} = 0.42$$

P_{ABE} is the shortest sub-path but leads to path P_{ABEFG}, which is not feasible because $w_2(P_{ABEFG}) > Q_2$. Thus, the algorithm cannot store just the shortest sub-path in each intermediate node. On the other hand, disregarding the condition on the length of the sub-paths would cause sub-path P_{ADE}, which leads to the shortest feasible path P_{ADEFG}, to be discarded in favour of P_{ACE}. Instead, by also comparing path lengths it is still possible to achieve a correct search space reduction and return the shortest path according to (2) within the constraints. Indeed, sub-path P_{ADE} is not dominated by P_{ACE} because $L(P_{ACE}) > L(P_{ADE})$ and therefore it is not discarded.

The worst-case complexity of SAMCRA is $O(kN\log(kN)+k^2mE)$, where k is the maximum amount of simultaneously stored paths. In [Van Mieghem and Kuipers, 2004], it is shown that if the QoS link weights $w_i(l)$ and the QoS constraints Q_i are integers, SAMCRA has a pseudo-polynomial-time complexity. The complexity of SAMCRA-B is that of SAMCRA, apart from a larger value of k because SAMCRA-B has to check one more condition and therefore less paths can be discarded.

4.1   Link cost function

This section illustrates the link cost function we introduce to improve the dynamic behavior of SAMCRA-B with respect to SAMCRA. The link cost $c(l)$ is defined as a function γ of the link utilization $\rho = \frac{C(l) - w_0(l)}{C(l)}$ (ratio of the reserved bandwidth to the total capacity):

$$\gamma(\rho) = \begin{cases} \dfrac{\gamma(\Delta) - 1}{\Delta}\rho + 1 & \text{if } \rho \leqslant \Delta \\[2ex] \gamma(\Delta)\dfrac{1 - \Delta}{1 - \rho} & \text{otherwise} \end{cases} \qquad (3)$$

The function $\gamma(\rho)$, depicted in Fig. 2, depends on two design parameters, Δ

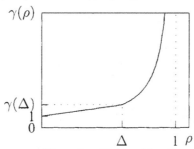

Figure 2.   Link cost function

and $\gamma(\Delta)$. The rationale behind such proposal is that a minimum-hop path approach is preferable when network load is low, since it prevents longer paths from consuming more resources. On the other hand, when network load is high, it is preferable to use the path with the maximum available bandwidth. Consuming all the available bandwidth on some links could cause future requests to be blocked. Such a twofold behavior may be achieved by appropriately setting each link cost depending on its resource occupation. The link cost function we propose is divided in two segments whose junction takes place in $(\Delta, \gamma(\Delta))$. For values of the link utilization ρ less than Δ, the link cost grows linearly. As soon as ρ becomes greater than Δ, the link cost tends to infinity as ρ approaches 1. With such a function, link costs are only slightly differing for low traffic loads. Low slope values of the linear segment let the routing algorithm behave similarly to the minimum-hop path routing. Instead, small load variations reflect in substantial link cost differences as soon as the load on the link increases beyond a specified threshold Δ. In this way, links having more available bandwidth are highly preferable.

Table 1.   Random variables used to specify network flows

Name	Description
IntArriv	Inter-arrival time between two successive flow requests
Source	Source node
Dest	Destination node
FlowDur	Flow duration
Bwd	Requested bandwidth
QoS$_i$	i-th additive QoS constraint

The values assigned to Δ and $\gamma(\Delta)$ determine the relative importance of the two approaches. We expect that their "optimal" values are dependent on the network topology and the traffic load. As an attempt, we have used $\Delta = 0.6$ and $\gamma(\Delta) = 1.5$ for the simulations shown in the next section. From now on, we will implicitly consider (3) as the link cost function of SAMCRA-B.

5.   Performance Studies

The performance studies of this section aim to compare the algorithms based on the minimum interference concept (New MIRA, TE-DB, MI-PA) to SAM-CRA and SAMCRA-B and to evaluate the possible gain achieved by using the new path length function (3). The experiments were carried out on several topologies generated by BRITE [Medina et al., 2000]. We used two router-level models, Barabasi-Albert and Waxman. All the topologies have 100 nodes and a different number of links per new node. For each topology, 10 nodes are randomly chosen to act as edge routers, the entry and exit points for the network traffic. The capacity of the links is uniformly distributed between 100 and 1024 units. We considered two additive QoS constraints ($m = 2$), the first uniformly distributed between 3 and 8 units, while the second ($w_2(l)$) uniformly distributed between 4 and 9 units. All links are symmetric, with respect to both capacity and QoS link weights.

We have developed a flow-level simulatorto analyze and compare the performance of different routing algorithms in a dynamic scenario. Our simulator makes use of several random variables to specify the characteristics of network flows (Table 1). For all the presented simulations, source and destination nodes are chosen uniformly among the set of edge nodes. We studied the performance of the routing algorithms in the generated topologies under different loads. Each test was repeated 20 times with different seeds for the random variables. For each of these 20 iterations, the algorithms under evaluation faced the same set of flow requests. Each iteration involved the generation of 120000 flows. The first 20000 were not considered in our analysis, as they represent a warm-up period needed by the network in order to reach a steady state regime.

For each iteration we computed the call blocking rate (CBR) and the bandwidth blocking rate (BBR) achieved by each algorithm:

$$CBR = \frac{\text{number of rejected flows}}{\text{total number of flows}} \qquad BBR = \frac{\sum_{\text{rejected flows}} \text{requested bandwidth}}{\sum_{\text{all the flows}} \text{requested bandwidth}} \ .$$

We also computed the throughput after the processing of each new flow request as the sum of the bandwidth requested by the flows crossing the network at that time. In order to get a smooth throughput curve, we first computed the mean over each window of 5000 throughput samples for each iteration and then the average of the corresponding values obtained from the 20 iterations. Finally, we measured the average processor time spent by each algorithm to select a path.

5.1   Large QoS constraints

The purpose of this subsection is to compare all the algorithms from the viewpoint of resource optimization. Since some of them select a path disregarding additive QoS constraints, we chose the QoS constraints large such that all algorithms can return a path that obeys these constraints. We have carried out a number of simulations using several topologies and different loads. In this subsection we illustrate three different tests that are representative of the different cases we observed. Table 2 shows how we set the random variables that specify a flow and the model and the number of links of the topologies we used. The results are presented in Figures 3a–3f. For each algorithm, we computed the mean μ and the standard deviation σ of the CBR from 20 iterations. Each bar shown in Figures 3a, 3c and 3e represents the interval $(\mu - \sigma, \mu + \sigma)$ related to the CBR achieved by each algorithm. In tests 1 and 2 (Figures 3a and 3c), SAMCRA-B achieves respectively a slightly larger CBR than the minimum and the minimum CBR. The CBR of New Mira and TE-DB is higher (around 30%) than the minimum, so as that of SAMCRA (below 10%). In test 3 (Figure 3e), instead, the minimum CBR is achieved by New MIRA, closely followed by TE-DB and SAMCRA-B. In all the simulations we have carried out SAMCRA-B achieves the minimum CBR or a CBR close to the minimum. The bandwidth blocking rate results (not shown here) are similar to CBR ones, except that the algorithms based on the maxflow concept (New MIRA and TE-DB) perform better in terms of BBR than CBR. This behaviour suggests that New MIRA and TE-DB accept those flows with larger bandwidth requirement.

While the CBR plot shows a mean value over all the iterations, the average throughput plot gives us information on the average behaviour during an iteration. Figures 3b, 3d and 3f indicate that the behavior of the algorithms from the

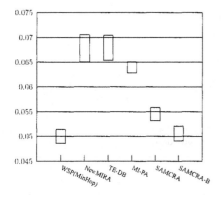

Figure 3a. Test 1 - Call blocking rate

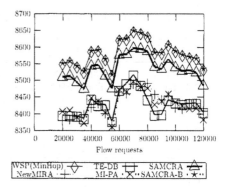

Figure 3b. Test 1 - Throughput

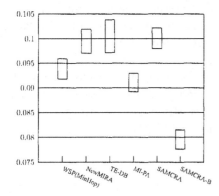

Figure 3c. Test 2 - Call blocking rate

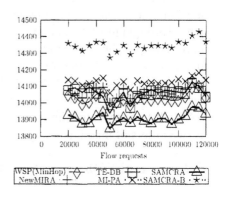

Figure 3d. Test 2 - Throughput

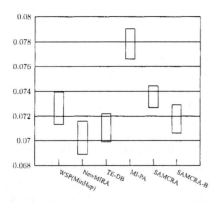

Figure 3e. Test 3 - Call blocking rate

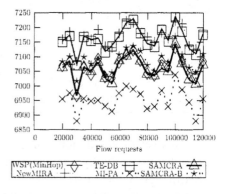

Figure 3f. Test 3 - Throughput

Table 2.   Scenario 1: flow and topology parameters

Test	1	2	3	
IntArriv	Exp(1/0.15)	Exp(1/0.11)	Exp(1/0.5)	
FlowDur	Exp(1/250)	Exp(1/320)	Exp(1/175)	
Bwd	U(1,10)	U(1,10)	U(1,10) with $P = 0.75$	U(80,100) with $P = 0.25$
QoS$_1$		U(792,800)		
QoS$_2$		U(891,900)		
Topology	Barabasi	Waxman	Barabasi	
Links	294	200	197	

viewpoint of throughput is similar to that in terms of CBR. In the sense that the algorithm achieving the minimum CBR also presents the maximum through-put. Throughput plots enable to ascertain that the difference in performance between algorithms is maintained during the whole iteration. The analysis of the average computation times reveals that SAMCRA approximately requires the same time ($\approx 5 \cdot 10^{-4}$s) as widest-shortest path. As expected, due to the less efficient search space reduction, SAMCRA-B ($\approx 9 \cdot 10^{-4}$s) is slower than SAMCRA. Instead, the time required by New MIRA and TE-DB ($\approx 6 \cdot 10^{-2}$s) is two orders of magnitude larger than that of SAMCRA.

5.2   Tight QoS constraints

Table 3.   Scenario 2: flow parameters

Test	4a	4b	4c	4d	4e
IntArriv			Exp(1/0.33)		
FlowDur			Exp(1/200)		
Bwd			U(1,10) with $P = 0.75$		
			U(80,100) with $P = 0.25$		
QoS$_1$	U(792,800)	U(30,50)	U(24,44)	U(22,42)	U(21,41)
QoS$_2$	U(891,900)	U(35,55)	U(29,49)	U(27,47)	U(26,46)

This set of simulations aims at comparing the algorithms which select a path taking explicitly into consideration additive QoS constraints: SAMCRA, SAMCRA-B and TE-DB. They are evaluated from the viewpoint of resource optimization as the QoS constraints become more stringent. We present five tests, which differ only in the QoS constraints (see Table 3). The topology is the same as that used in test 2. Figures 4a–4b shows the plots representing

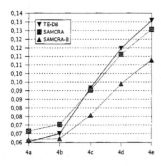

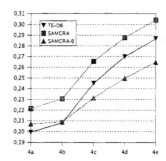

Figure 4a.   Call blocking rate   *Figure 4b.*   Bandwidth blocking rate

the average call and bandwidth blocking rates for each test. When QoS constraints are large enough (test 4a), the minimum CBR is achieved by TE-DB. But, as the QoS constraints become more stringent, SAMCRA-B performs the best. Moreover, the gap between the average CBR of SAMCRA-B and those of SAMCRA and TE-DB increases. This suggests that SAMCRA-B is less sensitive to the tightening of QoS constraints than SAMCRA and TE-DB are. Also, the CBR of SAMCRA is initially larger than that of TE-DB, but eventually it becomes smaller. This suggests that SAMCRA, too, is less sensitive to the tightening of QoS constraints than TE-DB. The same conclusions can be drawn from the viewpoint of BBR (Figure 4b). Figure 4b also confirms our insight regarding the fact that TE-DB performs better from the viewpoint of BBR than CBR. Finally, the path computation times are similar to those indicated in the previous section.

6.   Conclusions

We proposed a new path length function for SAMCRA and carried out simulation studies in order to compare SAMCRA-B to previous algorithms for dynamically routing requests having a bandwidth requirement and a number of constraints on additive QoS measures. Two scenarios have been analyzed, the first under loose QoS constraints and the other by the tightening of QoS constraints. For every test of the first scenario the call blocking rate of SAMCRA-B was the minimum or very close to the minimum. The simulations therefore revealed that the proposed path length function of SAMCRA-B (based on the current bandwidth availability) allows a considerable advantage over SAMCRA. The second scenario showed that SAMCRA-B performs better and better than the other algorithms (SAMCRA and TE-DB) when decreasing the QoS constraints. SAMCRA, too, reduces its gap from TE-DB as the QoS constraints become more stringent. If we also consider the analysis of path computation times, we can conclude that SAMCRA-B achieves the best performance at a low computational cost.

The scenarios covered by our simulations were necessarily limited and therefore the results only indicate a potential for SAMCRA with a properly chosen path length function. Further investigation is needed to confirm our claim.

Acknowledgments

This work has been partly supported by the European Union under the E-Next Project FP6-506869 and by the "Ministero dell'Istruzione, dell'Università e della Ricerca (MIUR)" in the framework of the FIRB Project "Middleware for advanced services over large-scale, wired-wireless distributed systems (WEB-MINDS)".

The research of Stefano Avallone is partly funded by the European Doctoral School of Advanced Topics in Networking (SATIN), the instrument employed by the E-Next Network of Excellence to invest in education of researchers for the European Research Area.

References

Ahuja, R.K., Magnanti, T.L., and Orlin, J.B. (1993). *Network Flows: Theory, Algorithms and Applications*. Englewood Cliffs, NJ: Prentice-Hall.

Banerjee, G. and Sidhu, D. (2002). Comparative analysis of path computation techniques for MPLS traffic engineering. *Computer Networks*, 40:149–165.

De Neve, H. and Van Mieghem, P. (2000). TAMCRA: A Tunable Accuracy Multiple Constraints Routing Algorithm. *Computer Communications*, 23:667–679.

Guerin, R., Williams, D., and Orda, A. (1997). QoS routing mechanisms and OSPF extensions. In *Proc. Globecom*.

Iliadis, I. and Bauer, D. (2002). A New Class of Online Minimum-Interference Routing Algorithms. *Networking 2002, LNCS 2345*, pages 959–971.

Kar, K., Kodialam, M., and Lakshman, T.V. (2000). Minimum Interference Routing of Bandwidth Guaranteed Tunnels with MPLS Traffic Engineering Applications. *IEEE Journal on Selected Areas in Communications*, 18(12):2566–2579.

Kuipers, F., Van Mieghem, P., Korkmaz, T., and Krunz, M. (2002). An overview of constraint-based path selection algorithms for QoS routing. *IEEE Communications Magazine*, 40(12):50–55.

Medina, A., Matta, I., and Byers, J. (2000). On the Origin of Power Laws in Internet Topology. *ACM Computer Communications Review*, 30(2).

Van Mieghem, P. and Kuipers, F.A. (2004). Concepts of Exact QoS Routing Algorithms. *IEEE ACM Transactions on Networking*, 12(5):851–864.

Wang, Bin, Su, Xu, and Chen, C.L.P. (2002). A New Bandwidth Guaranteed Routing Algorithm for MPLS Traffic Engineering. In *Proc. of IEEE International Conference on Communications, ICC 2002*.

IMPLEMENTATION OF AN IPV6 MULTIHOMING INGRESS FILTERING COMPATIBILITY MECHANISM USING AUTOMATIC TUNNELS

Carlos Barcenilla, Antonio Tapiador, David Fernández, Omar Walid and Tomás P. de Miguel
Department of Telematics Engineering, Telecom Engineering School (ETSIT), Technical University of Madrid (UPM), Madrid, Spain

Abstract: Nowadays, many organizations need to be multihomed in order to achieve fault tolerant Internet access. Unfortunately, the hierarchical nature of IPv6 addressing architecture poses some threats on multihoming. The IETF is designing a solution based on the discussion of several approaches to solve the problem. Ingress filters are part of the problem, so ingress filtering compatibility mechanisms are needed. This paper discusses the host-centric multihoming approach and describes an implementation of an ingress filtering compatibility mechanism based on automatic tunnels and anycast addresses. The implementation has proven to work properly, being easily developed and deployed.

Keywords: IPv6, multihoming, ingress filtering

1. INTRODUCTION

Internet connectivity has a strategic importance for a growing number of organizations nowadays. Their activity heavily depends on the reliability of their Internet connections, as an important part of their mission-critical processes are based on distributed applications running over Internet. In some cases, it is not exaggerated to state that the organization activity completely stops whenever its Internet connection goes down.

For that reason, reliability is an important requirement in organization's demands to Internet Service Providers (ISP). Apart from the use of highly reliable equipment (carrier class) and redundancy in ISP services, organizations try to improve the reliability of their Internet connectivity by getting service from two or more ISPs.

A site connected to Internet through two or more ISPs is commonly known as a *multihomed site*. Multihoming allows achieving fault tolerance: if the main connection goes down, the routing system reacts and redirects the traffic though one of the alternative connections. Besides, multihoming allows an organization to define its own *traffic engineering* policies, ranging from simple load balancing strategies to more complex approaches.

However, as implemented today, the advantages that multihoming presents for the organizations are transformed in drawbacks when they are observed from the Internet global routing system point of view. Multihoming has an important impact on the size of the global BGP routing tables (each multihomed site contributes with at least one prefix), increasing the global routing instability, as stated in several studies [Bu et al., 2002].

Many proposals have been made to address the multihoming problem in IPv6, but there is little work on implementation and validation of the feasibility of the proposals. The aim of this work was to implement and test one of the proposals we considered interesting. Therefore, we designed an implementation of an ingress filtering compatibility mechanism based on automatic tunnels and anycast addresses.

The article is organized as follows. Section 2 introduces the multihoming problem in IPv6 and the solutions proposed so far. Section 3 presents the basis of the host-centric multihoming approach, detailing the source and destination address selection procedures. Later, Section 4 describes the automatic tunneling proposal based on dynamic routing protocols and anycast addresses. Section 5 provides details about how we implemented and tested the solution over Linux and FreeBSD operating systems. Finally, Section 6 summarizes the main conclusions of the paper.

2.   MULTIHOMING IN IPV6

As already mentioned, the goal of multihoming is to provide solutions for the management of multiple Internet connections for a site, in order to achieve fault tolerance and support load balancing. Multihoming in IPv4 is traditionally achieved by means of the use of *provider independent* (PI) address ranges announced through all ISP connections of a multihomed site. For example, if an organization is multihomed to ISPs A and B (Fig. 1), their PI address prefixes are announced to A and B. In this way, in case of a failure in ISP A, external hosts may still connect to the multihomed site through ISP B, being the BGP interdomain routing responsible to react and provide failure tolerance.

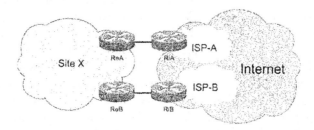

Figure 1. General multihoming scenario.

This technique can also be applied using *provider aggregatable* (PA) addressing. In this case, the site address prefix is assigned by one of the providers, and the other provider agrees to distribute it through its routing system.

In any case, although widely deployed, the use of this IPv4 multihoming technique raises important problems for the global Internet routing system, compromising its scalability.

On the other hand, IPv6, the new Internet network protocol designed by IETF, tries to solve the lack of addresses, widely increasing the address space for the next generation Internet. In addition, it provides multiple features and facilities, such as address auto-configuration, mobility, security or QoS capabilities. In order to improve the network scalability, the IPv6 routing architecture has been redesigned following a strongly hierarchical model. Address aggregation is the key design premise, requiring address delegation from providers to organizations.

Usually, organizations are supposed to be connected to the IPv6 network only in one point in the hierarchy, receiving only one address prefix from its provider. However, as stated before, an important number of organizations need two or more connection points to the network. For example, multinational organizations connected to providers in different countries or, as in the UPM case, university departments connected to production and experimental research networks. In this case, organizations inherit several IPv6 address prefixes, one from each connection.

Due to the strictly hierarchical nature of the IPv6 routing model, IPv4 multihoming solutions are not valid in IPv6 networks, as it is not possible to announce the prefix inherited from one provider through another ISP connection. That behavior would break the address aggregation scheme – 48-bit site prefixes typically assigned to organizations would be flooded into interdomain routing– and it would lead to unmanageable routing table sizes, especially in core routers (routers in the Internet core that do not have a default route in their routing tables), breaking the whole interdomain routing system. Therefore, in order to keep address aggregation, new solutions to multihoming scenarios are required for the IPv6 deployment.

An IETF working group, Multi6, [multi6] was formed to study the IPv6 multihoming problem and its proposed solutions. Its charter included studying multihoming common practices, defining multihoming goals and requirements, creating a multihoming functional architecture decomposition in IPv6, and defining architectural approaches to IPv6 multihoming solutions. This group has produced an RFC and several drafts, and it has recently been rechartered into a new IETF group, Shim6, which is trying to design a multihoming solution.

Many IPv6 multihoming solutions have been proposed [Tapiador et al., 2004][Dunmore, 2003] . Some of them may be complementary, as multihoming is a complex problem and its solution will probably come from the combination of some of them.

There are site-oriented solutions that propose a global solution to the entire multihomed organization as a whole [Hagino and Snyder, 2001]. On the other hand there are host centric solutions, which are focused in multi-addressed hosts. The most relevant work in this subject [Huitema, 2004] describes the multihoming problem from the host point of view.

Other solutions are based on:
• Network layer modifications, either implemented on the hosts, in the routers or both.
• Transport layer modifications.
• Addition of new layers.

Some of them, like MHAP   [Dunmore, 2003], have already been discarded. Solutions like LIN6 [Teraoka et al., 2003], MAST [Crocker, 2003] or HIP [Moskowitz et al., 2005] have been reviewed, and many of their ideas will be gathered in the multihoming Shim6 solution. This host centric approach will insert a new sub-layer (shim) inside the IP layer of the end systems. Packets traversing the network will use the multiple IPv6 available addresses at each host (so called locators) in order to establish new connections or maintain the existing ones after a network outage. But the shim layer will show steady addresses (ULIDs) to the upper layers. In that way, transport connections can survive locator changes, i.e. address changes. Maintaining state at both ends of the communication will be necessary.

To prevent address spoofing attacks, ISPs perform *ingress filtering* on packets leaving the site and entering the ISP's domain. Filters check that each packet's source address belongs to the prefix delegated to the site by the ISP. Packets not passing the check are dropped by the ISP's access router.

Among other issues, the Shim6 working group will have to work on solutions to avoid ISP ingress filters. These solutions for the ingress filtering problem are commonly called *ingress filtering compatibility mechanisms*.

The rest of this paper will deal with in the Host Centric multihoming proposal in a general manner, and with an ingress filtering compatibility mechanism we have implemented in a specific manner.

3. HOST CENTRIC MULTIHOMING

In *Host Centric Multihoming*, hosts choose the source and destination addresses of each packet with the aim of doing the best usage of available network resources. As it will be described later, address selection plays a key role in IPv6 multihoming due to the hierarchical nature of PA addressing and the presence of *ingress filters*.

3.1 Destination Address Selection

Before establishing a new communication, a host has to obtain the destination address to be used. Commonly, destination addresses are obtained from the DNS. DNS answers can contain multiple addresses for the same destination. But the DNS is not able to indicate which of these addresses is preferred to be used.

RFC 3484 [Draves, 2003] describes a destination address selection algorithm. While not very smart by default, this algorithm provides, at least, a way to avoid choosing the destination address randomly from the set obtained from the DNS.

To work smartly, this algorithm must be fed with policies. Policies can stem from the administrative policy of the site, and eventually be based on network state information.

Destination address selection influences the path packets will take in their way to the destination.

3.2 Source Address Selection

As multihomed hosts have several IPv6 addresses assigned, once the destination address is chosen, a source address selection algorithm must be performed.

The selected source address will be used as destination address for the reply traffic coming from the remote host. Thus, due to IPv6's hierarchical addressing architecture, the source address used in outgoing traffic determines the path the incoming traffic will follow.

As previously stated, ingress filters check that each packet's source address belongs to the prefix delegated to the site by the ISP. Packets not passing the check are dropped by the ISP's access router.

In order to avoid packets from being dropped by ingress filters, the routing system has to conduct the traffic to the proper *site-exit router*. This implies that the source address selection also determines the path of the outgoing traffic.

Given these considerations, host-centric multihoming has to deal with:
- Source address selection
- Ingress filtering compatibility mechanisms

There are many proposals for doing source address selection. RFC 3484 establishes a basic algorithm that defaults to the longest prefix match of the candidate source addresses and the destination address. To perform better selections, the algorithm introduces a policy table. However, as in the destination address selection case, this table has to be fed in order to be useful.

There are several ways to fill policy tables up; one of them[0] is a way to do it manually. However, to take full advantage of the policy table, entries should be added and deleted dynamically in reaction to network topology changes. A method for policy distribution from the ISP to the site-exit routers [Matsumoto et al., 2004] using an extension to DHCP for Policy Distribution [Troan and Droms, 2003] is proposed. From the site-exit routers to the hosts this approach proposes the usage of a new DHCPv6 option or an extension to the Router Advertisement message.

The NAROS [de Launois et al., 2003] approach establishes a protocol to ask a server which of the available source addresses is the best for a given destination. The NAROS server, based on administrative policies and complete routing information (e.g. obtained via BGP) can select the best address.

Another problem to solve regarding address selection is how to choose addresses in the presence of network failures such as access link problems or routing problems inside the ISP's network. Possible solutions to this kind of problems are discussed in *Host-Centric IPv6 multihoming* [Huitema, 2004].

There are also several proposals for ingress filtering compatibility mechanisms, which address different scenarios. The simplest mechanism is to relax source address filters to allow traffic sourced from any of the site's prefixes. Perhaps the best long term solution is to use a routing protocol that supports *Source Address Dependent* (SAD) routing [Bagnulo et al., 2004].

Standard routing protocols base their routing decisions on the inspection of the destination address; on the other hand, SAD routing protocols take into account both the source and destination addresses. In this way, the routing protocol itself can convey the packets to the correct site-exit routers, circumventing the ingress filters.

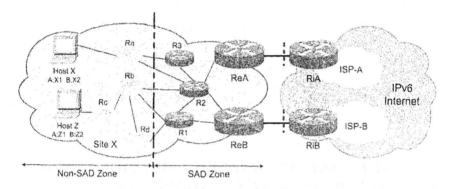

Figure 2. A domain with a mixed SAD and non-SAD routing. Once packets enter the SAD zone, they are conducted towards the proper site-exit router.

In the meantime, other transition mechanisms can be used. A site could have a mix of SAD and non-SAD routing capable routers. The site would be separated into two routing domains, one with SAD routing and the other with non-SAD (i.e. destination based) routing. SAD routing domain has to include at least all the exit routers and must be a connected domain. Non-SAD routing domain does not require routers to be connected, and in fact, it is possible to have several non-SAD routing domains. Once a packet enters the SAD routing domain, it is routed to the correct site-exit router (See Fig. 2).

If this mix is not possible, a full mesh of tunnels between exit routers can be implemented. If a packet arrives to a wrong exit router, it will be tunneled to the correct exit router as depicted in Fig. 3. As usual, a full mesh does not scale well if the number of routers is big and the configuration is done manually.

To handle the burden of tunnel creation there is a proposed solution[0] that detects exit routers and creates tunnels automatically. Each site-exit router is assigned a special anycast address called *site-exit anycast*. These addresses are derived from the site prefixes and routes to them are disseminated by the site's interior routing protocol (IGP). Exit routers can this way discover their peers and associated prefixes.

This method, which is the main topic of the present article, will be described in detail in the next section.

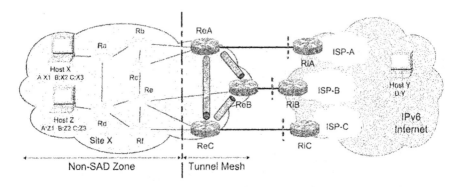

Figure 3. A domain with a full mesh of tunnels. If a packet arrives to an incorrect site-exit router, it is tunneled to the proper site-exit router.

4.   AUTOMATIC TUNNELING SOLUTION BASED ON IGP AND ANYCAST ADDRESSES

There are multiple multihoming scenarios depending on the organization's size. We may have big organizations with headquarters around the world, several ISPs servicing in each country and VPNs linking the various country networks. On the other side, we may have a multihomed laptop with wireless LAN and GPRS access.

We focus our work on site multihoming solutions. Thus, we are talking about an organization connected to several ISPs as a whole, and not single laptops connected to casual points.

Big organizations have enough negotiating power to ask the ISPs to relax ingress filters, but medium and small sized organizations don't. The solution discussed in this paper is intended for medium and small sized sites.

The solution solves scenarios as presented in Fig. 4. A site is connected to several ISPs. ISPs run ingress filters on their access routers. In addition, the site's IGP does not perform SAD routing. Therefore, packets won't always arrive to the right exit router for the source address being used.

For instance, if the multihomed *Host X* uses the ISP-C's source address and packets are routed through ISP-A, packets will be dropped by ISP-A's ingress filters.

So a mechanism for ingress filtering compatibility is needed (i.e. a mechanism that reconciles destination based routing with ingress filters). The solution introduced here is based on the automatic tunneling with the *site-exit anycast addresses* mechanism mentioned earlier.

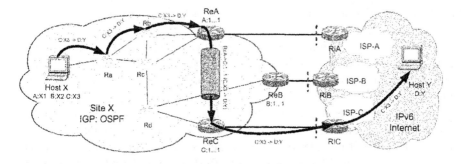

Figure 4. Scenario to be solved by the implementation. Site X is multihomed to three ISPs. If packets from Host X to Host Y reach ReA then they must be tunneled to ReC .

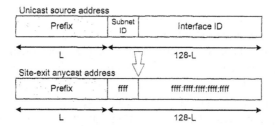

Figure 5. Site-exit anycast addresses can be obtained given a unicast address.

A *site-exit anycast address* is built by appending an "all 1" suffix to a prefix allocated to the site. If a prefix has a length of L, the last 128-L bits of the prefix will be set to 1 (see Fig. 5).

In this proposal, site-exit routers are assigned site-exit anycast addresses for the site prefixes for which they act as exit. Then, host routes generated from anycast addresses are injected into the IGP and disseminated throughout the site. So every router in the domain will know about the existence of these anycast host routes.

In the example shown in Fig. 4, exit router ReC is assigned the site-exit anycast address corresponding to prefix C (denoted as C:1...1 for simplicity). Supposing Site X is running the Open Shortest Path First (OSPF) IGP, a host route for C:1...1 will be injected into OSPF. The same happens with routers ReA and ReB, which are assigned A:1....1 and B:1...1, respectively.

Then, site-exit routers can detect which are the site prefixes tracing site-exit anycast host routes in their Forwarding Information Bases (FIBs). Having this data on hand, it's really simple to obtain the prefix associated to a site-exit anycast address: just replace the last 128-L bits from 1 to 0 and use L as the prefix length.

With this information, site-exit routers can divert packets toward the correct site-exit router. This diversion is achieved by tunneling packets to the site-exit anycast address associated to the source address prefix, as shown in Fig. 4.

Continuing the example depicted in Fig. 4, host route C:1...1 will be present in ReA's and ReB's FIBs, because it was distributed by OSPF. Then, ReA and ReB will be able to tunnel packets sourced with prefix C towards C:1...1, which is an address assigned to ReB. Both ReA and ReB have no idea where ReC is located, they have just discovered it by means of its site-exit anycast address.

Therefore, there are three tasks to perform at site-exit routers:
- Site-exit router advertisement
- Site-exit router and prefix detection
- Tunnel creation and destruction

It is important to take into account that for this mechanism to work, all the site's prefixes must have the same length (L). This is not an important limitation because it is stated that sites will be assigned 48-bit length prefixes. Therefore, the usual value of L will be 48.

In the example presented in this section, OSPF has been used as IGP. However, the solution is independent of the used IGP.

5.   IMPLEMENTATION DETAILS

We have implemented this solution on *Linux* and then ported it to *FreeBSD*. On *Linux*, an *USAGI* project kernel was used because it is the only package that provides IPv6-in-IPv6 tunnels and source based routing. On FreeBSD IPv6-in-IPv6 tunnels are available through the standard ifconfig tool, and source routing was achieved with either IP Filter or OpenBSD Packet Filter tools.

Most of the work was done on *Quagga,* which is a routing software package that implements OSPFv2, OSPFv3, RIP, and BGP routing protocols. It has been ported to several Unix-like operating systems such as GNU/Linux, FreeBSD, NetBSD and Solaris.

Quagga has a modular architecture composed of a main module called *zebra* and a set of secondary modules that implement individual routing protocols. In fact, these modules are called *bgpd, ripd, ospfd, ospf6d, and ripngd.* The main module is the only one that has a strong dependence on the platform, as it is in charge of communication with the kernel. An internal protocol known as the *Zebra Protocol* is used to communicate protocol modules with *zebra*.

To perform the tests, we relied on the VNUML virtualization tool [VNUML], which allows the creation of complex Linux based virtual network scenarios.

Many aspects influenced the way this implementation was done; among them the following are the most relevant:

- **Multiplatform:** Because *Quagga* is multiplatform, the solution could be easily ported to other OSs.
- **User-Level Implementation:** Since it is not necessary to write kernel code, the development and debugging are simplified. This also makes a more portable implementation.
- **Quagga's Platform:** *Quagga* is not only a routing package, but also a routing platform. It has an extensive function library that developers can take advantage of. *Quagga* is also able to detect routing events such as the addition of routes and interfaces, triggering handlers for these events.
- **Routing Protocol Independence:** Despite the fact that the current implementation is developed and tested using OSPF, developing the solution inside *Quagga's zebra* main module allows the use of other IGPs.
- **Management and Monitoring Interface:** *Quagga* has its own configuration and monitoring interface, which is similar to the command-line interface of *Cisco IOS*™. Having this command-line framework makes adding new commands more simple in order to integrate multihoming configuration in a single user interface.

5.1 Advertisement, Detection and Tunnel Handling

Site-exit routers announce themselves as such by adding the proper *site-exit anycast addresses* to their internal interfaces. These addresses reflect the prefixes for which each router will act as an exit.

To make such announcement, an exit router needs to know the following parameters:

- Length of the site's prefixes (L: usually 48).
- Set of internal interfaces.
- Set of prefixes for which the router will act as an exit.
- Given these parameters the router can:
- Identify the interfaces that the site-exit anycast addresses will be assigned.
- Generate the set of site-exit anycast addresses to advertise.
- Generate source-based default routes for the given prefixes.

In order to receive tunneled packets from other exit routers, the router must also enable a way to receive IPv6-in-IPv6 tunneled packets from any internal source.

After that, host routes derived from the site-exit anycast addresses must be injected into the IGP. In our test implementation, this step is performed by redistributing the routes into OSPF.

An exit router can detect the site prefixes announced by its peers. Because site prefixes are disseminated by the IGP, the detection can be done searching for site-exit anycast entries in the router's FIB. Site-exit anycast address entries in the FIB are represented by host routes. Therefore, the detection process has to look for entries whose prefix length is 128 and whose last 128-L bits are set to 1.

The site prefix associated to the site-exit FIB entry is obtained by setting the last 128-L bits of the entry to 0 and changing the prefix length from 128 to L.

When a new route is added or deleted from the FIB, *zebra* triggers event handlers that execute handling code. So that's the perfect place to put the *site-exit anycast address* detection code. Additionally, the detection is independent of the IGP being used.

Once the prefixes are detected, tunnels can be created. In our implementation, for each detected prefix, a tunnel is created. Each tunnel has the *site-exit* anycast address as the remote endpoint. As the local endpoint address, we use the address assigned to a virtual interface that never goes down (sometimes referred to as *loopback interface*). This way, the tunnel source address does not change over time.

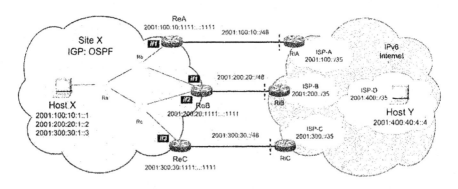

Figure 6. Scenario of the example of automatic tunneling configuration.

But creating the tunnel is not enough for packets to be rerouted to the proper site-exit router. A source-based default route has to be added to the FIB too. This route directs packets with source addresses in the range of the prefix through the recently created tunnel. As a result of that, packets will travel to the correct site-exit router.

When *zebra* is notified of FIB entry deletions, it also checks if the entry being deleted corresponds to a site-exit anycast route. If so, it destroys the tunnel and deletes the source-based default route.

5.2 Configuration Example

This subsection presents an example of multihoming configuration at site-exit routers. As shown in Fig. 6, a site connects to three ISPs through three exit routers. Each ISP assigns a prefix of length 48 to the site, so the site has three prefixes. Consequently, *Host X* inherits three addresses taken from these prefixes.

```
ReB's Configuration
multihoming
  ipv6 site prefix-length 48
  ipv6 automatic-tunneling
  ipv6 site internal-interface if1
  ipv6 site internal-interface if2
  ipv6 exit-prefix 2001:200:20::/48
```

Figure 7. Site-exit router configuration example for router ReB.

In order to configure multihoming capabilities several commands were added to *Quagga's* command-line interface. A new configuration section was introduced and named `multihoming`. This section holds the following commands:

- `ipv6 automatic-tunneling`
  Enables automatic tunnels usage.
- `ipv6 site prefix-length X`
  Defines the site's prefix length.
- `ipv6 exit-prefix X:X::X:X/M`
  Defines the site's prefixes for which the router acts as exit.
- `ipv6 site internal-interface IFNAME`
  Defines which are the site internal router interfaces.

A command called `show multihoming` was also added to display multihoming status. Fig. 7 presents the relevant configuration commands needed at each exit router for the example in Fig. 6.

6.   SUMMARY

The IPv6 multihoming problem has been discussed extensively inside the IETF technical community. The Multi6 IETF working group has set up the foundations of a future solution to the multihoming problem. It is now the task of the new Shim6 to design the solution that will be standardized. This new working group must not only design the so called *Shim6* protocol, but also mechanisms for ingress filtering compatibility, among other tasks.

The article has focused on the *host-centric* multihoming approach, which is based on address selection by the host itself. The implications of source and destination address selection were examined. Source address selection plays a key role because it determines the incoming path for reply traffic and in the presence of ingress filters it also determines the way packets take to leave the site.

Because ingress filters pose many threats to multihoming, there are multiple proposed ways to handle the problem. From relaxing the ingress filters to the setup of a static mesh of tunnels between site-exit routers.

We have implemented one of the proposed ingress filtering compatibility mechanisms. This mechanism uses anycast addresses to advertise site exit routers to their peers. In this way, site exit routers can tunnel packets to the correct exit routers if they are not the correct exit routers for some packets.

The implementation was done on Linux and FreeBSD, using the Quagga routing package. In the tests it performed its functions as expected, advertising and detecting the site exit routers, creating and destroying the tunnels, and redirecting the packets towards the correct exit router. This happened despite the different platform details. One advantage of this implementation is that it was done in user space, that way it was easily ported to FreeBSD from Linux. Deployment of this solution only needs changes on exit routers. At the time being it is not deployable on proprietary commercial routers.

ACKNOWLEDGEMENTS

We would like to thank all the partners involved in the Euro6IX project for their support and cooperative attitude.

REFERENCES

Bagnulo, M. et al. (2004). The Case for Source Address Dependent Routing in Multihoming, Lecture Notes in Computer Science, Volume 3266, 2004.

Bu, Tian, Gao, Lixin, and Towsle, Don (2002). On Characterizing BGP Routing Table Growth. Proceedings of IEEE Global Internet Symposium 2002.

Crocker, D. (2003). Multiple Address Service for Transport (MAST): An Extended Proposal. Internet draft draft-crocker-mast-proposal-01. IETF. September 2003.

de Launois, C. et al. (2003) The NAROS Approach for IPv6 Multihoming with Traffic Engineering, Proceedings of QoFIS 2003, Lecture Notes in Computer Science

Draves, R. (2003). Default Address Selection for Internet Protocol version 6 (IPv6), RFC 3484, IETF, 2003, http://www.ietf.org/rfc/rfc3484.txt

Dunmore, M. (Editor) (2003). Report on IETF Multihoming Solutions, version 2. Deliverable 4.5.1, 6NET Project. http://www.6net.org/publications/deliverables/D4.5.1v2.pdf

Hagino, J. and Snyder, H. (2001). IPv6 Multihoming Support at Site Exit Routers. RFC 3178, IETF, http://www.ietf.org/rfc/rfc3178.txt

Huitema, C. (2004). Host-Centric IPv6 Multihoming. draft-huitema-multi6-hosts-03, IETF, Work in progress

Matsumoto, A. et al. (2004) Source Address Selection Policy Distribution for Multihoming, draft-arifumi-multi6-sas-policy-dist-00, IETF Work in progress.

Moskowitz, R., Nikander, P., Jokela, P. and Henderson, T. (2005). Host Identity Protocol. Internet draft draft-ietf-hip-base-02. IETF. February 2005.

multi6. Site Multihoming in IPv6 (multi6). IETF Working Group. http://www.ietf.org/html.charters/multi6-charter.html

Tapiador, A. et al. (2004). A simple host centric solution for a network research multihoming environment. In Proceedings of EUNICE 2004

Teraoka, F., Ishiyama, M. and Kunishi, M. (2003). LIN6: A Solution to Multihoming and Mobility in IPv6. Internet draft draft-teraoka-multi6-lin6-00. IETF. December 2003.

Troan, O. and Droms, R. (2003), IPv6 Prefix Options for Dynamic Host Configuration Protocol (DHCP) version, RFC 3633, IETF. http://www.ietf.org/rfc/rfc3633.txt

VNUML Tool. http://www.dit.upm.es/vnuml

A BGP SOLVER FOR HOT-POTATO ROUTING SENSITIVITY ANALYSIS

B. Quoitin and S. Tandel
Computing Sciences and Engineering Department
University of Louvain-la-Neuve, Belgium
{ quoitin,tandel } @info.ucl.ac.be

Abstract   The interactions between the IGP and BGP routing protocols which are running inside an ISP's network are sometimes hard to understand. The problem becomes particularly complex when there are dozens of routers/links and several thousands of destination prefixes. In this paper, we present a publicly available routing solver to evaluate routing what-if scenarios. The solver is able to model the complete network of an ISP and given the external routes learned by this ISP, to compute the paths towards all the destination prefixes. We demonstrate the use of our routing solver, C-BGP, by showing the results of an analysis of the link/router failure sensitivity in a transit network. Based on the analysis' results, we can pinpoint links/routers whose failure has an important impact on the selection of BGP routes. The deployment of protection techniques that are used for optical links, SONET-SDH and MPLS should be considered for these links/routers.

Keywords: Interdomain routing, BGP, network design.

1.   Introduction

With today's needs for better Internet services, ISP's network operators increasingly care about the resilience and performance of their networks. They seek to build networks that will accomodate varying traffic load and be robust to link and router failures. However, achieving these goals is not easy since managing large IP networks requires a good understanding of the interplay of the intradomain and interdomain routing protocols.

There are two routing protocols that interact in a domain and their paths selection methods differ. Basically, the intradomain routing protocol such as IS-IS [Moy, 1998] or OSPF [Oran, 1990] is used to compute the paths between any two routers within the domain. The objective of the intradomain routing is to find the paths that best fit a previously selected metric which can be, for instance, the delay along the path or the bandwidth. Many network operators use the CISCO default metric, which is one over the bandwidth [CISCO, 2005].

On the other hand, the interdomain routing protocol, BGP [Rekhter et al., 2004; Stewart, 1999], is responsible for the selection of interdomain paths. That is, it selects the paths towards the networks that are outside the domain. The incentive behind the design of BGP was to provide reachability among domains and the ability for any domain to enforce its own routing policies, i.e. controlling what traffic enters and leaves the domain, and where. To the contrary of the intradomain routing protocol, BGP does not optimize a global metric [Huffaker et al., 2002] but relies on a *decision process* composed of a sequence of rules [Rekhter et al., 2004]. The routing decisions depend on local preferences, the length of the interdomain routes, the intradomain cost to the egress router and other tie-breaking criteria.

It is difficult for an operator to figure out the routing decisions performed by its routers in case of link/router failures or in case of configuration changes. Especially when the network is composed of dozens of routers and there are several thousands destination prefixes. For this reason, we propose an open-source routing solver that can be used by ISP network operators to study routing what-if scenarios based on routing information collected in their network. The solver takes as input the network topology, the IGP weight and the BGP routes learned by the ISP network. As output, the solver computes for each router the routes selected towards all the interdomain prefixes.

We use the solver to evaluate various routing scenarios, such as the sensitivity to link/router failures and IGP metric changes. In particular, we are able to pinpoint which links/routers cause the largest number of routing changes in case of failure and are thus eligible for the deployment of protection mechanisms [Vasseur et al., 2004].

The paper is structured as follows. First, we describe in Section 2 our routing model and how we implemented it. In Section 3 we describe a sample routing scenario: the analysis of the impact of IGP changes on BGP routing. Then we apply our scenario to an operational transit network and show our results in Section 4. Finally, we conclude in Section 6.

2.   Routing Model

In order to accurately model the routing in an ISP's network, we need to accurately model the path selection performed by the intradomain and interdomain routing protocols. That is, we must compute for each router the next-hop that would have been selected to reach each destination prefix, we have designed and implemented an open-source routing solver, C-BGP [Quoitin, 2003]. This solver models the topology of the network, the intradomain routes, the BGP route filtering and the complete BGP decision process without reproducing the time-consuming packet exchanges that occur between simulated routers in packet-level simulators such as SSFNet [Premore, 2001] or J-Sim [Tyan, 2002]. We are therefore able to model large ISP networks. We have also used C-BGP to perform simulations with up to 30.000 BGP routers.

A sketch of the solver's internals is provided in Fig. 1. The solver can be configured using a CISCO-like syntax and it can read standard input formats such as MRT dumps [Merit, 2005] and libpcap IS-IS trace [Tcpdump, 2005]. The solver provides convenient ways to analyze the results of its computations. A first possibility is to have a look at any routers's routing tables. Another possibility is to trace the route followed by packets sent by one router to another.

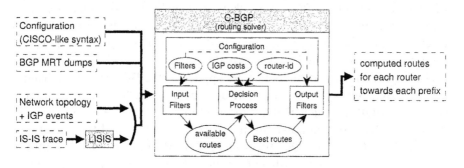

Figure 1.   Overview of the routing solver.

2.1   Topology and IGP Models

We represent the network as a graph where nodes are routers and edges are layer-three links between routers. We do not model the network's topology at the facility level. Each edge is weighted by the IGP metric of the corresponding link. The network graph can be built in many different ways, such as manually building a representation of an existing network, extracting information from an IGP protocol trace captured in the network, or even building a synthetic network. Our tool uses LISIS, written by Olivier Bonaventure (http://totem.info.ucl.ac.be), to read IS-IS traces in libpcap format.

The selection of paths by the intradomain routing protocol is modelled using the computation of the shortest paths based on the weight associated with each edge. In our model, we do not simulate the details of the intradomain routing protocol such as the propagation of the Link State Packets (LSPs). We compute the shortest paths in the solver using Dijkstra's SPF algorithm. These paths do not change until there is a weight change or a link/router failure. The model we have implemented currently supports a single area, the most common type of IS-IS deployment in large ISP networks.

In addition to the paths selected by the intradomain routes, the solver also supports the addition of static routes. These routes are typically used for peerings with neighbor domains or to direct traffic towards customers. The static routes do not participate in the intradomain routing protocol.

2.2   Models of the BGP routers

As explained earlier and shown in figure 1, our model contains the following information for each node that models a BGP router. First, an input and an output Adjacent Routing Information Bases (Adj-RIB-in/out) are used to store the BGP routes exchanged by the node with its neighbor BGP routers. The Adj-RIB-in contains the BGP routes that are available to this router. Second, a Local Routing Information Base (Loc-RIB) is used to store the best BGP routes selected by this node among the routes in the Adj-RIB-in. Finally, import and export filters are associated with each node.

The import and export filters that are applied to the BGP routes exchanged over the eBGP sessions. On commercial routers, those filters can be used to modify the BGP messages that are received or sent over the eBGP sessions. We studied BGP configurations from large ISP networks and found that they use complex BGP filters [Quoitin et al., 2003]. Besides the classical utilisation of the local-pref attribute for backup links and to prefer client routes over provider routes, those filters can contain complex operations on the BGP routes. Many ISPs rely on BGP communities for internal traffic engineering purposes or to allow their customers to influence the processing of their routes. Those various usages of the BGP communities [Quoitin and Bonaventure, 2002] must be accurately modelled. Another frequently used attribute is the MED. It should be possible to consider or ignore this attribute in the received routes on a per eBGP session basis and it should also be possible to selectively use it on outgoing eBGP sessions. Another construct that we found frequently was the utilisation of AS-Path filters containing regular expressions. For this analysis, it is clear that an accurate model of an ISP network must be able to reproduce all the complexities found in those filters.

To be able to apply our solver to large ISP networks, we have developed a flexible conversion tool that is able to convert the actual BGP configuration of each router in the solver's configuration language. Our conversion tool is able to convert most of the BGP related commands supported by commercial routers. The current version supports both Cisco (IOS) and Juniper (JUNOS) router, but it was designed to easily support other languages. By using this conversion tool, a model of a large ISP network can be built. Furthermore, it is possible to update the model each time a BGP configuration changes and in some networks those configurations can change frequently.

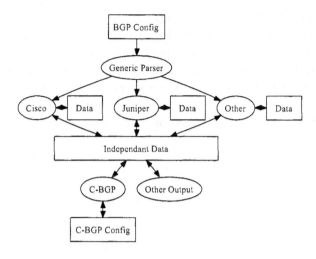

Figure 2. Overview of the converter.

Figure 2 represents the architecture of the converter. First a generic parser loads a specific parser in order to retrieve all the useful BGP commands. They are stored in an independent vendor data structure. Once the parsing has been done, the converter plugin converts this data in C-BGP configurations.

2.3 Computation of the Interdomain routes

Our model for the interdomain routing protocol relies on the computation of the paths that routers know once the BGP routing has converged [Griffin and Wilfong, 1999]. For this purpose, we model the propagation of BGP messages and accurately reproduce the route selection performed by each router [Rekhter et al., 2004; Stewart, 1999]. Even if we model the propagation of BGP messages, the simulation we perform is static since we are not interested in the transient states of routing, but only in its outcome. This is reasonable approach since the large majority of Internet routes are stable in time [Rexford et al., 2002; Uhlig et al., 2004].

The model works as follows. Once the network topology is available and the intradomain routes have been computed, the solver begins the propagation of route advertisements. The solver starts with an arbitrary BGP router and advertises the routes known by this router. These routes either come from a manual configuration of the router or from a capture of the routes contained in the BGP RIB (Routing Information Base) of the router being modelled. The C-BGP solver supports RIBs in MRT [Merit, 2005] format. For each route to be advertised, the solver builds UPDATE messages and sends them to the router's neighbors according to the output filters. For each BGP message to

send, the solver looks up in the router's routing table to find the link along
which the message must be forwarded to reach the next hop. The message
is forwarded on a hop-by-hop basis until it reaches its final destination. The
generated BGP messages are pushed on a single global linear first-in first-out
queue that guarantees that the BGP messages are received in sequence (see
Fig.3). In real routers, the BGP messages ordering is guaranteed by the TCP
connections underlying the BGP sessions. The solver does this for all the BGP
routers.

```
while (!msg_queue.empty()) {

    /* Get next message to process */
    (msg_type, dst, src, msg_content)= msg_queue.pop();

    /* Process message in destination router (dst) */
    if (msg_type == BGP_UPDATE) {

        route= msg_content;

        /* Does the destination router (dst) accept the route
           from the source router (src) */
        if (dst.in_filter(src, route) == ACCEPT)
            router.adj_rib_in[src].replace(route.prefix, route);
        else
            router.adj_rib_in[src].remove(route.prefix);

        /* Run the BGP decision process */
        dst.decision_process(route.prefix);

        /* Best route has changed, propagate to neighbors */
        if (dst.best_has_changed(route.prefix)) {

            foreach neighbor in (dst.neighbors) {

                /* Route can be redistributed to neighbor ? */
                if (router.out_filter(neighbor, route) == ACCEPT)
                    msg_queue.push(BGP_UPDATE, dst, neigbor, route);

            }
        }
    }
}
```

Figure 3.   Simplified algorithm for the BGP solver.

The solver continues the simulation by poping the first message from the
queue, and waking up the router corresponding to the current hop of the message. If the BGP message is a WITHDRAW, the router removes from the
corresponding Adj-RIB-in the route towards the withdrawn prefix, and runs
the decision process. If the BGP message is an UPDATE, the router checks if
the route it contains is accepted by its input filters. If so, the route is stored in
the Adj-RIB-in and the router's decision process is run. The decision process
retrieves from the Adj-RIB-ins all the feasible routes for the considered prefix,
compares them and selects the best one. The selection process implemented
in the C-BGP solver supports all the rules of the BGP decision process. The

router then propagates its new best route to its neighbors by pushing new BGP messages on the global linear queue. The solver continues until the message queue is empty, which means that BGP has converged.

In addition, the interdomain model implemented in the C-BGP solver supports route-reflectors [Bates et al., 2000]. Route-reflectors are special BGP routers that are deployed to decrease the number of internal BGP (iBGP) sessions required inside a network. The solver is thus able to model ISP networks with an iBGP hierarchy.

3.   Hot-Potato Routing Sensitivity

A sample application of our routing solver is the study of the sensitivity of a network to hot-potato routing. That is, we evaluate the impact of IGP changes on the selection of interdomain routes by BGP. This is important for an ISP for two main reasons. The first one is to predict which router will serve as an egress router to reach a given Internet prefix from a given ingress router. This choice is based on the routing information available through BGP, obtained from the various BGP peers of the domain, but it also depends on the internal paths from an ingress router to each of the peerings points (egress routers). Thus, this choice is sensitive to the internal paths computed by the intradomain routing protocol. The failure of a link, the failure of a router or a change in an IGP weight has an impact on the internal paths and the reachability. Therefore, it can have a dramatic impact on the BGP routing choices. As a consequence, such event can cause major traffic shifts or even cause Internet prefixes to become unreachable from certain ingresses.

The second reason is that changes in the intradomain routing of a domain may have an impact on the BGP routes that are announced outside the domain. An IGP event that seems unsignificant to the global Internet, as an IGP weight change, may be seen by all BGP routers in the Internet [Feldmann et al., 2004; Teixeira et al., 2004]. In addition, some ISPs use the BGP Multi-Exit-Discriminator (MED) attribute when they have multiple peering links with the same neighbor domain [Quoitin et al., 2003]. The MED is used to inform the neighbor AS of the quality of each ingress router. The MED value can for instance contain the IGP cost of the path between the ingress and the egress routers. The neighbor AS will select the route with the lowest value of the MED. In this case, each time the IGP cost of the intradomain path changes, a BGP UPDATE message will be issued to update the MED value.

We show an example domain in Fig. 4. This domain is composed of 4 routers, R1, R2, R3 and R4. The domain has two providers, ISP A which is connected to routers R1 and R2 and ISP B which is connected through R3. In addition, the domain has a single customer, AS2 which is connected to R4. We consider the traffic flows between the domain's customer and a remote

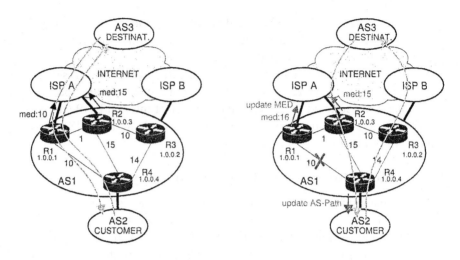

Figure 4.   Example network: impact of a link failure.

destination network, AS3. When all links are up and running, (left side of Fig. 4), AS1 learns equal quality BGP routes towards AS3 from its ISPs. This is common in the Internet today [Bonaventure et al., 2003]. The traffic sent by the customer to AS3 is received by R4 which forwards it to the closest egress router, R1, where it is handed to ISP A.

The traffic in the reverse direction enters the domain at R1. AS1 uses the MED attribute to indicate to ISP A the best ingress router to reach AS2's prefix. For this purpose, AS1 uses as MED value the IGP cost between the ingress routers and R4. ISP A will prefer the route with the lower value of the MED, which is through R1 in this case.

Now, if the link between R1 and R4 fails, the network will converge to the state shown in the right part of Fig. 4. R4 will select R3 as egress router to reach the prefix of AS3 since the closest egress router according to the IGP metric is R3. An update message is thus sent to AS2 in order to update the AS-Path. On the other hand, R1 and R2 advertise new BGP messages to ISP A in order to update the MED values. The best ingress router to reach AS2's prefix is now R2. The traffic coming from AS3 to AS2 now enters through R2.

3.1   Routing changes

Our methodology for studying the impact of IGP changes on the path selection is as follows. First, we build a representation of the network inside the routing solver, as explained in Sec. 2.1. We let the solver compute the routes in each router, then, we store a snapshot of the selected paths. This snapshot corresponds to the state of routing when everything is up and running.

We then apply our changes to the IGP: link failures, router failures or metric changes. We let the routing solver recompute the paths. Now, we compare the newly obtained routes to the snapshot. For each router and for each destination prefix, we classify the routing change as shown in Table 1.

Prefix up/down	The reachability of the prefix has changed. The prefix has either become up or down.
Peer change	The next-hop AS has changed.
Egress change	The egress router has changed, but not the nex-hop AS.
Intra Cost change	The cost of the intradomain path towards the egress router has changed.
Intra Path change	The intradomain path towards the egress router has changed, but the IGP cost remains the same.
No change	The route has not changed.

Table 1. Classification of routing changes.

The computational complexity of the analysis is directly proportional to the number of prefixes in the routing tables. A full BGP routing table can contain more than 180.000 prefixes. However, when considering the routes announced by all the neighbors of one domain, it appears that a lot of prefixes are learned from the same neighbors, with the same BGP attributes (local-preference, as-path, MED, next-hop) [Halabi, 2000]. The outcome of the decision process will be the same for these prefixes. Therefore, we group together the prefixes announced with the same attributes by the same neighbor routers in order to decrease the analysis time.

4. Case Study on the Géant network

In this section we describe the results of our evaluation of hot-potato routing sensitivity on the Géant [Dante, 2005] network (AS20965). Géant is the pan-European research network and it is operated by Dante. It carries research traffic from the european National Research and Education Networks (NRENs) connecting universities and research institutions. Géant has Points of Presence (POPs) in all the european countries. The graph that models Géant is composed of 23 nodes and 37 links. In addition, there are 48 peering links.

Using the methodology described in Section 3.1, we simulated all the single-link/single-router failures in Géant and observed the impact on the BGP routes selected by each Géant router. We obtained the Géant topology from an IS-IS trace collected on one router, in libpcap format. We also obtained a dump of the routes advertised through the iBGP by all the Géant routers , in MRT format. The IS-IS trace and the BGP dump are dated from the 1st of July, 2004.

We grouped the 140.334 prefixes in the BGP routing table in 403 clusters of prefixes learned from the same routers with the same attributes.

4.1   Routing changes

The results of the single-link failure analysis are shown in Fig. 5. On the x-axis, we show all the internal links of Géant. Upon request of Géant, we do not reveal the names of the routers. Instead, we label each router with a unique number. Each link is named from the two routers it connects. On the y-axis, we show the number of routing changes cumulated on all the Géant routers. The routing changes are classified according to Table 1. The links on the x-axis are ordered according to the number of routing changes caused by their failure. We observe that the failure of nearly 50% of the Géant links cause more than 100.000 routing changes. These links should probably be protected by the addition of parallel links, SONET-SDH protection or the use of MPLS protection tunnels [Vasseur et al., 2004].

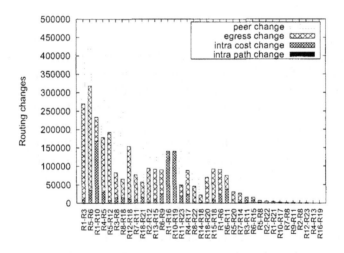

Figure 5.   Most sensitive single link failure.

In particular, the R1-R3 link causes more than 450.000 routing changes. This is due to its particular position in the Géant topology. Actually, the R3 router has a peering with an important peer AS as well as with many Géant POPs. Many POPs use R1 as a transit router to reach the R3 router. Therefore, removing the R1-R3 link causes all the above POPs to use another route to reach the prefixes received by R3. The other links that cause large numbers of routing changes also connect to important border routers. We can also observe that that there is nearly no routing changes in the *Intra Path change* class.

This is due to the absence of multiple equal cost paths between ingresses and egresses in Géant.

Fig. 6 shows the results of the single-router failure analysis. On the x-axis, we show all the routers of Géant. On the y-axis, we show the number of routing changes cumulated on all the Géant routers. The routers on the x-axis are ordered according to the number of routing changes caused by their failure. We observe that the impact of nearly half the Géant routers cause routing changes. The failure of a single router corresponds to the failure of all the links that are connected to this router. The consequence is that the routers whose failure cause the largest number of routing changes are the routers that connect to the most critical links identified in Fig. 5. Routers R5, R3, R18, R11 and R15 have peerings with important peers of Géant. Routers R1 and R6 are used by a large number of Géant POPs as transit routers to reach important destinations. We can also observe that a few routing changes concern losts of reachability. This occurs when routers that provide access to single-homed customers of Géant fail. The impact seems low in term of the number of prefixes but this means that the concerned customers of Géant have lost their connectivity to the research Internet unless they have another access through a commercial provider for instance.

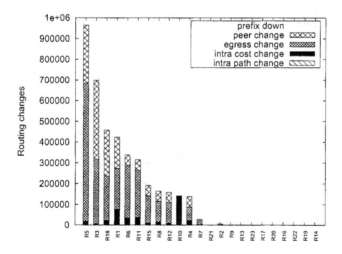

Figure 6.   Most sensitive single router failure.

4.2   Impact on traffic

In addition to studying the impact of failures on routing changes, we also evaluated the importance of traffic shifts caused by link failures. Indeed, when routes change some traffic flows may be forwarded along different intradomain paths. This will occur for traffic flows that are forwarded based on routes that have changed. Traffic shifts will modify the distribution of the traffic inside the network and change the load of some links. As a consequence, some links can even become congested.

For the purpose of evaluating the traffic shifts caused by link failures, we obtained a prefix-prefix traffic matrix from Géant. A router-router traffic matrix is not sufficient since we need to re-route the traffic flows based on the BGP routing tables. The traffic matrix was obtained by collecting Netflow statistics on all the external interfaces of Géant. We used a one-day traffic matrix and we accurately reproduced how the traffic flows are forwarded inside Géant. By traffic flow, we mean the amount of IP traffic sent from a source prefix to a destination prefix, without regards to the protocols that are used. In order to reproduce the forwarding of one flow, we use the routing tables computed by C-BGP after each link failure. Then, we proceed on a hop-by-hop basis. We know the ingress router that received the flow and we perform a lookup in its routing table in order to find the next-hop router. We continue with the next-hop routers along the intradomain path until we reach the egress router. We add the volume of the flow to all the links we traversed. We do this for all the flows and obtain the volume of traffic carried by each individual link.

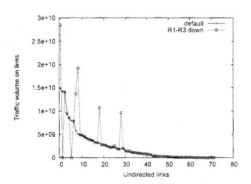

Figure 7.   Impact of the failure of R1-R3 on the links load.

We show in Fig. 7 and Fig. 8 the traffic volume carried by each link after the failure of links R1-R3 and R5-R6 respectively. In these figures, we distinguish the links directions since each direction may carry a different volume of traffic. On the x-axis, we show all the directed links ordered based on the volume of traffic they carry before the failure. The y-axis shows the amount of traffic carried by the corresponding link. In each figure, we show two curves. The first one, labelled "default", represents the links load when all the links are up and running. The second one represents the links load after the link failure.

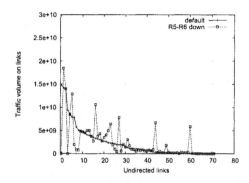

Figure 8.   Impact of the failure of R5-R6 on the links load.

Fig. 7 shows the links load after the failure of R1-R3. We observe that the traffic originally carried by the R1-R3 link now passes through other links. We also observe that the load of the previously most loaded link, which is R5-R6, has nearly doubled. Nevertheless, Géant links have enough capacity not to show congestion, but this demonstrates that link failures do cause important traffic shifts.

In Fig. 8, we show the links load following the failure of link R5-R6. We observe that the traffic shifts are less localized than with the failure of R1-R3. More links have their load changed. This may seem surprising since Fig. 5 shows that the number of routing changes due to the failure of R5-R6 is lower than the number of routing changes due to the failure of R1-R3. As explained in Section 3, this is due to the complex interaction of IGP, BGP and the traffic. The failure of R1-R3 and the failure of R5-R6 have not the same impact on the intradomain routes computed by the IGP. These routes are used by ingress routers to reach egress routers. Then, the ingress-egress routes are used by the BGP routes to cross Géant. Depending on which routes are used to forward important amounts of traffic, the impact will differ.

Finally, Fig. 9 shows a summary of the impact of all the link failures on the traffic. The x-axis shows all the link failures ordered based on the load of the most loaded link. The y-axis provides the following statistics: the median, 5th- and 95th-percentile as well as the mean load and the load of the most loaded link. First, we observe that in Géant, the failure of some links cause a large increase of the maximum link load. There is even a link failure that causes the maximum link load to nearly double. Second, we observe that in Géant, the shape of the links load distribution is not much impacted. Indeed, the median and the 5th and 95th percentile does not move much.

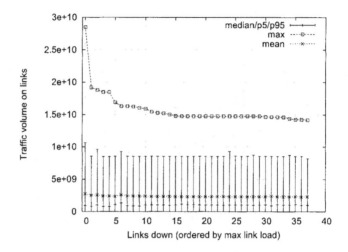

Figure 9.   Most sensitive single link failure.

5.   Related work

There are some prior works in the literature that are related to our project. First, our routing solver shares some similarities with AT&T's NetScope [Feldmann et al., 2000]. The aim of NetScope was to provide the networking industry with a software system to support traffic measurement and network modeling. NetScope was able to model the intradomain routing and study the implications of local traffic changes, configuration and routing. However, NetScope does not model the BGP and it is not publicly available.

The BGP emulator designed and implemented by Nick Feamster at the MIT [Feamster et al., 2004] is also similar to our routing solver. It computes the outcome of the BGP route selection process for each router in a single AS, based on a single snapshot of the network state. The BGP emulator relies on an algorithm that does not simulate the complex details of BGP message passing. It is however not publicly available and we do not know any utilisation of this tool for evaluating the impact of link/router failure.

Hot-potato routing has recently be studied in [Teixeira et al., 2004]. The paper describes the interaction between the IGP and BGP and proposes an analytical model of hot-potato routing. In addition, this paper proposes metrics to evaluate network sensitivity to hot-potato disruptions. These metrics can be used as tools to assist in the design of networks that are less sensitive to hot-potato disruptions. The model is able to compute the impact of hot-potato disruptions on the traffic matrix. However, the analytical model that is proposed does not take into account the iBGP hierarchy which is now frequent in many large ISP networks. The model does not take into account the BGP policies that are enforced by the ISPs. Finally, there is no publicly available implementation of the analytical model described in [Teixeira et al., 2004].

6. Conclusion

In this paper, we have described a pragmatic approach to study the interaction between an intradomain and an interdomain protocols in an ISP's network. We have implemented an open-source solver that is now available to network operators and to the research community. The solver is able to take input from a real ISP's network by relying on widespread file formats such as MRT dumps and libpcap IS-IS traces.

We also described a what-if scenario that can be evaluated by our solver. We showed how to evaluate the impact of link/router failures on the selection of BGP routes. This is an important problem faced by network operators and a hot research topic. Our tool makes possible the identification of the links/routers that are important for the routing and should be protected. We also studied the impact of failures on the traffic matrix and we showed that both the routing and the traffic points of view are important. We already performed additional analysis on Géant and Internet2 and we are currently collaborating with a large commercial transit network to apply our model to its network.

Other utilisations of the routing solver can also be envisaged. For instance, we could study the impact of a peering failure. An ISP could also use the tool to compare the addition of new peering links before signing a contract with a new provider or with a peer on an Interconnection Point. The solver could also be used to study the impact of route-reflectors on routing. In particular, it could help finding the best location to deploy route-reflectors. Finally, the impact of intradomain traffic engineering techniques such as [Fortz et al., 2002] on BGP could also be studied.

Acknowledgments

This work was supported by: the Walloon Government within the WIST TOTEM project (http://totem.info.ucl.ac.be), the E-NEXT European Network of Excellence and a grant from France Telecom R&D. We are grateful to Tim Griffin and Richard Gass from Intel Research and to Nicolas Simar from Dante for providing us with the Géant data. We also thank Olivier Bonaventure, Cristel Pelsser and Steve Uhlig for their insightful comments on the project.

References

Bates, T., Chandra, R., and Chen, E. (2000). BGP Route Reflection - An Alternative to Full Mesh IBGP. Internet Engineering Task Force, RFC2796.

Bonaventure, O., Trimintzios, P., Pavlou, G., Quoitin (Eds.), B., Azcorra, A., Bagnulo, M., Flegkas, P., Garcia-Martinez, A., Georgatsos, P., Georgiadis, L., Jacquenet, C., Swinnen, L., Tandel, S., and Uhlig, S. (2003). *Internet Traffic Engineering*, pages 118–179. Springer-Verlag. Chapter of COST263 final report, LNCS 2856.

CISCO, Systems (2005). Technical support & information. http://www.cisco.com.

Dante (2005). The GEANT Network. http://www.geant.net.

Feamster, N., Winick, J., and Rexford, J. (2004). A model of BGP routing for network engineering. In *Proc. of ACM SIGMETRICS*.

Feldmann, A., Maennel, O., Mao, M., Berger, A., and Maggs, B. (2004). Locating internet routing instabilities. In *ACM SIGCOMM2004*.

Feldmann, Anja, Greenberg, Albert, Lund, Carsten, eingold, Nick R, and Rexford, Jennifer (2000). Netscope: Traffic engineering for ip networks. *IEEE Network Magazine*.

Fortz, B., Rexford, J., and Thorup, M. (2002). Traffic engineering with traditional IP routing protocols. *IEEE Communications Magazine*.

Griffin, T. and Wilfong, G. (1999). An analysis of BGP convergence properties. In *Proc. of ACM SIGCOMM*.

Halabi, B. (2000). *Internet Routing Architectures (2nd edition)*. Cisco Press.

Huffaker, B., Fomenkov, M., Plummer, D., Moore, D., and Claffy, K. (2002). Distance Metrics in the Internet. In *Proc. of IEEE International Telecommunications Symposium (ITS)*.

Merit, Network (2005). MRT: multi-threaded routing toolkit. http://www.mrtd.net.

Moy, J. (1998). *OSPF : anatomy of an Internet routing protocol*. Addison-Wesley.

Oran, D. (1990). OSI IS-IS intra-domain routing protocol. Request for Comments 1142, Internet Engineering Task Force.

Premore, B. J. (2001). Ssf implementations of bgp-4. available from http://www.cs.dartmouth.edu/~beej/bgp/.

Quoitin, B. (2003). C-BGP, an efficient BGP simulator. cbgp.info.ucl.ac.be.

Quoitin, B. and Bonaventure, O. (2002). A survey of the utilization of the BGP community attribute. Internet draft, draft-quoitin-bgp-comm-survey-00.txt, work in progress.

Quoitin, B., Uhlig, S., Pelsser, C., Swinnen, L., and Bonaventure, O. (2003). Interdomain traffic engineering with BGP. *IEEE Communications Magazine*.

Rekhter, Y., Li, T., and Hares, S. (2004). A Border Gateway Protocol 4 (BGP-4). Internet draft, draft-ietf-idr-bgp4-26.txt, work in progress.

Rexford, J., Wang, J., Xiao, Z., and Zhang, Y. (2002). BGP routing stability of popular destinations. In *Proc. Internet Measurement Workshop*.

Stewart, J. (1999). *BGP4 : interdomain routing in the Internet*. Addison Wesley.

Tcpdump, The Group (2005). libpcap: packet capture library. http://www.tcpdump.org.

Teixeira, R., Griffin, T., Voelker, G., and Shaikh, A. (2004). Network sensitivity to hot potato disruptions. In *Proc. of ACM SIGCOMM*.

Tyan, H. (2002). *Design, realization and evaluation of a component-based compositional software architecture for network simulation*. PhD thesis, Ohio State University.

Uhlig, S., Magnin, V., Bonaventure, O., Rapier, C., and Deri, L. (2004). Implications of the topological properties of internet traffic on traffic engineering. In *ACM Symposium on Applied Computing*.

Vasseur, J.-P., Pickavet, M., and Demeester, P. (2004). *Network Recovery: Protection and Restoration of Optical, SONET-SDH, and MPLS*. Morgan Kaufmann.

A FRAMEWORK FOR COOPERATIVE INTER-DOMAIN QOS ROUTING

Alexandre Fonte,[1,3] Edmundo Monteiro,[1]
Marcelo Yannuzzi,[2] Xavier Masip-Bruin,[2] and Jordi Domingo-Pascual,[2]

[1] *University of Coimbra,*
Laboratory of Communications and Telematics,
CISUC/DEI, Polo II, Pinhal de Marrocos, 3030-290, Coimbra, Portugal
afonte,edmundo@dei.uc.pt

[2] *Universitat Politecnica de Catalunya,*
Departament d'Arquitectura de Computadors,
Avgda. Victor Balaguer, s/n-08800 Vilanova i la Geltru, Barcelona, Catalunya, Spain
yannuzzi,xmasip,jordid@ac.upc.es

[3] *Polytechnic Institute of Castelo Branco,*
Av. Pedro Alvares Cabral, n-12, 6000-084, Castelo Branco, Portugal

Abstract   Currently, a straightforward way to design BGP-based Traffic Engineering (TE) tools for stub Autonomous Systems (AS) is to rely on selfish routing mechanisms. Although TE tools can find an optimal solution, this optimum represents only a local optimum for outbound traffic. Indeed, this is one of the main limitations of the selfish routing approach. This approach makes the TE tools unaware of the effects of their route choices on transit AS throughout the chosen paths, due to uncoordinated routing decisions, and congestion can occur on distant intra- or inter-domain links. Thus, cooperation among AS is the key to avoid the performance degradation and routing instability caused by the selfish routing approach and it would be fundamental for the future QoS-aware Internet. With these objectives in mind this paper presents and discusses a framework for coordinated Inter-domain QoS Routing (QoSR) decisions among stub and downstream AS taking into account multiple traffic QoS constraints and routing preferences. The paper includes a description of the main mechanisms and algorithms that integrate the framework, and finally a discussion of the implementation issues.

Keywords: Inter-domain QoS routing, Cooperative inter-domain routing.

1. Introduction

Nowadays Internet Autonomous Systems (AS) are largely operated by commercial entities. Part of the inter-domain traffic exchanges are governed by Service Level Specification (SLS) reflecting AS business inter-relationships. Stub AS (AS that don't carry transit traffic) demand robust SLS from transit AS to satisfy the Quality of Service (QoS) requirements of user applications. However, mainly due to economical reasons, transit AS delay the deployment of mechanisms to support the provision of multi-level QoS-aware connectivity services.

On the stub AS side, an emergent approach to either protect traffic aggregates from QoS degradation or in general optimize traffic performance and business goals (e.g. transit costs) is to deploy on-line Traffic Engineering (TE) mechanisms. These TE mechanisms can be located at specialized Smart Routing Managers (SRM) entities (also called Overlay Entities - OE) [Rekhter, 1995; Yanuzzi, 02] working on top of the Border Gateway Protocol (BGP). SRMs are out-of-BGP-band autonomous routing agents able to perform intelligent path selections satisfying multiple QoS constraints (e.g., latency and throughput). They operate on shorter timescales and exploit as much as possible AS multihoming and BGP capabilities. Specifically, SRMs are able to change BGP attributes (e.g. LOCAL-PREFERENCE) on-the-fly, reflecting the required traffic exchanges.

The benefits of such SRM-based approaches, operating on shorter timescales, are evident from the technical and economical perspectives and so they are also being developed as commercial products [Dai, 2003; Internap, 2005; Cisco, 2005]. However, these tools also rely on the selfish routing approach and are focused on outbound traffic optimization. They allow stub AS to perform outbound traffic optimization but the optimum is only a local one since the routes (or transit providers) are greedily selected.

Selfish routing approaches make SRMs unaware of the effects of their route choices on transit AS (e.g. on tier-3 or tier-4 providers) throughout the chosen exit paths, due to uncoordinated routing decisions. Namely, congestion can occur on distant intra- or inter-domain links, since it is very difficult to generate accurate forecasts of traffic demands to support resource distribution optimization [Feldmann, 2001]. Recent theoretical results by T. Roughgarden and E. Tardos [Roughgarden, 2002] confirm these limitations. The study revealed that important performance losses can be introduced by local optimization mechanisms comparing to global optimization. The cited work also shows that when general link latency functions are used the price of anarchy (that is the worse-case ratio between the total latency for the selfish case and the one for global optimization) is unbounded.

Poor routing stability is another significant shortcoming of the selfish approach. Uncoordinated routing reactions attempting to face congestion could produce cycles of influence between AS and thus routing instability. In the worst case, selfish routing mechanisms can cause extensive route flapping that can seriously affect the performance of large parts of Internet [Griffin, 2002]. Furthermore, the currently available techniques to enable AS to react and repair the congestion problems by means of inbound traffic control are limited to BGP in-band techniques. These techniques can assign new MED (Multiple-exit Discriminator) values or prepend the AS paths to indirectly signal congestion by influencing their neighboring link choices. Unfortunately, those techniques require external BGP updates and operate typically on TE management cycles of several minutes or hours. For that reason, they reveal to be more effective for persistent congestion problems. Moreover, some studies have documented problems and limitations such as MED oscillation and coarse-grained traffic control, arising by using these techniques [Griffin2, 2002; Chang, 2005].

Being aware that uncoordinated routing decisions, that are inherent to selfish approach, are on the origin of the above mentioned problems, a solution to help SRMs to alleviate the congestion caused by their selfish actions is widely desirable, namely, a solution to coordinate routing decisions among SRMs on behalf of stub and transit AS. Ideally, one global authority (in other words a global coordination mechanism) would be designed to support and guide SRMs on finding global optimums. Unfortunately, given the size and the complexity of today's Internet, this is inconceivable. Consequently, alternative approaches must be sought to cope with selfishness that don't rely on a global authority or on a global policy repository, even at some additional costs on signaling. Moreover, it could be expect that those approaches would be simpler as well as involve considerably lesser deployment costs as global ones.

To address the above issues, this paper presents a conceptually simple out-of-BGP-band cooperative approach able to support coordinated inter-domain QoS routing decisions among stub and transit AS for the context (but not limited) of the future QoS-aware Internet. The particularity of this approach is that it allows finding 'social' optimums by honoring both individual stub and transit AS preferences (or constraints) regarding the carrying (or admission of new) traffic amounts of certain traffic class (TC) aggregates. To summarize, the proposed approach is motivated and well-suited to:

1 Protect stubs from SLS violations of TC aggregates;

2 Reduce selfish costs (i.e. performance losses and instability);

3 Improve the traffic exchanges predictability;

4 Improve network resources utilization;

The remaining sections are organized as follows. In Sect. 2, a brief analysis of the related work is given. Then, in Sect. 3, the proposed cooperative approach is described, including the basic concepts and the complete algorithm for coordinated routing decisions. In Sect. 4, some implementation considerations are discussed. Finally, in Sect. 5 the paper is concluded and some directions for future (already ongoing) work are discussed.

2.   Related Work

TE state-of-art is primitive [Feamster, 2003]. In previous work concerning intelligent routing schemes willing to control inter-domain traffic exchanges, two sets of TE mechanisms coupled with BGP have been proposed. The first set includes proposals for on-line and off-line BGP route optimization techniques. Among these proposals there are only few papers dealing with the design of algorithms for multi-objective (e.g. performance and cost) route optimization [Akella, 2003; Goldenberg, 2004]. The second set of mechanisms was designed to meet another central TE issue that is the attainment of smooth traffic distributions on egress links. In [Uhlig, 2004] this problem is addressed by using an evolutionary TE algorithm. One important aspect common to the cited works is that the proposed mechanisms operate on relatively large timescales of a few minutes to avoid frequent BGP route changes and the consequent BGP updates advertisements. This means that these techniques are not able to handle real-time metrics (e.g. in the order of magnitude of the network Round-Trip Time). In parallel to the cited scientific work, commercial products are also appearing. These products are globally known as smart (or optimized) edge routing and are able to operate on short timescales [Internap, 2005; Cisco, 2005]. In general commercial solutions try to select the most cost-effective routes or providers. In contrast with research tools, their internal details are unknown. For instance, their effective performance improvements and their impact on BGP performance is unclear. Another important common aspect is that these techniques behave as selfish routing schemes. On the other hand, solely two works attempt to coordinate route selections by using a negotiation strategy to avoid resource policy violations among AS [Mahajan, 2005; Winick, 2002]. However, both works are focused on the scenario of a pair of multi-connected ISPs (Internet Service Providers).

The proposal of the present paper differs from the above described techniques in the following aspects 1) it is based on a cooperative approach as part of (but not limited to) an overall solution to address inter-domain QoSR issues; 2) it is able to handle SLS violations by the automatic reconfiguration of BGP routers parameters; 3) it is focused on coordinated path selections; 4) it takes into account both individual stubs and transit AS preferences and constraints.

3.   Cooperative Approach

As stated previously the inter-domain QoSR framework proposed in this paper is based on SRMs working on top of BGP. Due to scalability concerns the proposed framework focuses on the control of routing between pairs of multi-homed stub AS [Yanuzzi, 02]. The key idea is that the peering SRMs belonging to remote stub AS, would like to co-operate in a reflective (mirroring) manner to share QoS measurement data and to manage traffic exchanges between both AS, such as the traffic goals of TCs en route to the remote stub can be fulfilled. Examples of such goals for a TC are the latency minimization and throughput maximization.

This cooperative approach for inter-domain QoSR allows the incremental deployment because it does not require cooperation with intermediate AS and most of the introduced complexity is located in the edges of the Internet. Unfortunately, similarly to the existing scientific and commercial SRM-based mechanisms, it suffers from the selfish shortcomings, described so far. This section presents an extension of this cooperative approach able to perform co-ordinated QoSR decisions.

3.1   Basic Concepts

As mentioned in Sect. 1, rather than assuming that a global authority or a global policy repository exists, our approach is based on a simpler route co-ordination strategy for finding 'social' optimums, that honors both individual stub and transit AS preferences (or constraints). The design of a routing mechanism relying on this approach is achieved by introducing extensions to SRM's route controller mechanisms to enable traffic adaptation making use of information on both QoS measures of TCs and the corresponding acknowledged transit AS routing preferences. For sure, it is assumed that stub AS are willing to sacrifice themselves for the benefit of the overall routing environment. Figure 1 illustrates a possible scenario for the cooperation among remote SRMs. The figure also illustrates the exchange of signaling messages carrying transit AS preferences. For clearness the SRMs mechanisms located in transit AS are omitted.

Let us assume that each multi-homed stub subscribes among K providers, several connectivity services for transit traffic classified into M TCs. Similarly to DiffServ (Differentiated Services) framework, we use the concept of TC, denoted as TC_n, where n is the class index and $n = 0, ..., M - 1$ for M TC, to divide the network traffic (e.g., premium, gold, silver and bronze) [Blake, 1998]. Moreover, we do not consider any special notation to distinguish among the paths used to route packets classified in each one of M TCs. We simply denote a path as $P_k, k = 1, ..., K$.

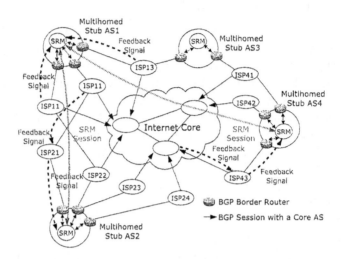

Figure 1.   Illustration of the proposed approach

Assuming that all QoS interconnections are established and also that default active paths to target destinations are inserted into local RIBs (Routing Information Base) (i.e., Local-RIB [Rekhter, 1995]) of stub's BGP routers, let us describe our route coordination strategy. Figure 2 outlines a useful model of the route coordination strategy. For simplicity, consider the case that an SLS violation or else that a significant QoS change occurs on a certain active path P_k carrying the traffic classified into a certain TC_n. Upon detecting one of these events, an ingress SRM performs the following steps:

1 First, it obtains all available QoS feasible paths $P_{k'}$ for the traffic aggregate affected, alternative to the active one P_k. In the descriptions we assume that a $P_{k'}$ is feasible if $\forall c_i(P_{k'}) < C_i, i = 1, 2, ..., m$, where c_i is the i_{th} additive QoS constant assigned to $P_{k'}$ and $C_i > 0$ the corresponding i_{th} constraint. We denote the set containing all $P_{k'}$ as A.

2 It then requests to the SRMs of transit AS throughout each path $P_{k'}$ their preferences regarding the admission of the affected TC aggregate, TC_n.

3 Next, after obtaining all preferences from transit AS it joins them together with the corresponding $c_i(P_{k'})$ constants, and map them into the parameters of the route rank function, $rank()$. The $rank()$ basically implements the SRM's route decision process and manages the SRM's route ranking tables for each TC_n to target prefix destinations.

4 Finally, after $rank()$ outputs the 'social' optimum path, it sets the local BGP routers to select this path. Of course, if the outputted path differs

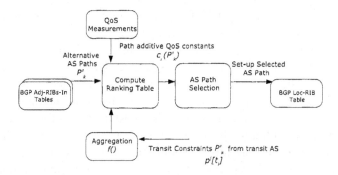

Figure 2. Model of the Route Coordination Strategy

from the current active path, it withdraws that path from BGP Local-RIBs. In principle, at this stage, the IP packets classified in TC_n are routed into the best QoS interconnection.

This process is continuously repeated, step-by-step, for each traffic aggregate affected by degradation. Concerning transit AS (as it will be detailed in next subsection) and besides giving feedback about preferences to stub SRMs, SRMs of transit AS have the job of coordinating link change decisions among neighbor AS as well.

There are some basic concepts concerning the overall approach and the design of this kind of coordinated routing mechanisms as follows.

AS Routing Preferences: For the effectiveness of our route coordination strategy, we assumed that the transit AS members of all available paths at stub (i.e., from all P_k and $P_{k'}$), are willing to co-operate by reporting their routing preferences. An AS routing preference is data structure similar to a cost, denoted as p^j, which represents the cost reported by j_{th} transit AS throughout a path P_k. It may reflect either the estimated overall congestion state of an AS on carrying a new traffic amount for a certain TC or (after admission) an estimation of the current AS's congestion state regarding the carrying the traffic aggregate. In practice, this concept easily allows transit AS to influence how traffic enters into their networks targeting to both maximize of their network utilization and to fix congestion problems.

Coordination Metric: We introduce the concept of a coordination metric to support transit AS on periodical generation and expression of their AS routing preferences. The coordination metric values are computed by an ordinal function $M()$. Thus, a given preference could be expressed as $p^j[t_i] = M(v^j)$. In terms of this notation $p^j[t_i]$ is the routing preference instance reported by the j_{th} transit AS at instant t_i for traffic classified in a certain TC; and v^j represents a given vector of internal information of that peer being mapped into p^j. As example, a natural $M()$ function is the Excess of Bandwidth Demanded

(EBD) for TC_n for all individual customers, denoted as E_n. Precisely, if at the provider j the sum of the bandwidth demanded for TC_n is D_n and S_n is the bandwidth supplied by the provider for a certain TC_n. So thus, $v^j = (D_n, S_n)$ and, then, the EBD reported to customers is given by $E_n = D_n - S_n$.

Furthermore, the coordination metric is an essential mechanism to handle the business constraints on the disclosure of internal information (e.g. internal configurations or even policy details). We suggest the use of functions $M()$, for which the problem of finding its inverse $M()^{-1}$, is computationally unfeasible.

Preference Aggregation and Feasible Outputs: At stub AS, SRMs consider that the gathering operation of the AS routing preferences along a certain QoS feasible path is well-succeeded when every preference from all AS members is gathered. The result of all well-succeeded gathering operations is a subset of alternative paths, i.e., $R \subset A$. It is assumed that all collected preferences $P^{k'} = \{p^1, ..., p^j, ..., p^n\}$, for a $P_{k'}$, where p^j is the AS routing preference from the j_{th} transit AS, are aggregated using a function $f()$. In case of additive routing preferences, the result of the aggregation denoted as $\zeta^{k'}$ and defined as $\zeta^{k'} = f(P^{k'})$, is equal to the sum of the p^j values of $P^{k'}$. For nonadditive routing preferences, $\zeta^{k'}$ can be the minimum (or maximum) among the p_k elements in $P^{k'}$. Alternatively, the cumulative routing preferences can be calculated hop-by-hop across transit AS throughout a $P_{k'}$. This has the advantage of reducing signaling and local processing cost. However, this complicate the location of congestion points. In our model, the subset R (including the associated $\zeta^{k'}$ values and $c_i(P_{k'})$) is the set of feasible outputs of the coordination mechanism. In other words, these paths are the elements of the SRM's route ranking table for TC_n to the target prefix destination.

Path Selection Triggering and Routing Optimization Problem: The following questions regarding the dynamic traffic adaptation process must be answered during the coordination mechanism design: *What is the approach followed for the path selection triggering? What is our routing problem? How can we solve it?*

As described so far, SRMs manage routing patterns by composing and updating multiple ranking tables. To achieve these objectives, first SRMs actively check QoS bounds and transit AS constraints from paths in BGP Adj-RIBs-In tables, whether they are installed into BGP Local-RIBs or not. Then, whenever a significant variation on any constraint value (e.g., on $c_i(P_{k'})$ constant or on a p^j value) is registered or in response to abnormal network operation events, the $rank()$ function is called and thus the path decision process is triggered to remove or insert a path into the ranking or simply to update the order of the paths.

Although, the proposed approach imposes higher CPU and memory consumption in the SRMs, as well as additional load on the network due to SRMs signaling messages, it is characterized by reduced response times, since all

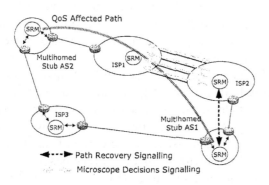

Figure 3.   SRM recovering a QoS affected Path

alternative paths are "pre-computed". To bound the implementation costs according to TE guidelines SRMs should focus on engineering the paths to a small fraction of the prefix destinations (e.g., popular prefix destinations or on stable traffic volumes) [Feamster, 2003].

Naturally, SRMs must be aware of traffic goals, of the precise routing problem and how to solve it. In other words, this means that SRMs must be able to select the feasible path $P_{k'} \in R$ that maximize its degree of satisfaction regarding *multiple independent objectives* (i.e., $c_i(P_{k'})$ constants and $\zeta^{k'}$), among the set of feasible outputs R. However, this MCP (Multi-constrained Path) problem is known as being NP-complete [Garey, 1979]. To cope with the NPcompleteness of m-constrained problems, researchers had focused on the development of polynomial time heuristics [Kuipers, 2002]. An SRM's route controller dealing the MCP problem should follow a similar approach, that is, to integrate a computationally efficient optimization algorithm.

3.2   Interactions between Smart Routing Managers

Rather than assuming an identical arrangement of AS independently of the existing inter-relationships (like BGP does), our out-band approach allows our interdomain QoSR model to adopt a different strategy to improve stability and scalability. We propose two levels of interactions between the SRMs. In the first level SRMs perform coordinated path change decisions, as described so far. Contrary, in the second level the SRMs perform coordinated link changes decisions to reallocate TC aggregates among links shared by pairs of AS. Figure 3 illustrates these interactions.

The clustering for the first level of interactions between SRMs is obtained by identifying the AS, which have previously agreed to perform coordinated path change decisions. One the other hand, the clustering for the second level interactions between SRMs is obtained by identifying pairs of dense AS, which have previous agreements to perform coordinated link change decisions. The later arrangement is motivated by recent tomography studies showing that transit AS are usually very dense and normally share among them multiple links [Map, 2005]. In both cases, the addresses of SRMs and their capabilities can be encoded in a new BGP attribute (e.g., an extended community attribute).

When coupling both levels of interactions, instead of immediately changing an affected traffic aggregate to an alternative path, an SRM explicitly spawns a QoS degradation warning message on the current path. Consequently, this requires the pairs of SRMs with second level relations to seek for alternative links able to improve the current offered QoS. This feature has the advantage of keeping the current path in the case of a successful recovery operation prerequired, avoiding thus unnecessary path shifts and the corresponding BGP updates. This process is supported by the BGP path concept to be agnostic of any detail about AS interconnections.

3.3   Coordinated Link Changes

In the coordinated link changes case, the ingress SRM adapts the TC aggregates among the alternative routing options (i.e. the alternative links) following a similar process to the path change case. In contrast, this is accomplished by exchanging of link preferences between the egress SRM and its peer.

Among all available routing options, the ingress SRMs must select the ones that don't hurt downstream peers of the egress AS. As depicted in Fig. 4, the routing option that implies the use of different egress points at the egress AS could be selected as the solution. Therefore, congestion therefore could occur in downstream peers of the egress AS along the select path the target prefix destination. This in turn could trigger a subsequent cascade of coordinated link decisions processes before achieving convergence. To avoid these effects and to alleviate BGP as well, one solution is the egress SRM to signal its peer to use only the equivalent links (i.e., the ones whose the traffic changes uses the same egress point) [Winick, 2002]. Alternatively, to produce the same effect and reduce signaling costs, we prefer to apply a condition to the alternative links (similar to the use of a drain plug) to obtain the subset of routes composed only by the routes which keep the current egress point. Finally, only the corresponding routing preferences are reported by the egress SRM to the ingress SRM. We call this subset the Null Effect Route Subset (NERS). In practice, NERSs are obtained simply passing the routes by a tuned filter.

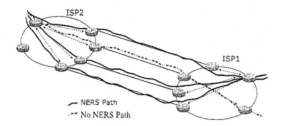

Figure 4.   Illustration of NERS paths

3.4   Algorithm for Coordinated Routing Decisions

The replacement process of routes impacted by performance degradations is accomplished in several steps. As described above, after path selection is triggered, SRMs star a new routing cycle. Upon that, this cycle finishes after a 'social' optimum path is computed and established. If no 'social' optimum path can be found we assume that SRMs can perform greedy route selections as a last chance to improve the QoS. Figure 5 shows the complete algorithm for coordinated routing decisions. The modularity and independency of exact implementation details about coordination metric computation, aggregation functions, traffic objectives and optimization algorithms and finally signaling, which are part of our mechanism, are fundamental requirements. Therefore, the presented algorithm mainly focuses on the flow of SRMs functions execution and on interactions between SRMs, themselves and BGP routers.

4.   Implementation Considerations

This section contains some considerations related of the SRMs functions needed to support the proposed cooperative approach. The section includes considerations related to QoS measurements, gathering of alternative paths, setting-up the selected path and signaling.

QoS Measurements: We assume that both remote SRMs have the knowledge of the existing SLSs, namely the QoS requirements for traffic exchanges among their stubs. To support path evaluation and SLS violation detection, we adopt a strategy based on active end-to-end measurements of QoS parameters. So thus, SRMs must incorporate efficient measurement methods following the recommendations of recent standardization efforts [Shalunov, 2004; Almes, 1999]. In the transit AS side, we assume that there is a general purpose measurement system to provide local traffic characteristics and periodically monitor the usage of the resources previously allocated to each service. This data is then used to compute AS routing preferences to be reported within feed-

```
1. Begin {Start Running the mechanism}                    1. Alternate Paths Computation to (dst);
2. Constraint Changes detected in Path to destination dst;  2. Begin
3. Recovery=Path Recovery Process (Path);                 3. PathOptions=Query Local BGP Routers (dst);
4.   if(Recovery==unsucceeded)                            4. QoSData=Query QoS History Database (PathOptions);
5.     AlternatePaths=Alternate Paths Determination(dst); 5. FeasiblePaths=Compute feasible Paths (PathOptions, QoSData);
6.     if(AlternatePaths=={})                             6. Return FeasiblePaths;
7.       NewPath=Path Ordering (AlternatePaths);          7. End.
8.       if(NewPath=={})
9.         Run Selfish Decision Process (AlternatePaths); 1. Preferred Path Computation (AlternatePaths)
10.      Else Set-up (NewPath);                           2. Begin
11.        Endif;                                         3. If(AlternatePaths =={})
12.      Endif;                                           4.   {Start one transaction foreach Alternate Path;}
13.    Endif                                              5.   Foreach Transaction
14. End. {Stop Running the mechanism}                     6.     Floods Request Preferences Messages to
                                                                  SRMs members of current target Alternate Path;
1. Path Recovery Process (Path);                          7.     Upon receive all reply preferences messages;
2. Begin                                                  8.     Incomingprefs=Retrieve all transit ASes preferences;
3. Send QoS Degradation Warning Message (Path);                  {Output List will contain the set of feasible Outputs}
4. Upon receiving message (type,Path) ;                   9.     OutputList=Aggregate(Incomingprefs);
5. If(type==WarningReply)&&(WarningReply->Trial Performed) 10.    EndTransaction;
6.   QoSEvaluation=Evaluate QoS performance (Path);       11.    if !(OutputList=={})
7.   If (QoSEvaluation==valid)                                   {Select from the OutputList a "social solution"}
       {Do nothing, the recovery operation was well-succeeded} 12.  NewASPathdst= Compute New Path (OutputList);
8.     Return Recovery=succeeded;                         13.    EndIf;
9.   Else Return Recovery=unsucceeded;                    14.  EndIf;
10.  EndIf                                                15. Return NewASPathdst;
11. EndIf                                                 16. End.
12. End
```

Figure 5.   Coordination Mechanism Algorithm

back signaling messages sent to stub SRMs. Recent efforts on developing of ISP-based capturing tools are found in [IPMON, 2005; ATT, 2005].

Gathering of an alternative path set: A fundamental requirement to deploy our out-band approach is that SRMs must have administrative control over BGP speakers and thus full access to the Routing Information Base (RIB), namely to the Adj-RIBs-In and the Loc-RIB databases. A precise definition of the terms Adj-RIBs-In and Loc-RIB can be found in [Rekhter, 1995]. Furthermore, in the QoS context the RIB must be extended to hold all P_k for all TCs into the QoS extended BGP Adj-RIBs-In table from peer at k_{th}-provider. The gathering of alternative paths able to accommodate a traffic aggregate affected by a strong QoS degradation is an essential function. These paths and the corresponding next-hops are thus retrieved from those QoS extended Adj-RIBs-In, depending on the QoS measurements history.

Setting-up the Selected Path: The final step of the proposed mechanism is to set-up the selected path as the active path. This can easily be done by installing the route into the QoS extended BGP Loc-RIB table. Rather than this, our proposal is to enable SRMs to modify the IP forwarding tables directly. This enables to create a soft state routing allowing SRMs to rollback routing decisions and to avoid overload BGP routers during instability episodes. The new routes are inserted into the BGP Loc-RIB only when they are considered as stable.

Signaling: Communication between SRMs is asynchronous and of limited network bandwidth. A signaling protocol is required. This must include requests, replies and acknowledgments to gather AS routing preferences, QoS data sharing or other actions. Messages are sent to individual or groups of SRMs. In addition, recent recommendations in the proposal of an IP signaling protocol with QoS extensions, should be taken into account in the deployments [Hancock, 2004].

5.   Conclusions and Future Work

In this paper, we have proposed an cooperative framework for coordinated inter-domain QoS routing decisions. The particulary of our framework is to rely on out-BGP-band routing mechanisms and signaling to support stubs on finding 'social' optimums by honoring both individual stub and transit AS preferences. We believe that this kind of approach is the only way to allow predictable inter-domain traffic exchanges between AS and to support robust SLSs in the Internet environment. As discussed in the paper, two main set of open issues are still part of our research agenda. First, we intent to design a specific coordination metric, and efficient traffic optimization algorithms to find 'social' optimums. Secondly, to ensure scalability, it is essential to build hierarchical SRMs organizations and to define their relations in order to design a signalling protocol for SRMs data sharing and actions' requests and acknowledges. Finally, in a simulation environment based on J-Sim [Jsim, 2005] and Infonet BGP suite [Infonet, 2005], we plan extensive simulations contrasting the behavior of the described cooperative approach with current in-band BGP mechanisms. The results collected will enable the evaluation of the strengths and limitations of the contributions and will lead to refinements.

Acknowledgment

This work was partially funded by the European Commission through Network of Excellence E-NEXT (contract FP6-506869) under SATIN Grant *Study of Coordination Mechanisms and Signaling Protocols for Inter-domain Quality of Service Routing in a Distributed Overlay Entities Architecture.*

References

A. Akella, B. Maggs, S. Seshan, A. Shaikh, and R. Sitaraman. *A measurement-based analysis of multihoming.* In Proc. of ACM SIGCOMM 2003, August 2003

G. Almes, S. Kalidindi, M. Zekauskas, *A one-way delay metric for IPPM*, IETF, RFC 2679, September 1999

Network Measurement Tools. http://www.research.att.com/. Web page accessed at August 2005.

S. Blake, D. Black, M. Carlson, E.Davies, Z. Wang and W. Weiss, *An Architecture for Differentiated Services*, RFC 2475, December 1998.

Cisco Systems, Optimized Edge Routing. http://www.cisco.com/. Web page accessed at August 2005.

R. Dai, D. Stahl, and A. Whinston. *The economics of smart routing and QoS.* In Proc. of the Fifth Inter. Workshop on Networked Group Comm. (NGC'03), 2003.

Internap Network Services. *Internap Flow Control Platform.* http://www.internap.com/. Web page accessed at August 2005.

R. Chang and M. Lo, *Inbound Traffic Engineering for Multihomed ASs Using AS Path Prepending.* IEEE Network, March/April 2005.

N. Feamster, J. Borkenhagen, and J. Rexford. *Guidelines for interdomain traffic engineering.* ACM SIGCOMM Comput. Commun. Rev., 33(5) : 19 to 30, 2003.

A. Feldmann, A. Greenberg, C. Lund, N. Reingold, J. Rexford, and F. True, *Deriving traffic demands for operational IP networks: Methodology and experience.* IEEE/ACM Trans. Networking 9, June 2001.

M. Garey and D. Johnson, *Computers and Intractability, A guide to the theory of NP-Completeness.* Freeman, San Francisco, 1979.

D. Goldenberg, L. Qiu, H. Xie, Y. Yang, and Y. Zhang. *Optimizing cost and performance for multihoming.* In Proc. of ACM SIGCOMM 2004, August 2004

T. Griffin. *What is the Sound of One Route Flapping?* IPAM talk, 2002

T. Griffin, and G. Wilfong. *Analysis of the MED Oscillation Problem in BGP.* In Proc. of the 10th IEEE International Conf. on Network Protocols (ICNPŠ02), 2002

R. Hancock, G. Karagiannis, J. Loughney and S. Bosh. *Next Steps in Signalling.* IETF, Internet-draft, November 2004

Infonet Suite Homepage. http://www.info.ucl.ac.be/ bqu/jsim/. Web page accessed at August 2005.

IP Monitoring Project (IPMON). http://ipmon.sprint.com/. Web page accessed at August 2005.

J-Sim Homepage. http://www.j-sim.org. Web page accessed at August 2005.

F. Kuipers, P. V. Mieghem, T. Korkmaz, and M. Krunz, *An Overview of Constraint-Based Path Selection Algorithms for QoS Routing*, In IEEE Communications Magazine, December 2002

R. Mahajan, D. Wetherall and T. Anderson. *Negotiation based routing between neighboring domains.* In Proc. of NSDI, May 2005.

The Internet Mapping Project. http://research.lumeta.com/ches/map/. Web page accessed at August 2005.

Y. Rekhter, T. Li. *A Border Gateway Protocol 4 (BGP-4).* IETF, RFC 1771, March 1995

T. Roughgarden and E. Tardos. *How bad is selfish routing?* Journal of ACM, 49(2):236 to 259, 2002.

S. Shalunov, B. Teitelbaum. *One-way active measurement protocol (OWAMP) requirements.* IETF, RFC 3763, April 2004

S. Uhlig, O. Bonaventure, *Designing BGP-based outbound traffic engineering techniques for stub ASes.* ACM SIGCOMM CCR, October 2004

J. Winick, S. Jamin, and J. Rexford. *Traffic engineering between neighboring domains.* http://www.research.att.com/jrex/papers/interAS.pdf, July 2002.

M. Yannuzzi, A. Fonte, X. Masip, E. Monteiro, S. Sanchez, M. Curado, J. Domingo. *A proposal for inter-domain QoS routing based on distributed overlay entities and QBGP.* In Proc. of WQoSR2004, LNCS 3266, October 2004

IPV6 DEPLOYMENT, NOT ONLY A NETWORK PROBLEM

Omar Walid Llorente, Tomás P. de Miguel Moro, and
David Fernández Cambronero
Universidad Politécnica de Madrid, Spain
omar@dit.upm.es, tmiguel@dit.upm.es, dfernandez@dit.upm.es

Abstract   The new IPv6 and the current IPv4 will coexist for many years. A wide range of techniques have been designed to make the coexistence possible and to provide an easy network transition. An organization involved in the IPv6 transition should address not only network issues but also final user applications. The management of the different services must also be revised. This is specially relevant in academic institutions where educational, production and research networks live together in the same environment. This document is intended to give the reader a more comprehensive and accurate picture about the IPv6 transition procedures that may be accomplished by the different University members to introduce IPv6 smoothly and successfully.

Keywords: IPv6 transition, IPv6 addressing plan, IPv4/IPv6 integrated management, IPv6 campus transition

1.1   Introduction

The current version of IP has not changed substantially since RFC 791 in 1981. To address the requirements of the New Generation Internet, the new IPv6 protocol has been designed. The new IPv6 and the actual IPv4 will coexist for many years. A wide range of techniques have been designed to make the coexistence possible and to provide an easy network transition. However, when an organization adopts IPv6, many issues should be taken into account. Although IPv6 is a network protocol, transition is not only a network issue.

IPv6 is not an update back-compatible with IPv4, but instead a complete new network protocol oriented to radically change (or upgrade) the way our computers and electronic devices collaborate one with each other. There are a lot of new features related to the new protocol, but the more relevant ones are the huge addressing capability and the more efficient hierarchical addressing and routing structure. IPv6 is able to address 2^{128} hosts and networks, what comes to be approximately like our current public addressing capacity elevated to the fourth power: $[Internet(IPv6)] \simeq [Internet(IPv4)]^4$. This large address space has been created to allow multiple levels of subnetting and address allocation, from the Internet backbone to the individual subnets within an organization.

Thanks to this range of available unique public identifiers, virtually everybody will be able to use end-to-end communications with their electronic devices, avoiding the current use of proxies and network address translators (NATs). The main benefits of the end-to-end model are threefold: the privacy is greatly enhanced; the performance of the communication is augmented; and the eventual network problems can be handled by both ends allowing the upper protocols to control the new situation in a way that better fits the user application (i.e. changing the data rate or transferring the connection to a new network interface).

If the question is about how will an IPv6 router will manage the huge number of networks that will be deployed with the current processing capabilities of the hardware, the problem is solved by using a more efficient hierarchical route path distribution: in the new network protocol, the network prefix will be assigned not to the final user organization, but to the Internet Service Provider (ISP) it will use. The new problem that arises is that the organization (and the final user) will have a different network prefix from each one of the ISPs hired by it. Network administrators will have to consider what solution fits their network best, among the many proposed.

1.1.1   Transition to IPv6

One of the main concerns about the new protocol is the way in which it can be introduced in existing organizations. IPv6 was thought to allow gradual migration, but protocol transitions are not easy, and the one from IPv4 to IPv6 is not the exception. Protocol transitions are typically deployed by installing and configuring the new protocol on all nodes within the network and verifying that all host and router operations work successfully. Although this might be easily managed in a small organization, the challenge of making a rapid protocol migration in medium and large organizations is very difficult. This is specially relevant in universities where advanced network researches are combined with administrative tasks and basic academic nodes, together in the same IP network.

It is then clear that the transition from the current IPv4 networks to the new IPv6 scenario will be a time consuming process during which both protocol versions will coexist. To put the new protocol in reality, there are many methods to choose from, either of which allows the access between IPv4 and IPv6 systems. The most recommendable ones are:

- IPv6 Protocol Translation (NAT-PT). Like IPv4 Network Address Translation (NAT), but with IP protocol translation also.

- Tunneling connections. This method allows the use of IPv4 packets to transport IPv6 ones and vice versa.

- Dual Stack Transition Mechanism (DSTM). Permits the use of both protocols at the same time by means of installing two different protocol stacks over the physical network drivers. The device is assigned an address of each type for each stack.

- Application Layer Gateways (ALGs). For example, an HTTP cache server that can fetch pages over IPv6 and transmit them to the client application using IPv4.

NAT-PT has at least the same constraints of the NAT approach in IPv4 networks, including requiring different translators for the different applications to be translated (i.e., one for HTTP, another for FTP and other for IRC) in the worst case. Although tunneling allows the user to have a real experience in IPv6 without noticing the intermediaries, it has various constraints from the administration point of view (like establishing and maintaining the tunnels, tracing the problems and managing the routing tables for the different connections, besides of the processing and memory requirements for the routers).

The ALGs, apart of interfering with the Application Level, may not allow the user a real IPv6 experience. On the contrary, DSTM is a method that does allow the user to feel a real IPv6 experience because it brings the new protocol to the user desktop with all the implied consequences. The main problem in DSTM is that it needs, for the Layer 3, two pieces of software capable of adequately managing both the old and the new protocol at the same time. This is its main advantage too: the user can still use both protocols simultaneously, each one with the required or supported applications.

1.1.2 Planning is the key

It is natural that the IPv6 transition process will be long in time. It is natural too that it won't be a costless one. Much less if the necessities of the organization do not fit within the initial planning.

As IPv6 transition planners, our first effort has to be oriented to being able to bring the new protocol to the users in an 'easy way'. Not only for them, but also for the network managers. For example, allowing the user to experiment the IPv6 benefits while using the same equipment or by reducing the number of changes that the internal and external networks will suffer.

As previously presented, there are a number of technical approaches for making the IPv6 transition available, each one with its own advantages and drawbacks. But even if only one transition mechanism is chosen for all the network, many configuration alternatives are available. Besides, the actual network technology used, the services offered and the operating priorities in each Campus to access the Internet may introduce some other considerations in the sense of available bandwidth, traffic interference, operative system and application software upgrading requirements, functionality, etc.

All these points will draw a different roadmap on each case to achieve the aim of being IPv6 aware, but from our experience, this task will not be overwhelming if the initial planning criteria are good enough. We consider that IPv6 is something that the end users cannot skip, empowering not only them and their applications but their work too. Therefore, putting IPv6 on their hands has to be a clear priority and has to be carefully planned.

1.2   Network level transition

Although there have been a tremendous number of different physical network technologies used in Campuses all around the world, nowadays, from a physical point of view, and as a de facto standard, the Ethernet (802.3) and its derived or related protocols (802.11b, 802.11g, 802.1q) are established as the actual LAN and WAN protocols for the majority of the Universities and High Schools.

This consideration, in addition to the fact that the Dual-Stack option is widely available on most modern OSs (like Windows XP, GNU/Linux, FreeBSD and many others), if taken into account, can polarize our design in two different ways: 1) to add IPv6 to the currently deployed networks creating a full DSTM network, and 2) to create a new, isolated and initially experimental network tree where the IPv6-only option is considered[1].

Which one of these methods is the best for each case is a common sense decision that has to be made taking into account the special circumstances of each organization and its users. Our experience points out that both approaches can be used in the same environment if it is necessary, but complexity is a factor to decrease.

From our point of view, the best approach for the IPv6 Transition Process in academic organizations is the full DSTM one. The main reason is that with this method, it is always possible to deploy the new protocol step by step and network by network, and then slowly adapt each host to the use of both protocols by upgrading or configuring its Operative System. This offers more control on the situation to the administrative personnel and greatly reduces the initial costs of the IPv6 deployment.

---

[1] The 2nd option can be configured in several ways: 2.a) By using a different interface in each host to access the separate IPv6 network, and 2.b) by using the same interface but another logical LAN (if 802.1q or LAN tagging it is available in the network core) to access the separate IPv6 network.

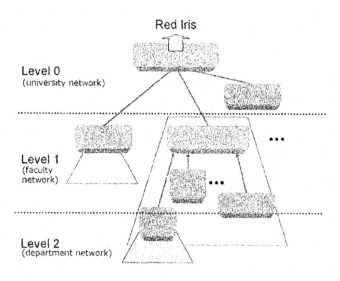

Figure 1. UPM network topology

1.2.1 Addressing plan

The Technical University of Madrid (UPM) network is organized as a star-shaped structure. Interconnection is provided by means of Giga-Ethernet links between all University High Schools, University Institutes and the Central Network Administration Department (CCUPM). Internet connectivity is provided by the Spanish Academic Network ISP (called RedIRIS) using another Giga-Ethernet link between CCUPM and the regional (Madrid) node of RedIRIS.

The UPM network is a multi-level topology (see Figure 1). At the first level is the CCUPM router which links University subnets with the rest of the Internet Academic Network. The second topology level is composed of all Faculty routers. Behind the Faculty level there is the department or research group topology level. This lower level is composed by one or more subnets connected through a firewall to protect internal users from external attacks.

RFC 3513 defines the IPv6 protocol addressing architecture. As it is described in section 2.5, an IPv6 address is composed of 128 bits divided into:

- a Subnet Prefix, that identifies the subnet (link, in IPv6 terminology) where the system is connected, and is common to all the stations connected to it.

- an Interface Identifier, which identifies a station inside a network, and must be different for every system connected to it.

RFC 3513 in section 2.6, states that, with very few exceptions, the interface identifier must be 64 bits long, and must be derived from MAC address using the EUI-64 format.

The large size of the interface identifier is not due to the number of stations connected to a subnet, as it happened in IPv4. The cause is the simplification of the autoconfiguration mechanisms derived from this length, since the generation of a unique identifier derived from MAC address (48 bits long) is very simple. Therefore, the autoconfiguration mechanism simplicty prevails against the efficient usage of bits, which is not critical in IPv6 due to the large addressing capability.

The RIPE-267 document defines the actual address assignment policy in Europe. Basically, it is proposed to assign 32 bits long prefixes (/32) to IPv6 Internet providers. Regarding prefix assignment to ISP users, the RIPE document follows IAB/IESG (RFC 3177) recommendations, consisting in:

- As a general practice, assigning 48 bits (/48 prefix) to each ISP user, except large size users who will occasionally receive shorter prefixes (/47 or even shorter).

- Assigning 64 bits (/64 prefix) only if it is justified by a design decision of assigning a single subnet, for instance, a mobile network inside a car or an ADSL residential network.

- Assigning 128 bit addresses (/128 prefix) in case of being sure of having a single device connected (for instance, a PPP connection through telephone network).

It is preferred to sacrify address space in order to improve the network management efficiency and to simplify the address management, which is very expensive in actual IPv4 based networks. The idea of having a single address allocation in most of the cases underlies this assignment policy, which would cover current and long term needs, against usual high cost reassignments performed nowadays.

In addition to that, the studies performed (RFC 3177, section 4) suggest that despite the high misuse of addressing space no addresses shortage will occur, even according to the more pessimistic forecasts.

According to the previous recommendations, RedIRIS has been delegated by RIPE 2001:720::/32 prefix. And, in the same way, RedIRIS IPv6 addressing plan establishes the assignment of a /48 prefix to each University. As the prefix assigned to UPM by RedIRIS is not known at the moment, it will be referred to in this document in the following way: 2001:720:XXXX::/48.

Once such network prefix is assigned to the Campus, the main objective has to be to assign subnetwork prefixes for the different Campus users in a way that could allow subsequent assignments to be contiguous to the previous ones. This is important because managing one IPv6 network prefix is much simpler than administering and configuring more than one.

The way this is done is the following: to assign sparse prefixes to the subsequent hierarchical levels by leaving blank (unassigned) spaces between them. Of course, the network mask lengths have to be proportional to the number of final subnetworks and users.

If UPM is assigned a /48 prefix, there are 16 bits for subnetting that are available for making /64 final user subnetworks. These 65536 /64 subnets can be distributed in the following way:

- 64 very big schools if 6 bits for each school /54 prefix are used, having 4*256 possible /64 subnets into each school, or

- 128 big schools using a /55 prefix, having 2*256 possible /64 subnets into each school, or

- 256 medium size schools using a /56 prefix, having 256 possible /64 subnets into each school.

Studying the different school needs and according to our estimations, the best approach in our case may be the following:

- 16 type A schools, each one with a /53 prefix network (each center with 4 blocks of 256 /64 subnets assigned and 4 more blocks to assign in the future), and

- 16 type B schools, each one with a /54 prefix network (each center with 2 blocks of 256 /64 subnets assigned and 2 more blocks for future use), and

- 16 type C schools, each one with a /55 prefix network (each center with 1 block of 256 /64 subnets assigned and 1 more block not assigned), and

- 32 type D schools, each one with a /56 prefix network (each center with 1 block of 256 /64 subnets assigned).

Using this addressing structure, which represents a total of 48 + 32 different schools or centers (see Table 1), it is possible to give to the more than 32 UPM institutions an adequate IPv6 prefix and thus to all their current and future users, hosts and networks.

1.2.2   Routing issues

There are many IP routers that are IPv6 capable. Probably most of the ones deployed for IPv4 are capable of managing IPv6 packets by upgrading their software. And many times even without upgrading them. As a matter of fact, it

Table 1.   UPM prefix delegation schema

Center type	Address format	Prefix Length
A	0CCCCBBBnnnnnnnn	/53
B	10CCCCBBnnnnnnnn	/54
C	110CCCCBnnnnnnnn	/55
D	111CCCCCnnnnnnnn	/56

may be quite inexpensive today (forgetting the administration costs) to deploy a PC based IPv6 router if an open-source OS -like FreeBSD, GNU/Linux or any other- is used for routing one or both protocols into our networks. Other commercial solutions of the most important firms are widely available too.

As previously stated, if Dual-Stack infrastructures are to be deployed, it may be crucial to have routers capable of managing IPv4 and IPv6 packets without loosing performance. If this is not achieved, our users may be obliged by the circumstances to avoid using IPv6, thus wasting all the efforts done.

The main activities that an IPv6 router has to perform, besides the usual ones like forwarding IP packets and re-distributing routes (Inter-domain Gateway Protocols, EGPs, and Intra-domain Gateway Protocols, IGPs), are to generate Router Advertisement (RA) packets. This is done in order to inform the hanging nodes which prefix is assigned to the network or subnetwork and to permit the Stateless Autoconfiguration of the IPv6 devices connected to take place.

Managing RA configuration is an easy task if only a router per network is deployed. In other cases, as in multihoming, it is necessary to configure the routers to export the correct prefixes and the nodes to import, understand and manage all the RAs learned.

In large organizations, the route distribution protocols (EGPs and IGPs) play a very important role. Usually, the EGPs are imposed by our ISPs. Therefore, few changes can be made regarding this aspect. What has to be planned in any case for the migration is the IGP protocol, if needed (many times, as is our particular case, the static-route deployment approach may be good enough if the organization is not too dynamic or unstable).

If the IGP is necessary, and the one used to manage IPv4 routes does not support IPv6, a decision has to be made: to deploy a different and independent routing protocol for IPv6 or to upgrade to a new IPv4 and IPv6-capable routing protocol. It is widely recommended, because of its mature state and high compatibility, to use IS-IS [IS-IS] as IGP protocol even when OSI environments and TCP over IPv4/IPv6 have to live together.

Depending on the particular details of the migration, it might be considered to have (even when deploying DSTM) two different routers, one for each IP protocol. This approach permits to avoid collisions and interference between the two IP version packets, specially if the new technology is not well known or stable.

1.3 Services transition

Ordinary users see the Internet through the applications they use daily for their work, from electronic mail to the WWW navigation. In general, users get great benefits from all Internet services, even the simplest ones such as FTP or Telnet. This section deals with the concerns of services migration.

1.3.1 Transition is not only a network problem

Existing applications cannot use IPv6 without previous modifications. One of the reasons is that TCP/IP network architecture is not perfectly layered. For example, upper layer applications usually use IP addressing to identify destination nodes and their traffic flows. Although many times symbolic names are provided, standard communication libraries based on socket interfaces use only IP addresses. Therefore, IP address management should be maintained as part of the application and complemented with the Domain Name System (DNS) management.

Besides, the new IPv6 addresses' structure forces the use of a new transport layer interface (the IPv6 sockets layer interface). Hence, from the applications point of view, the IPv6 deployment requires changes in the existing code and -maybe- the addition of new communication design concepts. The necessary changes to allow the IPv6 operation of any networked application are not deep nor specially difficult but have to be done by the main developer team, or at least, if the source code is available, by any interested group in the matter (usually public founded projects, research teams or universities).

In the case of the usual academic application set, there are a lot of applications already ported or at least IPv6-capable. A very good link related to IPv6 applications and protocol support is [Bieringer, 2005]. For the reader to have a sight of the status, [IPv6 status] is recommended.

As a very short summary, the most important networked applications and protocols of our environment that lack IPv6 support are the following:

- SAMBA/NetBIOS[2]: File transfer protocol used for sharing data, authenticating and integrating Windows and Unix users, printers and computers.

---

[2]There is a non-official IPv6 patch available for 2.2.5 version of samba system, but it doesn't provide IPv6 interaction between GNU/Linux and Windows OSs.

- NFS: Networked filesystem used to share files efficiently in (originally Unix-like) local networks.

- Active Directory (AD): Windows based authentication and resource integration system.

- Vulnerability scanners: the most usual way of testing the exposure of our organization to security problems.

Other applications that do not have good enough support on IPv6:

- IP filtering: In a potentially aggressive environment such as Internet, some kind of adequate filtering policy has to be provided. But, in IPv6, only one stateful packet-inspection implementation is available for the task. Other solutions are still in an experimental stage. Options like translation at network level (NATs) or proxys at application level go against the end-to-end paradigm of IPv6 and should be deployed only in very specific environments.

- Event logging apps: Only one server (mysyslog) of the many Unix syslog protocol implementations has native IPv6 support. Maybe this is not a problem in a Dual-Stack transition approach.

- Webmail interfaces: In [IPv6 status] only one webmail implementation is IPv6 aware. This may be a problem if a fully functional IPv6-only network is the transition method chosen.

- Instant messaging (IM): currently only the IRC protocol is fully supported, but it is expectable that other popular instant messaging systems will be available soon. Euro6IX project ([euro6ix]) has this item among its many aims.

1.3.2   IP filtering, security and other issues

As previously stated, unlike with routing protocols, the IPv4 and IPv6 filtering solutions are nor widely available nor fully-operational in most of the cases. Nevertheless, security of the new network has to be at least as important as in the old one. Indeed if a mixed (dual-stack) environment is going to be deployed.

Stateful IPv6 packet-inspection filtering is nowadays only performed by Cisco products in the commercial world. In the open-source world this is done by the connection-tracking capabilities of netfilter ip6tables and USAGI kernel extensions, that point to be in experimental status. See [Bieringer, 2004] for a recent status report and detailed explanations.

Other security consideration that has to be taken into account is that, at the time of this writing, there are not any security auditing tools (like there are for

IPv4, as saint, nessus, etc) capable of testing IPv6 systems further, in addition to checking for open ports (like nmap).

Besides, if we consider that, because of the universal availability of global IPv6 addresses and their derivation from the -unique- physical interface MAC field and because the addresses would be neither masked nor shielded anyhow, it is possible to track the interface -and thus the user- all over the world since the day the interface is connected to the Internet for the first time.

To solve this problem, it has been proposed that some kind of random address assignation has to be provided. Some different approaches have already been proposed to do that IPv6 address assignation, but yet neither one is standardized or mandatory.

Of course, all these pointed problems and many more will be hopefully addressed in the future, but today they have to be subject of attention from the administration point of view and will be part of the job to implement the practical solutions for them.

Since the support of IPSec is mandatory in the IPv6 stack, a native virtual private network has been provided. The problem here comes from the point that if we agree that firewalls are needed for IPv6 and given that the end-to-end connection and the end-to-end security are mandatory, what kind of policy has to be deployed in order to permit or disallow encrypted connections that are opaque (IPSec tunnel mode) for the firewall? Here lies a big dilemma between allowing end-to-end encrypted connections from and to any IPv6 devices, or only to some ones that are previously known and allowed.

In other way, given the hierarchical routing structure designed for IPv6 and the fact that the network prefix will be no more owned by the final user nor by the organization but by its Internet Service Provider, it has been noticed that any networked organization that wants to have high network reachability will have to be connected to 2 or more ISPs, thus managing more than one global network prefix. The issues that cover this matter are commonly referred to as multihoming. Multihoming is not a new concept, but in IPv6 it has some implications that it does not have in IPv4 environments (derived from the fact that the prefix has to vary if the ISP changes). There are some experimental solutions proposed by different R&D teams that the initial planning of the IPv6 transition should study.

Support to mobility is one of the main advantages of the IPv6 protocol and it has a lot of implications in hardware to be deployed, inherited prefixes, published routes, end-to-end security and authentication, IP connection tracking and application independence of the real IP address used by the IP stack. Careful analysis is necessary if it is mandatory to have mobility in the new network.

Other services like Authorization, Multicast, Quality of Service (QoS) and Traffic Engineering (TE) techniques have to be adapted in many cases if the network protocol changes, so a careful study of the available options has to be done.

1.3.3   install.hosts tool: the integrated management of IPv4 and IPv6 networks

It is important to notice that only upgrading or porting the applications will not suffice for supporting the whole new protocol. Management tasks will be duplicated if special efforts are not planned to minimize the administration of DNS records, along with firewalling policies and wireless infrastructure, among other duties. Our approach to this problem was to update our management tools to support both protocols and to configure the different services mentioned. Besides, the task of maintaining both networks (IPv4 and IPv6 based) can be overwhelming if any kind of automatic configuration is not used to simplify the human part of the job and minimize the human mistakes.

We have integrated the configuration of the IP assignation to a name in DNS with the management of DHCP/DHCPv6 systems and with the actualization of wireless infrastructure hardware (MAC) access lists, among other functionalities. This approach has been completely developed at the Department of Telematic Systems Engineering at the Technical University of Madrid, using a one-pass, perl based script system to which IPv6 capabilities have been added [Latorre, 2004]. The main script name is install.hosts, and its main database is text based and refered to as tabla.numeros. Its main functions are:

- To create the IPv4 and IPv6 direct/reverse DNS address records for ISC [ISC] bind servers deployed. Other DNS registers, like MX, CNAME, etc are configured as well automatically.

- To create the DHCP/DHCPv6 config files for stateful address configuration for ISC [ISC] DHCP server and DHCPv6 sourceforge [DHCPv6] servers.

- To upgrade the Wi-Fi infrastructure access lists (ACLs) for MAC address filtering.

- To update the IPv4 and IPv6 filtering rules and host/network databases (using fwbuilder [fwbuilder] XML format for both IP protocols), cross-check MAC and IP addresses for each filtered host and auto-disabling obsolete/non-related rules.

- To distribute all the changes to the different systems affected and to restart the services when needed.

- To update the IPv4 NIS server configuration.

- Other minor tasks, like /etc/hosts, /etc/ethers and /etc/networks files generation or automatic accounting reports.

The main advantage of the system is its simplicity, allowing to do many complex management tasks in a easy, efficient and quick way.

For example, to do the most usual tasks (simple tasks like adding or deleting one host to or from an existing network) network managers have to edit only the main database file and then run the main script. When more complex tasks have to be done (like creating a new subnet or domain name) it is necessary to edit the main script, the headers and the library files on which the system relays, and then run the main script. It is fair to say that although this work is not so easy and have to be done by specially skilled staff, the management system helps a lot comparing with the manual configuration of the related individual services. Fortunately, that kind of tasks are much less usual.

The possibility of doing the usual changes in an easy way can be seen as an added advantage of this integrated management system: work can be divided into profiles depending on the skills of the personnel without compromising the reliability of the management process.

1.4 Conclusions

The IPv6 transition is a process which ends when all nodes within a network install and configure the new protocol. Although this might be easily managed in a small organization, the challenge of making a rapid protocol migration in medium and large organizations is much more difficult. This is specially relevant in Universities where advanced network researches are combined with administrative tasks and basic academic nodes.

We can recommend four steps in the transition of Universities and Campus networks to IPv6: 1st) To set up dual stack on backbone routers; 2nd) Rationally, to extend dual stack to the end-user networks and hosts and to finish the corporative applications migration in the dual environment; 3rd) To start removing IPv4 from end-users subnets providing at least a tunneling method to maintain communication with old IPv4-only nodes; 4th) Finally, all systems are IPv6 and IPv4 is removed from all routers.

Some clues that have been presented in this paper are:

- IPv6 transition is a slow process.

- Users want to maintain old services.

- Users don't care about the technology itself, only about the benefits it brings for them.

- Migration is not only a network transition problem, but a service upgrading one. There are two main kinds of services to be migrated in the process: the services oriented to the final users, and the services to manage and configure the network.

- Our experience is positive and this can only get better: Welcome to the IPv6 world!

References

P. Bieringer, "IPv6 & Linux". 1st Global IPv6 Summit. August 2004.
   http://www.bieringer.de/pb/lectures/PB-IPv6-Brazil-2004.pdf
Peter Bieringer page on IPv6, http://www.bieringer.de/linux/IPv6/
J. Bound (ed.), "IPv6 Enterprise Network Scenarios". IETF Internet Draft. July 2004.
   http://www.ietf.org/internet-drafts/draft-ietf-v6ops-ent-scenarios-05.txt
Current Status of IPv6 Support for Networking Applications,
   http://www.deepspace6.net/docs/ipv6_status_page_apps.html
DeepSpace6, http://www.deepspace6.net/
DHCPv6 project at Sourceforge, http://sourceforge.net/projects/dhcpv6/
A. Durand, S. Roy, and J. Paugh, "Issues with Dual Stack IPv6 on by Default". IETF Internet
   Draft. July 2004.
   http://www.ietf.org/internet-drafts/draft-ietf-v6ops-v6onbydefault-03.txt
Euro6IX: European IPv6 Internet Exchanges Backbone. http://www.euro6ix.org
Firewall Builder project, http://www.fwbuilder.org
C. Huitema, R. Austein, S. Satapati, and R. van der Pol, "Unmanaged Networks IPv6 Transition
   Scenarios". IETF Request for Comments 3750. April 2004.
   http://www.ietf.org/rfc/rfc3750.txt
Intermediate System to Intermediate System (IS-IS) IGP protocol IETF charter,
   http://www.ietf.org/html.charters/isis-charter.html
Internet Systems Consortium, Inc. (ISC), http://www.isc.org/
Latorre Sebastián, D. "Gestión de cortafuegos en redes departamentales IPv6". Career Final
   Project. ETSI Telecomunicación. Universidad Politécnica de Madrid. July 2004.
M. Lind, V. Ksinant, S. Park, and A. Baudot, P. Savola, "Scenarios and Analysis for Introducing
   IPv6 into ISP Networks". IETF Request for Comments 4029. March 2005.
   http://www.ietf.org/rfc/rfc4029.txt
MIPL: Mobile IPv6 for Linux. http://mobile-ipv6.org/
P. Nikander, J. Kempf, E. Nordmark, "IPv6 Neighbor Discovery (ND) Trust Models and Threats".
   IETF Request for Comments 3756. May 2004.
   http://www.ietf.org/rfc/rfc3756.txt
E. Nordmark, and R. E. Gilligan, "Basic Transition Mechanisms for IPv6 Hosts and Routers".
   IETF Internet Draft. March 2005. http://www.ietf.org/internet-drafts/draft-ietf-v6ops-mech-
   v2-07.txt
M-K. Shin, Y-G. Hong, J. Hagino, P. Savola and E. M. Castro, "Application Aspects of IPv6
   Transition". March 2005. http://www.ietf.org/rfc/rfc4038.txt
J. Wiljakka (ed.), "Analysis on IPv6 Transition in 3GPP Networks". IETF Internet Draft. Octo-
   ber 2004. http://www.ietf.org/internet-drafts/draft-ietf-v6ops-3gpp-analysis-11.txt

TOPOLOGY DISCOVERY USING AN ADDRESS PREFIX BASED STOPPING RULE

Benoit Donnet
Timur Friedman
Laboratoire LiP6/CNRS
Université Pierre & Marie Curie
{benoit.donnet, timur.friedman}@lip6.fr

Abstract   Recently, a first step towards a highly distributed IP-level topology discovery tool has been made with the introduction of the Doubletree algorithm. Doubletree is an efficient cooperative algorithm that allows the discovery of a large portion of nodes and links in the network while strongly reducing probing redundancy on nodes and destinations as well as the amount of probes sent. In this paper, we propose to reduce more strongly the load on destinations and, more essentially, the communication cost required for the cooperation by introducing a probing stopping rule based on CIDR address prefixes.

Keywords: Topology discovery, Cooperative algorithm, Doubletree, CIDR

1.   Introduction

This is a time when highly distributed applications are in full expansion. Among others, we can cite *SETI@home* [Anderson et al., 2002] (probably the first one and the most famous), *FOLDING@home* [Larson et al., 2002] and the *Human Proteome Folding Project* [Bonneau et al., 2004].

The network measurement community is not an exception to this fashion. Some measurement tools have already been released as daemons or screen savers. In particular, in France, we have *Grenouille* [A. Schmitt et al., vice], a monitoring tool for broadband networks. More recently, we saw the introduction of *NETI@home* [Simpson and Riley, 2004], an application collecting network performance statistics from end-systems.

Tools allowing for topology discovery at the IP level, based on *traceroute* [Jacobsen, 1989], are becoming more distributed. There is a number of well known systems, such as *skitter* [Huffaker et al., 2002], *RIPE NCC TTM* [Georgatos et al., 2001] or *NLANR AMP* [McGregor et al., 2000], skitter being probably the most extensive one as it considers a set of between 20 and 30 monitors tracing towards a million destinations. The two others, TTM and AMP, consider a larger number of monitors (on the order of one or two hundreds) but they trace in full mesh, avoiding to probe outside their own network. However, the need to increase the number of traceroute sources in order to obtain more complete topology measurement is felt [Clauset and Moore, 2004; Lakhina et al., 2003].

The idea of placing a tracerouting tool inside a screen saver, an idea first suggested by Jørg Nonnenmacher as reported by Cheswick et al. in [Cheswick et al., 2000] should allow one to quickly obtain a structure of a considerable size. Following this idea, a publicly downloadable measurement tool within a daemon, DIMES [Shavitt and Shir, 2005], has been released in September 2004. At the time of writing this paper, DIMES counts 4644 agents distributed across 78 countries.

Such a large structure has, however, inherent scaling problems. For instance, if all the monitors trace towards the same destination, it could easily appear as a distributed denial of service (DDoS) attack. Furthermore, such a system must avoid consuming undue network resources. However, before the development of the *Doubletree* algorithm [Donnet et al., 2005b], little consideration had been given to how to perform large-scale topology discovery efficiently and in a network-friendly manner.

Based on the tree-like structure of routes in the internet, Doubletree acts to avoid retracing the same routes through these structures. The key to Doubletree is that monitors share information regarding the paths that they have explored. If one monitor has already probed a given path to a destination then another monitor should avoid that path. We have found that probing in this manner can significantly reduce load on routers and destinations while maintaining high node and link coverage.

In this paper, we aim to improve Doubletree in order to more strongly reduce the impact on destinations. We propose to replace a stopping rule based on destination addresses with a stopping rule based on the *CIDR address prefixes* [Fuller et al., 1993] of destinations. The idea is to aggregate the destinations set into subnetworks, i.e. we filter each destination address and associate them to a subnetwork with the use of the CIDR address prefixes. Each monitor will probe all the destinations in each subnetwork. Futher, this proposal should also allow to reduce the amount of communication required by Doubletree. Indeed, instead of shareing a set of (interface, destination) pairs, monitors will share a set of (interface, prefix_destination) pairs.

The rest of the paper is organized as follow: in Sec. 2, we introduce our prior work on the Doubletree algorithm. In Sec. 3, we present our methodology and our results. In Sec. 4, we present related work. Finally, in Sec. 5, we conclude and discuss further works.

2.   Prior Work

Our prior work [Donnet et al., 2005b] described the inefficiency of the classic topology probing technique of tracing routes hop by hop outwards from a set of monitors towards a set of destinations. It also introduced Doubletree, an improved probing algorithm. Data for our prior work, and also for this paper, were produced by 24 skitter monitors on August 1st through 3rd, 2004. Of the 971,080 destinations towards which all of these monitors traced routes on those days, we randomly selected a manageable 50,000 for each of our experiments.

Considering first the inefficiency, we note that only 10.4% of the probes from a typical monitor serve to discover an interface that the monitor has not previously seen. An additional 2.0% of the probes return invalid addresses or do not result in a response. The remaining 87.6% of probes are redundant, visiting interfaces that the monitor has already discovered. Such redundancy for a single monitor, termed *intra-monitor redundancy*, is much higher close to the monitor, as can be expected given the tree-like structure of routes emanating from a single source. In addition, most interfaces, especially those close to destinations, are visited by all monitors. This redundancy from multiple monitors is termed *inter-monitor redundancy*.

While this inefficiency is of little consequence to skitter itself, it poses an obstacle to scaling far beyond skitter's current 24 monitors. In particular, inter-monitor redundancy, which grows in proportion to the number of monitors, is the greater threat. Reducing it requires coordination among monitors.

Doubletree is the key component of a coordinated probing system that significantly reduces both kinds of redundancy while discovering nearly the same set of nodes and links. It takes advantage of the tree-like structure of routes in the internet. Routes leading out from a monitor towards multiple destinations form a tree-like structure rooted at the monitor. Similarly, routes converging towards a destination from multiple monitors form a tree-like structure, but rooted at the destination. A monitor probes hop by hop so long as it encounters previously unknown interfaces. However, once it encounters a known interface, it stops, assuming that it has touched a tree and the rest of the path to the root is also known.

Both backwards and forwards probing use stop sets. The one for backwards probing, called the *local stop set*, consists of all interfaces already seen by that monitor. Forwards probing uses the *global stop set* of (interface, destination) pairs accumulated from all monitors. A pair enters the stop set if a monitor visited the interface while sending probes with the corresponding destination address.

A monitor that implements Doubletree starts probing for a destination at some number of hops h from itself. It will probe forwards at $h + 1$, $h + 2$, etc., adding to the global stop set at each hop, until it encounters either the destination or a member of the global stop set. It will then probe backwards at $h - 1$, $h - 2$, etc., adding to both the local and global stop sets at each hop, until it either has reached a distance of one hop or it encounters a member of the local stop set. It then proceeds to probe for the next destination. When it has completed probing for all destinations, the global stop set is communicated to the next monitor.

The choice of initial probing distance h is crucial. Too close, and intra-monitor redundancy will approach the high levels seen by classic forward prob-ing techniques. Too far, and there will be high inter-monitor redundancy on destinations. The choice must be guided primarily by this latter consideration to avoid having probing look like a DDoS attack.

While Doubletree largely limits redundancy on destinations once hop-by-hop probing is underway, its global stop set cannot prevent the initial probe from reaching a destination if h is set too high. Therefore, we recommend that each monitor set its own value for h in terms of the probability p that a probe sent h hops towards a randomly selected destination will actually hit that destination. Fig. 1 shows the cumulative mass function for this probability for skitter monitor apan-jp. For example, in order to restrict hits on destinations to just 10% of initial probes, this monitor should start probing at $h = 10$ hops. This distance can easily be estimated by sending a small number of probes to randomly chosen destinations.

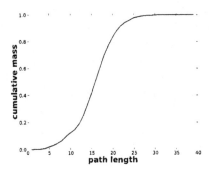

Figure 1.   Cumulative mass plot of path lengths from skitter monitor apan-jp

For a range of p values, compared to classic probing, Doubletree is able to reduce measurement load by approximately 70% while maintaining interface and link coverage above 90%.

One possible obstacle to successful deployment of Doubletree concerns the communication overhead from sharing the global stop set among monitors. Tracing from 24 monitors to just 50,000 destinations with $p = 0.05$ produces a set of 2.7 million (interface, destination) pairs. As pairs of IPv4 addresses are 64 bits long, an uncompressed stop set based on these parameters requires 20.6MB.

A way to reduce this communication overhead is to use *Bloom filters* [Bloom, 1970] to implement the global stop set. A Bloom filter summarizes information concerning a set in a bit vector that can then be tested for set membership. An empty Bloom filter is a vector of all zeroes. A key is registered in the filter by hashing it to a position in the vector and setting the bit at that position to one. Multiple hash functions may be used, setting several bits set to one. Membership of a key in the filter is tested by checking if all hash positions are set to one. A Bloom filter will never falsely return a negative result for set membership. It might, however, return a false positive. For a given number of keys, the larger the Bloom filter, the less likely is a false positive. The number of hash functions also plays a role.

In [Donnet et al., 2005a], we show that, when $p = 0.05$, using a bit vector of size 10^7 and five hash functions allow nearly the same coverage level as a list implementation of the global stop set while reducing only slightly the redundancy on both destinations and internal interfaces and yielding a compression factor of 17.3.

To reduce the load on destinations, we already investigated the concepts of *capping* and *clustering* [Donnet et al., 2005a]. The capping aims to impose an explicit limit on the number of monitors that target a destination. The clustering may be seen as a specialization of the capping by dividing the monitors into clusters, each cluster focusing on a different destination list. The real problem in theses mechanisms is how to assign monitors to destinations. In [Donnet et al., 2005a], we chose to work randomly but future work might reveal that a topologically informed approach provides better yield.

3. Doubletree with CIDR

3.1 Methodology

Skitter data from the beginning of August 2004 serves as the basis of our work. This data set is composed of traceroutes gathered from 24 monitors scattered around the world: United States, Canada, the United Kingdom, France, Sweden, the Netherlands, Japan and New Zealand. All the monitors share a common destination list of 971,080 IPv4 addresses. Each destination is probed in turn by each monitor. To cycle through the destination list, it can takes a few days, usually three. For our studies, in order to reduce computing time and hard disk space to a manageable level, we decided to work on a limited destination subset of 50,000 items randomly chosen amongst the whole set.

We conduct simulations based on the skitter data, applying Doubletree, as described in [Donnet et al., 2005b]. A single experiment uses traceroutes from all 24 monitors to a common set of 50,000 destinations chosen at random. Each data point represents the average value over fifteen runs of the experiment, each run using a different set of 50,000 destinations. No destination is used more than once over the fifteen runs. We determine 95% confidence intervals for the mean based, since the sample size is relatively small, on the Student t distribution. These intervals are typically, though not in all cases, too tight to appear on the plots.

We use $p = 0.05$, which is a value that belongs to the range of p values that our previous work identified as providing a good compromise between coverage accuracy and redundancy reduction. We test all prefixes length from /8 to /24, as well as lengths /28 and /32 (i.e. full IPv4 addresses).

Each monitor probes each destination and records in the global stop set (interface, destination_prefix) pairs instead of (interface, destination) pairs. Compared to classic Doubletree, we only change the global stop set stop rule. Each result considered is compared, in Sec. 3.2, with classic Doubletree and skitter.

3.2   Results

Fig. 2 shows the main performance metric for a probing system: its coverage of the nodes and links in the network. It illustrates how the nodes and links coverage vary in function of the prefix length. A value of 1.0 (not shown here) would mean that application of Doubletree with the given prefix length had discovered exactly the same set of nodes and links as skitter. As already pointed out in our previous work, the use of Doubletree implies a small accuracy loss in the link and node coverage compared to skitter. The lowest level of performance is reached for the /8 prefix. In our data set, on average, there are thirteen /8 subnetworks. As these subnetworks are quite large, monitors are stopped early in their probing. The loss of accuracy, however, is not so dramatic. The link coverage is 0,742 instead of 0,823 and node coverage is 0,897 instead of 0,924. We believe that the coverage level is still high due to the way exploration is performed by the first monitor to probe the network. Indeed, this first monitor uses an empty stop set (by definition of Doubletree) and is thus never stopped in its exploration. We further note that performance improves with prefix length until reaching nearly the same accuracy as classic Doubletree with /24 prefixes.

We believe that the loss of accuracy, compared to classic Doubletree, is essentially located within the subnetworks containing destinations but also inside the core of the network, where duplicated links (and the associated nodes) are missed due to the prefix based stopping rule. Typically, probes reach a very few number of destinations in each subnetwork but, in general, they are stopped at the ingress routers. We miss thus essentially the vast majority of destinations located in a given subnetwork. However more nodes and links may be missed

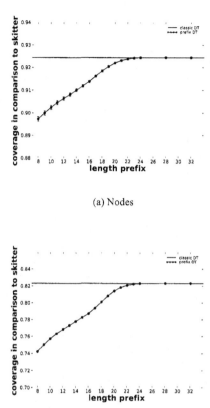

(a) Nodes

(b) Links

Figure 2. Coverage when using prefixes

if the network structure of the subnetwork is more complex, i.e. the subnetwork is not only composed of an ingress router that connects destinations with the rest of the network.

Doubletree aims also to reduce the load on routers. It would be a concern if the redundancy were to increase when introducing a prefix based stopping rule. The ordinates in Fig. 3(a) specify the gross redundancy on router interfaces, i.e. the total number of visits. The ordinates in Fig. 3(b) represent the inter-monitor redundancy. Inter-monitor redundancy, as defined in [Donnet et al., 2005b], is the number of monitors that visit a given interface. The maximum inter-monitor redundancy on destinations, not shown here, is 24. As the extreme values are the most worrisome, we consider redundancy on the 95th percentile interface.

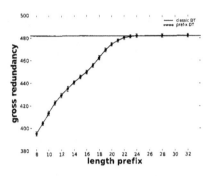

(a) Internal interfaces: gross

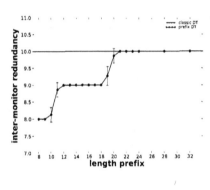

(b) Destinations: inter-monitor

Figure 3.   Redundancy on 95th percentile interfaces when using prefixes

As shown by Fig. 3, the redundancy is not increased when using prefix based stopping rule. Further, for low prefix lengths, the redundancy is reduced for both destinations and routers.

Fig. 4 compares global stop set size. Fig. 4(a) shows the number of keys recorded in the global stop set (in log-scale) as a function of CIDR block prefixes. Fig. 4(b) shows the global stop set size in megabytes.

We can see that there is a strong reduction for low prefixes. For instance, if we consider a /8 prefix, the global stop set will only contain, in average, 302,854 keys. As each key is recorded as a 64 bit value, it corresponds to a stop set of around 2.31MB. Compared to the classic Doubletree, there is a compression factor of 8.9.

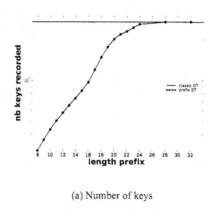

(a) Number of keys

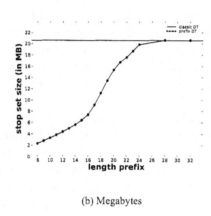

(b) Megabytes

Figure 4.   Global stop set size when using prefixes

In addition to the mechanism presented in this paper, we could also implement the global stop set as a Bloom filter without losing much coverage accuracy [Donnet et al., 2005a, Sec. 3].

	/8	/16	/24	/32
Prefix DT	2.31	7.40	19.87	20.61
Prefix DT with BF	0.361	0.689	1.192	1.192
Classic DT		20.61		
Classic DT with BF		1.192		

Table 1.   Global stop set size comparison (in MB)

Table 1 compared the global stop set implemented as a set of pairs and as a Bloom filter. It also compares classic Doubletree with the mechanism presented in this paper. Concerning Bloom filters, we follow Fan et al's suggestions [Fan et al., 1998, Sec. V.D] for tuning the vector size and the number of hash functions to use.

We see that coupling the prefix based stop rule with a Bloom filter implementation of the global stop set introduces a very strong reduction in the global stop set size. For instance, using a /8 prefix stop rule gives, compared to classic Doubletree, a compression factor of 57.1.

4.   Related Work

Very little work has been conducted on efficient measurement of the overall internet topology. This is in contrast to the number of papers on efficient monitoring of networks that are in a single administrative domain (see for instance, Bejerano and Rastogi's work [Bejerano and Rastogi, 2003]). The two problems are extremely different. An administrator knows their entire network topology in advance, and can freely choose where to place their monitors. Neither of these assumptions hold for monitoring the internet with end-host based software. Since the existing literature is based upon these assumptions, we need to look elsewhere for solutions.

Govindan and Tangmunarunkit [Govindan and Tangmunarunkit, 2000] have proposed the idea of starting traceroutes far from the source. Using a probing strategy based upon IP address prefixes, the *Mercator* system conducts a check before probing the path to a new address that has a prefix P. If paths to an address in P already exist in its database, Mercator starts probing at the highest hop count for a responding router seen on those paths. No results have been published on the performance of this heuristic, though it seems to us an entirely reasonable approach in light of our data.

The Mercator heuristic requires that a guess be made about the relevant prefix length for an address. That guess is based upon the class that the address would have had before the advent of CIDR.

Finally, Some authors [Siamwalla et al., 1998; Burch and Cheswick, 1999] have already suggested the idea of guiding topology discovery at IP level according to BGP information. They use BGP backbone routing tables in order to determine the destinations of traceroutes. For each prefix in the tables, they repeatedly generate a random IP address within that prefix. With the traceroute results to these destinations, they build a router adjacency graph. By probing only one destination per prefix, this technique may miss several nodes and links.

5. Conclusion

In this paper, we present an improvement to the Doubletree probing algorithm. By using stop rules based on address prefixes, we show that we are able to reduce load on destinations while maintaining an acceptable level of coverage accuracy. Further, if we use this simple mechanism with a global stop set implemented as a Bloom filter, we still reduce the global stop set size to very low proportions.

The next prudent step for future work would be to test the algorithms that we describe here on an infrastructure of intermediate size, on the order of hundreds of monitors. We have developed a tool called *traceroute@home* that we plan to deploy in this manner.

We also aim to improve Doubletree in order to guide probing with a higher level information. We plan to develop and experiment algorithms allowing Doubletree to realise more accurate exploration through the use of AS level topology and AS path information.

Acknowledgments

The authors are member of the traceroute@home project. This work was supported by: the RNRT's Metropolis project, NSF grants ANI-9986397 and CCR-0325701, the e-NEXT European Network of Excellence, and LiP6 2004 project funds. Mr. Donnet's work is supported by a SATIN European Doctoral Research Foundation grant.

Without the skitter data provided by kc claffy and her team at CAIDA, this research would not have been possible. They also furnished much useful feedback. Marc Giusti and his team at the Centre de Calcul MEDICIS, Laboratoire STIX, Ecole Polytechnique, offered us access to their computing cluster, allowing faster and easier simulations. Finally, we are indebted to our colleagues in the Networks and Performance Analysis group at LiP6, headed by Serge Fdida, and to our partners in the traceroute@home project, Mark Crovella, José Ignacio Alvarez-Hamelin, Alain Barrat, Matthieu Latapy, Philippe Raoult and Alessandro Vespignani, for their support and advice.

References

A. Schmitt et al. (ongoing service). La météo du net.

Anderson, D. P., Cobb, J., Korpela, E., Lebofsky, M., and Werthimer, D. (2002). SETI@home: An experiment in public-resource computing. *Communications of the ACM*, 45(11):56–61.

Bejerano, Y. and Rastogi, R. (2003). Robust monitoring of link delays and faults in IP networks. In *Proc. IEEE Infocom*.

Bloom, B. H. (1970). Space/time trade-offs in hash coding with allowable errors. *Communications of the ACM*, 13(7):422–426.

Bonneau, R., Baliga, N. S., Deutsch, E. W., Shannon, P., and Hood, L. (2004). Comprehensive de novo structure prediction in a systems-biology context for the archaea halobacterium. *Genome Biology.*

Burch, H. and Cheswick, B. (1999). Mapping the internet. *IEEE Computer,* 32(4):97-98.

Cheswick, B., Burch, H., and Branigan, S. (2000). Mapping and visualizing the internet. In *Proc. 2000 USENIX Annual Technical Conference,* San Diego, California, USA.

Clauset, A. and Moore, C. (2004). Traceroute sampling makes random graphs appear to have power law degree distributions. Technical Report arXiv:cond-mat/0312674 v3, University of New Mexico.

Donnet, B., Friedman, T., and Crovella, M. (2005a). Improved algorithms for network topology discovery. In *Proc. PAM 2005,* Boston, USA.

Donnet, B., Raoult, P., Friedman, T., and Crovella, M. (2005b). Efficient algorithms for large-scale topology discovery. In *Proc. ACM SIGMETRICS 2005,* Banff, Canada.

Fan, L., Cao, P., Almeida, J., and Broder, A. Z. (1998). Summary cache: A scalable wide-area web cache sharing protocol. In *Proc. ACM SIGCOMM.*

Fuller, V., Li, T., Yu, J., and Varadhan, K. (1993). Classless inter-domain routing (CIDR): an address assignment and aggregation strategy. RFC 1519, Internet Engineering Task Force.

Georgatos, F., Gruber, F., Karrenberg, D., Santcroos, M., Susanj, A., Uijterwaal, H., and Wilhelm, R. (2001). Providing active measurements as a regular service for ISPs. In *Proc. Passive and Active Measurement Workshop (PAM).*

Govindan, R. and Tangmunarunkit, H. (2000). Heuristics for internet map discovery. In *Proc. IEEE Infocom.*

Huffaker, B., Plummer, D., Moore, D., and Claffy, k (2002). Topology discovery by active probing. In *Symposium on Applications and the Internet,* Nara City, Japan.

Jacobsen, V. (1989). traceroute.

Lakhina, A., Byers, J., Crovella, M., and Xie, P. (2003). Sampling biases in IP topology measurements. In *Proc. IEEE Infocom '03.*

Larson, S. M., Snow, C. D., Shirts, M., and Pande, V. S. (2002). FOLDING@home and GENOME@home: Using distributed computing to tackle previously intractable problems in computational biology. In *Computational Genomics.*

McGregor, A., Braun, H.-W., and Brown, J. (2000). The NLANR network analysis infrastructure. *IEEE Communications Magazine,* 38(5):122–128.

Shavitt, Y. and Shir, E. (2005). DIMES: Let the internet measure itself. cs.NI 050699, arXiv.

Siamwalla, R., Sharma, R., and Keshav, S. (1998). Discovering internet topology. Technical report, Cornell University, Ithaca, NY 14853.

Simpson, Jr., C. R. and Riley, G. F. (2004). NETI@home: A distributed approach to collecting end-to-end network performance measurements. In *Proc. Passive and Active Measurement Workshop (PAM).*

PART THREE

MOBILE AND WIRELESS NETWORKS

PRACTICAL EVALUATION OF A NETWORK MOBILITY SOLUTION

Antonio de la Oliva, Carlos Jesús Bernardos and María Calderón
Universidad Carlos III de Madrid
Avda. Universidad, 30 28911 Leganés
Madrid (SPAIN)
{ aoliva,cjbc,maria } @it.uc3m.es

Abstract   As the demand of ubiquitous Internet access and the current trend of all-IP communications keep growing, the necessity of a protocol that provides mobility management increases. The IETF has specified protocols to provide mobility support to individual nodes and networks. The Network Mobility (NEMO) Basic Support protocol is designed for providing mobility at IP level to complete networks, allowing a Mobile Network to change its point of attachment to the Internet, while maintaining ongoing sessions of the nodes of the network. All the mobility management is done by the mobile router whilst the nodes of the network are not even aware of the mobility.

The main aim of this article is evaluating the performance of the NEMO Basic Support protocol by using our implementation. We also discuss the design of an implementation of the NEMO Basic Support protocol.

Keywords: Network Mobility, NEMO, experimental evaluation

1.   Introduction

We are witnessing how the number of devices that are connected to the Internet through wireless devices is continuously growing. The forthcoming 4G is expected to bring a new generation of portable, always-connected devices that are able to connect to the Internet through heterogeneous technologies.

Current standard Internet protocols, such as IPv4, do no support transparent *mobility*. This is because IP was not designed taking into account mobility. Terminals were considered to be fixed, and the IP address plays the role of both identifier and locator in a network, so a change of the address (needed when connecting to a different subnet) implies a change of the identifier which breaks ongoing transport connections. Protocols such as DHCP [Droms, 1997] enable *portability* (i.e., a terminal can change its point of attachment and obtain connectivity, but all its connections should be restarted). By *mobility*, we mean enabling the transparent movement of nodes, without breaking ongoing connections and allowing the nodes to be reachable through a permanent IP address. Mobile IP [Johnson et al., 2004] is an IETF protocol designed to enable node mobility.

Nevertheless, supporting the movement of nodes is not the only problem that should be faced. Ubiquitous networking is becoming more and more common, so it is expected to have not only mobile nodes but also mobile networks. When the mobility problem is extended to support the movement of a complete network, we found that mobility management has to be provided to every device inside the network, even if these devices cannot afford the computational load that mobility implies. To provide mobility support to these networks, a protocol based on Mobile IP has been designed. This protocol is called Network Mobility (NEMO) Basic Support protocol [Devarapalli et al., 2004].

We have implemented in Linux a first prototype of the NEMO Basic Support protocol. This implementation has allowed us to study the performance of the protocol in several scenarios. Both the design of the implementation and a performance evaluation of the protocol (using the prototype) are presented in this paper.

The paper is structured as follows. A brief introduction to the basic concepts of Mobile IP and the NEMO Basic Support protocol are introduced in section 2. Section 3 explains the design of the implementation, detailing all the functionality, the tools used and the structure of the implementation. An analysis of the NEMO Basic Support protocol performance is presented in section 4, describing the testing scenarios used, in section 4.1. Finally, some conclusions and future work, are presented in section 5.

2.   Background

Providing mobility at IP-level is difficult because, as we have pointed previously, IP addresses play the role of identifier and locator. Routing in IP is hierarchical, and IP addresses are configured taking into account the network that the nodes are attached to. Routers in a network forward packets based on the destination address and the information stored in their routing tables. When a node changes its point of attachment, packets addressed to that node are delivered (using normal IP routing) to the network it was connected to. In order to be able to receive packets at its new location, the node should configure an IP address belonging to the address space of the new network, but this implies changing also the addresses that transport protocols use (IP addresses are part of transport addresses), which breaks established sessions.

There are some situations in which not only a single node moves, but a complete network does. This will become more and more usual as the demand for ubiquitous Internet access in public transportation systems increases. A new Working Group (WG) within the IETF called NEMO was created to deal with the problem of complete networks that move as a whole. This WG has defined an extension of Mobile IP: the NEMO Basic Support protocol [Devarapalli et al., 2004], that enables Network Mobility support (see [Ernst and Lach, 2004] for the terminology).

In more precise terms, a Network that Moves (NEMO) - a mobile network - can be defined as a network whose attachment point to the Internet varies with time. The router within the NEMO that connects to the Internet is called the Mobile Router (MR). It is assumed that the NEMO has a Home Network where it resides when it is not moving. Since the NEMO is reachable through the Home Network, the Mobile Network has configured addresses belonging to an address block assigned to the Home Network. These addresses remain assigned to the NEMO when it is away from home. Naturally, these addresses only have topological meaning when the NEMO is at home. When the NEMO is away from home, packets addressed to the Mobile Network Nodes (MNNs) will still be routed to the Home Network. Additionally, when the NEMO is away from home, i.e., it is in a visited network, the MR acquires an address from the visited network, called the Care-of Address (CoA), where the routing architecture can deliver packets without additional mechanisms.

The goal of the network mobility support mechanisms is to preserve established communications between the MNNs and external Correspondent Nodes (CNs) through movement. Packets of such communications will be addressed to the MNNs addresses, which belong to the Mobile Network Prefix (MNP), so additional mechanisms to forward packets between the Home Network and the NEMO are needed. The basic solution for network mobility support [Devarapalli et al., 2004] essentially creates a bi-directional tunnel between a special node located in the Home Network of the NEMO (the Home Agent, HA), and the Care-of Address of the MR (fig. 1(a)).

This basic solution is derived from the solution proposed for host mobility support, MIPv6 [Johnson et al., 2004], without including the Route Optimisation support. Actually, the protocol is similar and the mobility signalling (i.e., Binding Update (BU) message) is extended to inform the Home Agent about the IP address of the NEMO side of the tunnel (that is, the CoA of the MR), through which the HA has to forward the packets addressed to the Mobile Network Prefix.

In addition to the triangular routing problem (all packets pass through the HA), also present in Mobile IPv6, the NEMO Basic Support protocol introduces the so-called *pinball* routing, that appears when nesting is considered. A Mobile Network can be attached to another Mobile Network, thus forming nested chains of networks (fig. 1(b)).

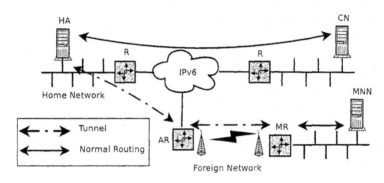

(a) Without Nested Operation

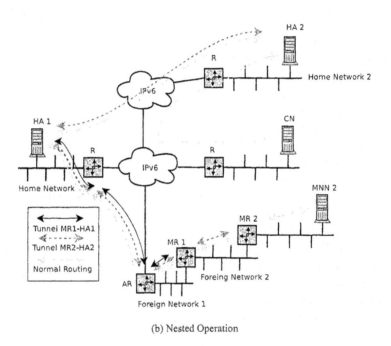

(b) Nested Operation

Figure 1.   Example of NEMO Basic Support protocol operation

3.   Implementation design

We have developed a first implementation of the NEMO Basic Support protocol [Devarapalli et al., 2004]. It supports the movement of a MR to different foreign networks, working also with nested networks. Besides the protocol operation, we have also implemented a tool for displaying the information stored in the different data structures that the MR and HA maintain (making easier the debugging of the implementation). The implementation has been developed for the Linux kernel 2.6.x branch.

The NEMO Basic Support protocol is completely implemented in user space, because in this way the development is easier and quicker than doing that in the kernel. In addition, the program is expected to work even when the kernel is upgraded, without requiring major changes. Nevertheless, some kernel support is needed in order to recognise the messages introduced by the protocol. Otherwise, the kernel would send ICMPv6 [Conta and Deering, 1995] error messages triggered by the reception of one of those signalling messages. Basically, the kernel should identify the BU and Binding Acknowledgement (BA) messages and their reception should not trigger any special treatment, as they are processed by the user space implementation of the NEMO Basic Support protocol. This is done by modifying the kernel code in the IPv6 stack that process the IPv6 extension headers. This has been implemented in kernel linux-2.6.7, but should work without major changes in any kernel linux-2.6.x (a patch with these minor modifications has been created).

A single program implements both HA and MR functionalities, being selected by a flag in the configuration file.

The implementation only supports implicit mode BUs. That is, the Mobile Router does not include a Mobile Network Prefix Option in the Binding Update. The Home Agent determines the Mobile Network Prefix(es) owned by the Mobile Router by manual configuration mapping to the Mobile Router's Home Address (HoA). A file is used to store these mappings.

The software requirements are: a Linux machine with kernel linux-2.6.x (tested with linux-2.6.7), support for IPv6-in-IPv6 tunnels enabled (used for the HA-MR bidirectional tunnel) and the pcap (http://www.tcpdump. org/) library (used for the capture and processing of the mobility related signalling).

3.1 MR operation

Movement detection is one of the main tasks of the Mobile Router. Mobile IPv6 does not impose any specific method to do that, but a simple movement detection mechanism is defined, based on IPv6 Neighbour Discovery [Narten et al., 1998]. This basically consists in listening to Router Advertisements (RAs). When the MR detects a new router advertising an IPv6 prefix different from its Home Prefix, the mobility management subroutine is launched.

At a first step, the routing table entries which correspond to the interface which has been moved, are deleted, because these routes are not useful anymore. All the routing table and interface's address modification is done using Netlink [Dhandapani and Sundaresan, 2005] sockets. By using this tool, we can manage the routing functionality of a Linux box by transferring information between kernel and user space. It consists of a standard sockets based interface for user processes, and an internal kernel API for kernel modules.

Afterwards the IPv6 address of the interface is removed and a new one is configured. This address is the CoA and is formed by the new prefix advertised (included in RAs) on the foreign link plus the EUI64 [Hinden and Deering, 1998] of the interface. The EUI64 is built from the MAC address of the interface. Finally, a default route to the HA address, using the previously detected router on the new link as next hop, is inserted in the routing table.

After that, a BU must be sent to the HA informing of the current location of the MR (CoA). This BU is basically the same defined by Mobile IPv6, including a flag that indicates that it has been sent by a MR. Raw Sockets are used to send the signalling packets. By using this type of sockets we can build the entire IPv6 packet. We have followed this approach because normal sockets does not work well while changing the routing table and the interface address. The tunnel must not be created before a BA has been received, so the program waits for a BA arrival. The program uses the capturing methods of the pcap library to wait for a BA reception. When the BA arrives, it is processed and if everything is correct, the tunnel is set up. The ip6_tunnel module and a modified version of ipv6tunnel (from http://www.mipl.mediapoli.com/) are used for the creation, management and removal of IPv6-in-IPv6 tunnels.

In order to be able to reconfigure the MR's routing table when it comes back home, the routing table is stored.

While the MR is away from home and it is not moving among different visited foreign networks, it periodically sends BUs to refresh the binding between the MR's HoA and MR's CoA at the HA.

3.2   HA operation

The HA waits for the reception of BUs that indicates that a MR has moved. Again, the pcap library is used to capture these packets and retrieve the required information. When a BU is received, it is processed, checking if it fits in one of the following categories: a new BU from a MR that was at home (a new binding has to be created), a BU from a MR that was already away from home but has moved again (an existing binding has to be changed), a BU from a MR that is not at home and refreshes its binding information (the lifetime and sequence number of an existing binding has to be updated) or a de-registration BU (an existing binding has to be removed because the MR is again at home).

When a BU indicating that a MR has moved away from home is captured, several configuration steps are performed. First, the configuration file containing the HoA-MNP bindings is searched for the HoA included in the received

BU. If it is found, a new entry is added to the HA's Binding Cache (BC)[1]. Then the routes to the MR's MNP are removed from the HA's routing table. A new bidirectional IPv6-in-IPv6 tunnel is set up, and a default route to the MR through this tunnel (i.e., using the newly created tunnel interface) is added. After that, a BA is sent to the MR.

When the received BU is one refreshing an existing binding, the lifetime field and sequence number of the BC entry are updated accordingly. If no BU is received refreshing an existing binding before the lifetime expires, the BC entry is removed and the original configuration is reestablished.

Finally, if a de-registration BU is captured, the BC entry is removed and the original configuration is reestablished.

A visualisation tool, used to make easier the development, debugging and use of the implementation has been also developed. This tool, called *nemodiag*, prints the information of the MR's Binding Update List (BUL) or the HA's BC on the screen. To facilitate the development of this application and the management of these tables by the processes that refresh them, we have used shared memory.

4. Performance Evaluation

The NEMO Basic Support protocol [Devarapalli et al., 2004] provides transparent network mobility support, but presents some performance issues. The triangular routing phenomena due to the MR-HA tunnel adds delay and packet overhead. This problem is exacerbated when nesting is involved. In order to experimentally evaluate the severeness of these problems, some practical tests and analytical studies have been performed.

The experimental tests are focused on evaluating how the delay introduced by the triangular routing affects to the performance of applications. We have chosen TCP as the protocol to be studied, because it is representative of most of the traffic exchange in the Internet. Besides, the end-to-end delay affects the effective throughput of TCP applications. The analytical studies are focused in the packet overhead effects on several kinds of data traffic.

4.1 Testbed Description

In order to test the correctness of our implementation, and perform some measurements to analyse the performance of the NEMO Basic Support protocol, a testbed was deployed. The testbed is shown in fig. 2.

---

[1]The HA maintains a data structure where the information about the association between the MR's HoA and CoA is stored. The BC stores the HoA, the CoA, the sequence number of the last BU received and the lifetime of the binding.

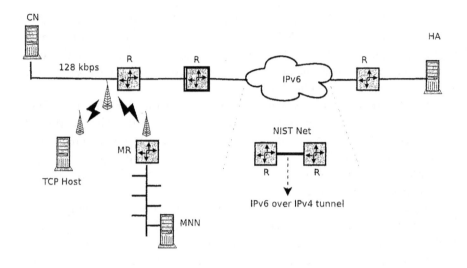

Figure 2.   Testbed

All the machines are Linux boxes, with kernel linux-2.6.7, except two intermediate routers that run linux-2.4.22. The routers are Linux boxes configured to this purpose. Our implementation is installed only in the HA and the MR.

In order to simulate a real IPv6 network between the HA and the network that the MR is visiting, and be able to modify some characteristics of this traversed network (e.g., latency, bandwidth, etc) the NIST Net network emulator tool (http://www-x.antd.nist.gov/nistnet/) was used. This tool was also used to restrict the bandwidth of the path between the CN and the network that MR is visiting. NIST Net allows a single Linux PC, set up as a router, to emulate a wide variety of network conditions. This software runs only in IPv4 and with linux-2.4.x kernels. Therefore, in order to use it in our testbed, we had to set up IPv6-in-IPv4 tunnels to use it. The use of tunnels does not have any important effect on the tests, as just a very small delay due to the encapsulation is added, and actually it reflects the real situation of the IPv6 deployment, with several IPv4 clouds.

The traffic traces were collected at the CN and analysed with tcptrace (http://jarok.cs.ohiou.edu/software/tcptrace/tcptrace.html). Tcptrace is used to analyse the data collected and generate TCP graphics and statistics about the traffic.

4.2   Effect of the Delay

In addition to the obvious effect that the delay has on performance (e.g., on real time applications), there is another aspect we have to take into account

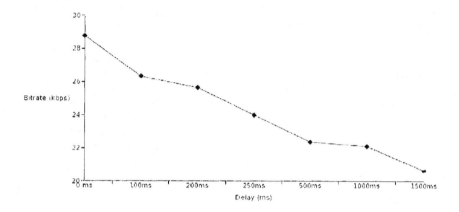

Figure 3. MR's operation: Throughput vs Added Delay

when TCP is used. TCP throughput is affected by the end-to-end delay, therefore when a physical communication channel is shared between several TCP flows, the ones that have lower RTTs obtain a higher throughput.

In order to study the effect of the network mobility support on TCP, we have performed tests setting the bandwidth between the CN and the visited network to 128kbps (using the NIST Net emulator). Besides, the delay between the visited network and the Home Network is also varied by using the NIST Net emulator. This scenario allows us to make several tests with different delays, simulating different *distances* (i.e., RTTs) between the Home Network and the visited network.

The test basically consists in obtaining traffic traces on the CN, when a MNN is downloading a file located at the CN, while another computer attached to the same visited network downloads the same file four times simultaneously. All the five TCP flows share the available bandwidth (limited to 128kbps), and only the TCP flow sent to the MNN is affected by the introduced delay. This allows us to evaluate how the different delays and the NEMO Basic Support protocol affects the overall performance perceived by users of the TCP applications.

The effect of a higher delay in the TCP application is clear: the effective throughput decreases as the delay increases. Therefore, the available throughput for the other TCP flows (that have smaller RTTs) is bigger than the throughput of the MNN, because of the added delay introduced by the triangular routing.

A graph displaying the mean throughput of a MNN downloading a file located at the CN for different delays in the HA-MR path is shown in fig. 3. These results are as expected, showing how the delay affects the TCP throughput when several sessions are sharing the same physical bandwidth.

Traffic Type	Packet size (bytes)	Description
TCP	40	Minimum TCP packet size.
TCP	552	TCP without path MTU discovery
TCP	1500	Maximum Ethernet payload
UDP VoIP GSM	33	UDP-RTP packets coded with GSM
UDP VoIP G723.1	20	UDP-RTP packets coded with G723.1
UDP VoIP G711	240	UDP-RTP packets coded with G711
UDP VoIP LPC10	7	UDP-RTP packets coded with LPC10
UDP VoIP iLBC 20ms	38	UDP-RTP packets coded with iLBC
UDP VoIP iLBC 30ms	50	UDP-RTP packets coded with iLBC

Table 1.   Traffic Types

4.3   Effect of the Packet Overhead

The use of the NEMO Basic Support protocol also increases the packet overhead, because of the tunnelling used between the HAs and MRs (this effect is even worse when nesting is involved). In this section we briefly study the overhead introduced by the NEMO Basic Support protocol, by comparing it with the overhead produced by plain IPv4 and IPv6.

The NEMO Basic Support protocol introduces a 40-byte extra IPv6 header to each packet in the HA-MR bidirectional path. Nesting introduces a 40-bytes extra headers for each level of chaining. The different types of traffic analysed are summarised in the table 1. Fig. 4 shows graphically the packet overhead for different kinds of IP payloads.

Nowadays, approximately the 83% of the total Internet traffic is TCP and other 13% is UDP [McCreary and K.Claffy, 2000], so fig. 4 is a good representative of how the NEMO protocol and the use of nested networks (up to 3 levels) would affect to most of the traffic that traverses today the Internet.

VoIP traffic is characterised for using small payload sizes, so the overhead in VoIP packets is very severe. This is specially important because of the expected use of VoIP in the forthcoming 4G communication networks.

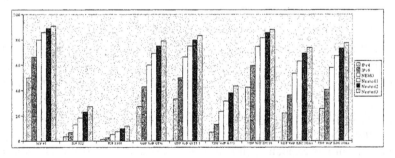

Figure 4.   Overhead percentage by traffic types

Fig. 4 shows that even for payloads as small as 552 bytes, the overhead is not worthless (approximately 16%). When the number of nesting levels increases, the overhead grows dramatically. The overhead for 40-byte TCP packets (e.g., ACKs), is of a 80% without nesting; a 2-level nesting increases the overhead up to the 90%. These results show the necessity of a route optimisation mechanism for NEMO. The impact of using the NEMO Basic Support protocol for VoIP communications is very high (60% of overhead in average), so special care, and special design decisions, have to be taken if the NEMO Basic Support protocol (without using any route optimisation) is going to be used in VoIP networks.

To exemplify the impact of this packet overhead, we use the iLBC [Andersen et al., 2004] codec, used by skype (http://www.skype.com/) software. The iLBC (internet Low Bitrate Codec) is a free speech codec suitable for robust voice communication over IP. The codec is designed for narrow band speech and results in a payload bit rate of 13.33 kbps with an encoding frame length of 30 ms and 15.20 kbps with an encoding length of 20 ms. Eq. 1 and Eq. 2 are the analytical expressions of the packet overhead (iLBC payload over UDP/RTP) when IPv6 (Eq. 1) or the NEMO Basic Support protocol[2] (Eq. 2) are used. Table 2 summarises the bitrate needed to use the iLBC codec (over UDP/RTP) with IPv4, IPv6 and the NEMO Basic Support protocol (with different levels of nesting). It should be noted that a typical 64 kbps connection would be unable to support a VoIP communication of a 2-level nested mobile network. This supports our argument that route optimisation mechanisms for NEMO, are needed.

$$\frac{(40(IPv6) + 8(UDP) + 12(RTP) + 38(iLBC)) * 8\frac{bits}{byte}}{0.020} \tag{1}$$

$$\frac{(NL * 40(NEMO) + 40(IPv6) + 8(UDP) + 12(RTP) + 38(iLBC)) * 8\frac{bits}{byte}}{0.020} \tag{2}$$

	IPv4	IPv6	NEMO (no nesting)	NEMO (NL=2)	NEMO (NL=3)
BR (kbps)	31.2	39.2	55.2	71.2	87.2

Table 2. iLBC bitrates

5. Conclusions and future work

The demand of ubiquitous Internet access (e.g., in public transportation systems) is increasing. Therefore, mechanisms that enable complete IP networks to be mobile without breaking ongoing connections of the nodes of the network are needed. The IETF NEMO WG has come up with an IP-level network

---

[2]NL=Nesting Levels. L=1 means a single mobile network, L=2 means 2 nested mobile networks and so on.

mobility solution: the NEMO Basic Support protocol, that enables a network to change its point of attachment.

In this paper we have developed an implementation of the NEMO Basic Support protocol for Linux, and we have used that to experimentally evaluate the performance of the protocol. The NEMO Basic Support protocol basically consists in setting a bidirectional tunnel between the MR and its HA. This tunnel adds both end-to-end delay and packet overhead. This delay can be unsuitable for some real-time applications, but also affects the overall TCP performance, as it has been practically showed in this paper. Besides, the added packet overhead increases the bandwidth requirements for applications. As an example, typical 64 kbps links would not be able to handle VoIP Skype calls of a node belonging to a two-level nested network.

The aforementioned inefficiencies need to be mitigated in order to facilitate the deployment of mobile networks. Therefore, work in route optimisation solutions would be a hot research topic in the near future.

Acknowledgments

The work described in this paper is based on results of IST FP6 Integrated Project DAIDALOS. DAIDALOS receives research funding from the European Community's Sixth Framework Programme. Apart from this, the European Commission has no responsibility for the content of this paper. The information in this document is provided as is and no guarantee or warranty is given that the information is fit for any particular purpose. The user thereof uses the information at its sole risk and liability.

References

Andersen, S., Telio, A. Duric, Astrom, H., Hagen, R., Kleijn, W., and Linden, J. (2004). Internet Low Bitrate Codec. RFC 3951.

Conta, A. and Deering, S. (1995). Internet Control Message Protocol (ICMPv6) for the Internet Protocol Version 6 (IPv6). RFC 1885.

Devarapalli, Vijay, Wakikawa, Ryuji, Petrescu, Alexandru, and Thubert, Pascal (2004). Network Mobility (NEMO) Basic Support Protocol. RFC 3963.

Dhandapani, Gowri and Sundaresan, Anupama (2005). *Netlink Sockets, Overview*. http://qos.ittc.ukans.edu/netlink/html/.

Droms, R. (1997). *Dynamic Host Configuration Protocol*.

Ernst, T. and Lach, H-Y. (2004). Network Mobility Support Terminology. draft-ietf-NEMO-terminology-02.txt.

Hinden, R. and Deering, S. (1998). IP Version 6 Addressing Architecture. RFC 2373.

Johnson, D., Perkins, C., and J.Arkko (2004). Mobility Support in IPv6. RFC 3775.

McCreary, S. and K.Claffy (2000). *Trends in wide area IP traffic patterns - A view from Ames Internet Exchange*. CAIDA, Tech. Rep.

Narten, T., Nordmark, E., and Simpson, W. (1998). Neighbor Discovery for IP Version 6 (IPv6). RFC 2461.

ERROR-AWARE SCHEDULING AND ITS EFFECT ON EFFICIENCY AND FAIRNESS

Pablo Serrano, David Larrabeiti, Manuel Urueña
Universidad Carlos III de Madrid
Departamento de Ingeniería Telemática
Av. Universidad 30, E-28911 Leganés, Madrid, Spain
{pablo,dlarra,muruenya}@it.uc3m.es

Antonio G. Marques
Departamento de Ciencias de la Comunicación
Universidad Rey Juan Carlos
Cl Tulipán s/n E-28933 Mostoles, Madrid, Spain
antonio.garcia.marques@urjc.es

Abstract   This paper describes a mechanism to adapt an existing wireline scheduling algorithm for a WLAN Access Point, by taking into account the error ratio affecting each flow. This enhancement is based on the idea of weighting flows according to their error ratio. Users connected over error-prone channels get their bandwidth share increased, up to a point where the overall efficiency breaks down, and the mechanism is reverted. The cost of this mechanism in terms of fairness is also addressed.

Keywords: Efficiency, Fair Queuing, WLAN.

Introduction

In wireless networks, time and location-dependent signal attenuation, interference, fading and noise result in a different error ratio for each flow sharing a packet switched link. This has motivated an intense research activity in wireless scheduling in the last years.

Wireless scheduling addresses the problem of how to provide a weighted fair allocation of bandwidth even under changing channel conditions (an excellent review on this topic is given in [Bharghavan et al., 1999]). These and more recent proposals (see [Raghunathan et al., 2002; Liu et al., 2003; Wong et al., 2003; Wang and Chin, 2001]) are based on the capability to probe the channel before transmission: flows that do not receive the corresponding bandwidth

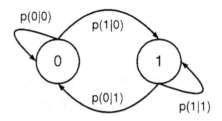

Figure 1.   Gilbert Cell

Table 1.   Gilbert Cell parameters

Flow	$p(0|0)$	$p(1|1)$
1, 2	0.1	0.9
3, 4	0.538	0.846
5	0.9	0.1

share *now* will receive it *later*. This assumption is not applicable to WLAN, where no probing mechanism is available.

We propose to adapt an existing conventional fair scheduling mechanism [Zhang, 1995] for WLAN, by taking into account the error ratio affecting each flow. This error ratio estimation serves as a basis for the development of two complementary mechanisms: flow compensation and throttling. Compensation aims to increase fairness, whereas throttling tries to keep up an acceptable overall efficiency.

One main problem of compensation is that it may yield to very low goodputs, if applied unrestrictedly. Unlike previous works, compensation is not only bounded in terms of *allocated rate* but also in the *amount of time* a flow is granted a preferential treatment. Furthermore we introduce throttling of flows suffering from high loss channels in an attempt to prop up efficiency, and determine its effect on fairness.

In WLAN-specific scenarios, available algorithms like [Vaidya et al., 2000; Banchs and Perez, 2002] deal with distributed QoS provisioning by modifying 802.11b [IEEE, 1999] behavior. Our work considers a centralized scenario, dealing with the Access Point (AP) operation in presence of Mobile Nodes (MN).

The rest of this paper is organized as follows. The target scenario is introduced in Section 1. Section 2 describes the proposed scheduler extension. Simulation results and conclusions are given in Sections 3 and 4.

1. Scenario

We focus on a 802.11b scenario, where no prioritized MNs with different channel conditions share a common medium in order to transmit from and to an AP. We consider the transmission of packets from the AP to the MNs. Each MN is associated with one and only one flow identifier at the AP (although this could impose scalability restrictions, APs deal with an affordable number of nodes). We aim to provide a fair allocation to all these users, but taking into account channel efficiency.

We make three assumptions about this scenario:

- Retransmission mechanisms are not implemented. Whether lower or upper layers should deal with retransmission is a passionate discussion (see [Saltzer et al., 1984] for a classical review of the topic). However, if retransmissions need to be implemented, it would be straightforward: if a packet needs n retransmissions prior to its receipt, it would be considered (from the point of view of the scheduler) as $n - 1$ transmissions with error and 1 successful transmission.

- Collisions are not taken into account, as we are only interested in packet errors due to bad channel conditions.

- Only one transmission rate is available (although with multiple rates available fair *temporal* access to the medium could be provided, instead of fair bandwidth allocation).

The channel is modeled as a two-state Markov Model (or *Gilbert Cell*, Fig. 1), following the empirical characterization of [Khayam and Radha, 2003]. The '0' state means that a packet gets lost, and the '1' state means that the packet gets through. The $p(i|j)$ is the probability of transition from state j to state i. The error probability is then: $P(0) = p(0|1)/(p(0|1) + p(1|0))$

2. The Algorithm

We can build our algorithm on top of almost any available wireline scheduling algorithm, by enhancing their functionality via a *configuration interface*. A new entity, called EAS (error-aware scheduler), modifies the wireline scheduler by sending a weight vector ($\{\omega_i\}$) and a throttling vector ($\{\theta_i\}$) (see Table 2 for a summary of notation). These vectors, sent from the EAS to the scheduler, support the implementation of compensation and throttling, respectively:

- The *compensation* is implemented by dynamically assigning weights to flows. Flows that need compensation are given higher weights (during some packets) than error-free flows.

- On the other hand, θ_i represents the number of turns to be lost by a packet from flow i: assume flow i has a Head of Line packet of size L_i,

Table 2. Variables and parameters of the algorithm

Term	Definition
N_F	Number of flows
$bytesErr_i$	Bytes transmitted with error since activation of compensation
$\hat{\rho}_i$	Mean packet probability error since activation of compensation
ω_{comp}	Weight reserved for compensation
ω_i	Weight given to flow i
ϵ_i	Number of consecutive errors of flow i
Ω	Threshold for maximum compensation
θ_i	Number of rounds for a flow i to be skipped
Θ	Maximum θ_i allowed for all i

and $\theta_i > 0$. When the next flow to dequeue is i, the scheduler computes L_i as work given to i and decrements θ_i by one. Only when $\theta_i = 0$ the packet is actually dequeued.

The EAS re-configures the Scheduler in a real-time fashion, by processing the received ACK (or its absence) after each transmission. Then it performs the *compensation/throttling* calculation. Our scheme generalizes easily to any scheduling algorithm, by implementing the described configuration interface (the work in [Ramanathan and Agrawal, 1998] also enjoys this feature).

2.1   Compensation

In order to define a compensation mechanism, we have decided to limit the maximum fraction of bandwidth (or weight, ω_{comp}) available for compensation (following the philosophy of [Ramanathan and Agrawal, 1998]).

If the compensation mechanism is triggered for a given flow, this flow has always a minimum weight guaranteed, given by $\omega_{i0} = (1 - \omega_{comp})/N_F$ (we impose $\sum_{i=1}^{N_F} \omega_i + \omega_{comp} = 1$). Compensation is proportional to lost bytes, and it vanishes with subsequent successful transmission. Flows with a high number of consecutive errors ($\epsilon_i > \Omega$) are not given any compensation; i.e. we consider them *irrecoverable errors* which will damage goodput of less error-prone channels. This way, the compensation mechanism is given by :

Give flow i the weigth ω_i, according to

$$\omega_i := \begin{cases} \omega_{i0} + \Delta\omega_i, & \epsilon_i \leq \Omega \\ \omega_{i0}, & \epsilon_i > \Omega \end{cases}$$

where

$$\Delta \omega_i := \omega_{comp} \times \underbrace{\frac{bytesErr_i}{\sum_{i=1}^{N_F} bytesErr_i}}_{\omega_{comp} \ partition} \times \underbrace{\hat{\rho}_i}_{damping}$$

Both the counter $bytesErr_i$ and the mean packet error probability ($\hat{\rho}_i$) start to measure from the first packet loss. If ϵ_i surpasses Ω, the compensation stops and they are both reinitialized to zero. Also, when $\Delta\omega_i/\omega_i \leq 0.1$, the compensation is finished (and counters are re-initialized). This way, not only the rate of compensation is bounded (via ω_{comp}), but also the amount of compensation (implicitly): either a flow perceives a low number of errors (and then $\hat{\rho}_i$ imposes the reduction of $\Delta\omega_i$), or it perceives a great number of errors (and thus $\epsilon_i > \Omega$ and compensation is deactivated).

2.2   Throttling

Starting from a number of consecutive errors ($\epsilon_i > \Omega$), the compensation mechanism will not give any increment of weight to flow i. But even in these situations, flows with very ill-behaved links will keep on wasting the radiolink during an error burst. In this case, we propose not only to give not any compensation, but also to *throttle* these flows in an adaptive manner (the more consecutive errors acquired, the more rounds a flow will be passed by if there is any are other flow in the system).

We start to throttle from the $\Omega + 1$-th consecutive packet error, in order to detect a series of packet losses. In order to avoid starvation, Θ limits the maximum number of rounds a packed can be passed by. Then, θ_i is given by:

$$\theta_i := \begin{cases} 0, & \epsilon_i \leq \Omega \\ \epsilon_i - \Omega, & \Omega < \epsilon_i \leq \Theta + \Omega \\ \Theta, & \epsilon_i > \Theta + \Omega \end{cases}$$

It should be taken into account that throttling *passes by* a flow. But if no other flow is competing for the link, the algorithm will be unnoticeable (although being active). Hence, in over-provisioned links no throttling will take place: only in scenarios where flows compete aggressively for the link the algorithm will really favor well-behaved channels.

3.   Simulation Results

The simulations were carried out with OMNeT++ [OMNeT++, 2003], a discrete-event simulator. With $N_F = 5$, we have five sources and five MNs, connected to the AP via five Gilbert Cells. We defined three kinds of channels associated to these MNs (see Table 1):

- Channels with little probability of errors (high quality links), modeling MNs close to the AP: Flows 1, 2.

- Channels whose model was taken from measurements of [Khayam and Radha, 2003] (average quality links): Flows 3, 4.

- Channels very error-prone (low quality links): Flow 5.

We implemented two MNs associated to the first channel type, two of the second type, and one of the third type (later on we will change the proportion of channel types, but not the number of MNs).

Transmission rate for the wireless link is 2 Mbps. The scheduling algorithm is SCFQ ([Golestani, 1994]). Traffic interarrival is exponential, and packet length is uniformly distributed between 1000 and 1500 bytes. All MNs are sent the same amount of traffic, considering three distinct cases: 282.84 kbps, 400 kbps and 564 kbps, for an aggregate of 1.41 Mbps, 2 Mbps and 2.82 Mbps respectively. This way we can analyze the performance in under and oversubscribed environments, covering a 3 dB range. The simulation run procedure was implemented following the two sequential method of [Nakayama, 1994]. A minimum of $m = 10$ batch means were collected for a 90% of confidence interval of $\epsilon = 0.1$ relative size (with a previous warm-up period, sized 5 batch means).

First the simulation results for the compensation algorithm alone are presented (Section 3.1), which achieves greater fairness at the expense of degrading system overall efficiency. In Section 3.2 the counterpart of compensation is shown: throttling, which improves system performance by reducing bandwidth of flows with errors. Finally, in Section 3.3 the performance of the complete algorithm is presented.

3.1   Compensation-only Algorithm

First we define the efficiency or goodput (the efficiency is actually the goodput normalized by the nominal rate) as the ratio $\frac{bytesAcked}{totalBytesTransmitted}$. Figure 2 shows the obtained system goodput vs Ω for two transmission rates and two values of ω_{comp} (being $\Omega = 0$ the case when no algorithm is active). In an oversubscribed scenario (2.82 Mbps of incoming traffic) and with $\omega_{comp} = 0.4$, goodput reduces noticeably with the maximum number of consecutive errors allowed, Ω. The explanation of this behavior is straightforward: the algorithm is giving flows with error-prone channels more and more bandwidth (up to 40% of channel capacity), and thus the proportion of error-free frames is diminishing ($\Delta\omega_i$ is assigned proportional to the number of bytes with errors). With $\omega_{comp} = 0.1$ the diminishing on goodput is less noticeable, since it bounds the amount of channel given to compensation. On the other hand, when incom-

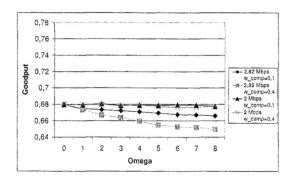

Figure 2. Goodput vs Ω, compensation only

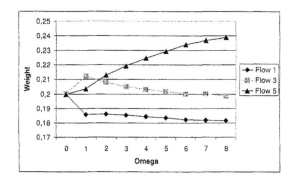

Figure 3. ω_i vs Ω, compensation only

ing traffic is 2 Mbps, the compensation mechanism is not noticeable, because flows are not always competing for the medium.

Figure 3 shows the mean ω_i obtained for different values of the maximum number of consecutive errors allowed (for $\omega_{comp} = 0.4$ and 2.82 Mbps). The flow with the greatest error probability (fifth flow) obtains a 25% of improvement over its nominal weigth, just because almost every packet transmitted to it is lost. And even with such an effort, this flow will only perceive a tiny improvement on its particular goodput. Thus, compensation by its own might lead to resource squandering. This issue is addressed by throttling.

3.2 Throttling-only Algorithm

In this case we will show the throttling performance with $\Omega = 0$, so every packet error is punished. Thus, by incrementing the maximum throttling allowed (via Θ) we are improving system performance (see Fig. 4), because the more a flow perceives consecutive errors, the more rounds it will be skipped (and error-free channels will monopolize the system). But throttling is adaptive

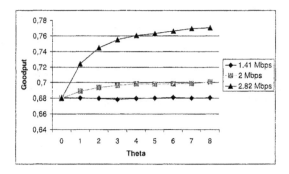

Figure 4.   Goodput vs Θ, throttling only

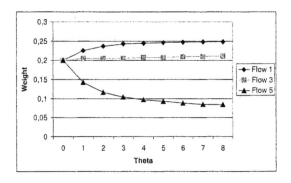

Figure 5. ω_i vs Θ, throttling only

in nature, as it has been discussed on Section 2.2: only when flows compete aggressively for the medium (2.82 Mbps) its behavior is noticeable. Thus, in undersubscribed scenarios (1.41 Mbps), despite all rounds a packet should be passed by due to errors, if no other flow is competing for the channel, it will be transmitted.

By looking at the mean values of ω_i (Fig. 5), it is clear that the increase of goodput comes from the decrease of ω_5, the weight assigned to the flow with the worst channel. Compensation mechanism guarantees a minimum fraction of bandwidth to all flows (ω_{i0}), but if the throttling mechanism is triggered this value will be lowered (the maximum number of throttling can be fixed via Θ: the minimum ω_i at any moment is $\omega_{i0}/(\Theta + 1)$).

3.3   Complete Algorithm

In order to analyze the performance of the complete algorithm, first we are going to give values to Ω and Θ (instead of performing a sweeping on all possible values). Even with $\Theta = 1$, bandwidth of flows with error-prone channels is

Table 3. Probability of n or more consecutive errors

Flow	1	2	3	4
1,2	10^{-1}	10^{-2}	10^{-3}	10^{-4}
3,4	0.25	0.1345	**0.0724**	0.0389
5	0.9	0.81	0.729	0.656

reduced to a maximum of half of its original value, while allowing a noticeable improvement on goodput (Fig. 4).

On the other hand, Ω aims to distinguish between flows with recoverable errors, and flows associated to an error-prone channel. Table 3 shows the cumulative probabilities for n or more errors of all flows. Second row values are taken from the empirical characterization ([Khayam and Radha, 2003]), and thus we choose them so as to perform the discrimination. This way, with $\Omega = 2$, the probability for a flow of the second kind to be throttled is less than 10% (see the highlighted value), which is a reasonable threshold.

Figure 6 shows the system goodput for four values of ω_{comp}, being again $\omega_{comp} = 0$ the case where the mechanism is inactive. The independence between goodput and ω_{comp} comes from the fact that only throttling provokes the goodput rise, while compensation aims to support a fair allocation of resources. Again, only in an oversubscribed scenario (2.82 Mbps) the improvement is noticeable, due to the adaptive nature of throttling.

The system increases overall efficiency. In order to measure properly the impact on fairness, a quantity is needed. Based on the concept of proportional fairness [Kelly, 1997], the following measure is defined:

$$Fairness = \sum_{i=1}^{N_F} log\left(\frac{bytes ACK_i}{Simulation\ Time}\right) \quad (3)$$

This is the *cost* paid for the efficiency increase: if the mechanism aims to improve goodput by throttling aggressively flows with error-prone links, this punishment will be taken into account in Eq. 3 (preventing flow starvation).

For the $\omega_{comp} = 0.6$ case, the efficiency rises from 0.68 to 0.72, while fairness (calculated via Eq. 3) varies from 51.0 to 50.9. Thus we have almost a 6% of increment on efficiency, while the reduction on fairness is just 0.2%. Thus, less error frames appear in the system, although it keeps on providing almost the same proportional fairness.

3.4   Different Distribution of Channel Conditions

In order to analyze the performance of the algorithm in different scenarios, the proportion of channel types is modified from the original one (described in Table 1). Instead of two users with a *high quality* channel (HQ), two with

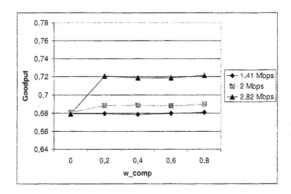

Figure 6. Efficiency, complete algorithm

Table 4. Goodput Improvement for Different Distributions of Channel Types

N_{LQ}	N_{AQ}					
	0	1	2	3	4	5
0	0.00	-0.01	-0.01	-0.01	-0.01	-0.01
1	0.07	0.07	0.07	0.08	0.08	
2	0.13	0.13	0.14	0.14		
3	0.17	0.17	0.17			
4	0.16	**0.15**				
5	-0.01					

a *average quality* channel (AQ) and one with a *low quality* channel (LQ), all possible combinations of $N_F = 5$ flows were simulated. Then, both the improvement introduced by the algorithm and its effect on system fairness were measured, and compared to the situation where the mechanism was inactive.

Results for efficiency are shown on Table 4, where the number of AQ channels increases to the right, and the number of LQ channels increases downwards (the number of HQ channels is implicit, $N_{HQ} + N_{AQ} + N_{LQ} = 5$). For example, the 0.15 value (highlighted) corresponds to a scenario with no MN with a HQ channel, 1 MN with an AQ channel and 4 MNs with LQ channels. It is evident that goodput improvement rises with the number of LQ channels. When all channels are equal, the goodput remains almost the same. There is an average relative improvement on efficiency of 8%.

On the other hand, the algorithm provokes a 0.16% average relative decrease of fairness. Figure 7 shows the achieved trade off between fairness and goodput, for all considered scenarios. The relative decrease of fairness is almost unnoticeable (at most, 0.25%), while the improvement on goodput is never less than 5%, when there is room for improvement.

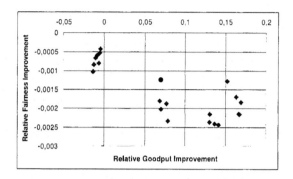

Figure 7.   Goodput improvement vs Fairness improvement for different distributions of channel types

4.   Conclusions

In WLAN environments the absence of channel probing mechanism prevents direct application of most wireless fair scheduling algorithms. Moreover, even if they were applicable, the compensation mechanisms implemented may provoke resource squandering, because a flow may deserve endless compensation. In this work we have presented a mechanism to adapt wireline scheduling algorithms to WLAN Access Points, by implementing a bounded (in terms of bandwidth and time) compensation mechanism, and a throttling mechanism. This novel type of double-bounded compensation, and the application of throttling to flows associated with error-prone channels, has been shown to perform well on scenarios with different distributions of link quality.

Acknowledgments

This work has been partly supported by the European Union under the e-Photon/ONe Project (FP6-001933) and by the Spanish Research Action CI-CYT CAPITAL (MEC, TEC2004-05622-C04-03/TCM). We also thank the reviewers of this paper for their valuable comments.

References

Banchs, A. and Perez, X. (2002). Distributed fair queuing in ieee 802.11 wireless lan. In *IEEE International Conference on Communications (ICC 2002), New York, April 2002.*

Bharghavan, V., Lu, Songwu, and Nandagopal, T. (1999). Fair queuing in wireless networks: issues and approaches. In *Personal Communications, IEEE, Vol.6, Iss.1, Feb 1999 Pages:44-53.*

Golestani, S. (1994). A self-clocked fair queueing scheme for broadband applications. In *Proceedings of IEEE INFOCOM 94, pages 636-646, Toronto, CA, June 1994.*

IEEE (1999). Ieee 802.11b, part ii: Wireless lan medium access control (mac) and physical layer (phy) specifications: Highspeed physical layer extension in the 2.4 ghz band.

Kelly, F. (1997). Charging and rate control for elastic traffic. *European Transactions on Telecommunications, 8*, pages 33–37.

Khayam, Syed A. and Radha, Hayder (2003). Markov-based modeling of wireless local area networks. In *Proceedings of the 6th international workshop on Modeling analysis and simulation of wireless and mobile systems*, pages 100–107. ACM Press.

Liu, Yonghe, Gruhl, S., and Knightly, E.W. (2003). Wcfq: an opportunistic wireless scheduler with statistical fairness bounds. In *Wireless Communications, IEEE Transactions on, Vol.2, Iss.5, Sept. 2003 Pages: 1017- 1028.*

Nakayama, M. (1994). Two-stage stopping procedures based on standardized time series. In *Management Science 40, 1189–1206.*

OMNeT++ (2003).

Raghunathan, Vijay, Ganeriwal, Saurabh, Schurgers, Curt, and Srivastava, Mani B. (2002). E2wfq: An energy efficient fair scheduling policy for wireless systems. In *International Symposium on Low Power Electronics and Design (ISLPED'02), Monterey, CA, pp. 30-35, August 12-14, 2002.*

Ramanathan, Parameswaran and Agrawal, Prathima (1998). Adapting packet fair queueing algorithms to wireless networks. In *Mobile Computing and Networking*, pages 1–9.

Saltzer, J. H., Reed, D. P., and Clark, D. D. (1984). End-to-end arguments in system design. *ACM Trans. Comput. Syst.*, 2(4):277–288.

Vaidya, Nitin H., Bahl, Paramvir, and Gupta, Seema (2000). Distributed fair scheduling in a wireless LAN. In *Mobile Computing and Networking*, pages 167–178.

Wang, Kuochen and Chin, Yi-Lon (2001). A fair scheduling algorithm with adaptive compensation in wireless networks. In *Global Telecommunications Conference, 2001. GLOBECOM '01. IEEE, Vol.6, Iss., 2001 Pages:3543-3547 vol.6.*

Wong, W.K., Zhu, Haiying, and Leung, V.C.M. (2003). Soft qos provisioning using the token bank fair queuing scheduling algorithm. In *Wireless Communications, IEEE [see also IEEE Personal Communications], Vol.10, Iss.3, June 2003 Pages: 8- 16.*

Zhang, H. (1995). Service disciplines for guaranteed performance service in packet-switching networks. In *Proc. IEEE, vol. 83, Oct 1995, pp. 1374-96.*

A QOS-AWARE AD HOC WIRELESS NETWORK FOR ISOLATED RURAL ENVIRONMENTS

Javier Simó
Fundación EHAS
ETSIT, Ciudad Universitaria s/n
28040 Madrid (Spain)
jsimo@ehas.org

Joaquín Seoane
DIT, Universidad Politécnica de Madrid
ETSIT, Ciudad Universitaria s/n
28040 Madrid (Spain)
jsp@dit.upm.es

Rodrigo de Salazar
Fundación EHAS
ETSIT, Ciudad Universitaria s/n
28040 Madrid (Spain)
no_id@hotmail.com

Abstract   Ad-hoc wireless networks are constituted by routers enabled to establish wireless links among them in a mesh topology. This kind of networks are becoming very popular because of their potential, low cost and ease of deployment, specially when IEEE 802.11b wireless technology is used. There has been a lot of research in the design of protocols and algorithms for improving the performance of this kind of networks. However, real implementations and testbeds are scarce, and even those few well known interesting experiences are not QoS-aware and their implementation details are not consistent. This paper presents the design of a 802.11b multi-hop QoS-aware mesh network specifically designed for isolated rural environments. This proposed network is used as a testbed for driving some initial experiments that aim to measure its performance when supporting both elastic and real-time traffic. The evaluation includes guidelines for a QoS-aware deployment of the network and recommendations for further work that can improve these results.

Keywords: 802.11, QoS, ad-hoc wireless networks, VoIP, developing countries

1.   Introduction

Wireless ad hoc networks have been the subject of many researches during the last years. A wireless ad hoc network is constituted by several computing devices communicated with each other through wireless links, that cooperate for configuring a multi-hop ad hoc network automatically. Each node of the network can be the client, the server or an intermediate router within a communication, and one or several of them can eventually be for the others a gateway to other networks like the Internet or the PSTN (public switched telephone network). At the IP level, the address that each node gives to itself must be unique, but not necessarily similar to the others. Multi-hop routes are created by special dynamic routing protocols adapted to the special characteristics of this kind of networks.

Many researches in this field are concerned by the mobility of nodes; in these approaches, dynamic routing protocols are designed or chosen considering that topology changes very quickly. Unfortunately, few researches focus on static ad hoc networks. These networks require routing protocols that take into account the real quality of wireless links in the metrics due to the fact that typical hop count is not enough in them [De Couto et al., 2002]. Quality-of-Service (QoS) is another interesting aspect often referred from a theoretical point of view in researches about ad hoc networks [De Couto et al., 2003; Mohapatra et al., 2003; Ge et al., 2003].

Contrasting with the quality and quantity of theoretical research, there are few software packages implementing IP auto-configuration, ad hoc routing protocols and QoS architectures, and even those few products are not well tested. Moreover, real testbeds of static ad hoc networks as in [Aguayo et al., 2003] are very scarce, procedures used in them for routing and address configuration are not good enough for real applications, and none of them is concerned by QoS, as far as we know.

In the EHAS group [EHAS Foundation, 2003], we work on telecommunication technologies adapted to isolated rural environments in developing countries, and specifically with health facilities and their communication to hospitals [Martínez et al., 2004a; Martínez et al., 2004b]. Deploying reliable and sustainable communication networks in such environments needs some challenging implementation considerations: firstly, several wireless technologies allow easy, cheap and infrastructure-free communication links and thus they are highly suitable for these scenarios; such installations will be generally difficult to access and therefore unsupervised, meaning that maintenance and system administration might be minimized; secondly, lack of reliable electric sources means that such terminals require low-power consumption, and thirdly, low population density in such areas makes advisable the use of low-cost links.

This paper presents the development of a wireless solar-powered router designed to perform QoS-aware ad hoc routing in outdoor installations. This system is an embedded computer with a QoS-aware routing software powered by solar panels, having one or several WiFi cards provided with external antennas. A network can be easily deployed by installing some units in previously fixed positions so that antennas are well oriented and line-of-sight is assured between two systems supposed to be connecting to each other. IETF's zero-conf proposals have been used for IP self-configuration [Cheshire et al., 2005], a DiffServ-like simplified QoS architecture based on Linux advanced traffic control permits the QoS-aware packet switching [Blake et al., 1998; Nichols et al., 1998; Heinanen et al., 1999; Jacobson et al., 1999], and a free software implementations of the AODV ad hoc routing protocol has been used. The first prototype has been produced using a x86 embedded computer, but the software has been integrated in such a way that cross-compiling the same software for other platforms is straight-forward. A second version of it is previewed using a XScale platform, which will reduce power consumption approximately from 3W to 0.8W, so that the whole system will become smaller and much cheaper.

The network designed has also served as a testbed permitting the evaluation of different dynamic routing protocols and technical procedures for partial QoS support. A first experiment permitted to evaluate and compare several ad hoc routing protocols already implemented for Linux. Once that IP addressing and routing where solved, a second experiment permitted to test our simplified DiffServ-like implementation, which gave us some usable results about the network performance and the optimal configuration of queuing disciplines that permit a good coexistence between elastic and real-time traffic.

The final results of this work are intended to be used in real installations by the EHAS program.

2. The link level in wireless ad hoc networks

The choice of the most appropriated wireless technology for this project is determined by the next three constraints: the use for long distances, the use of a free band and a very low cost of devices. All this make 802.11b the most appropriated technology at this moment; however, it has several important limitations proved by other researches: the MAC cannot assure a good performance when different connexions share the channel, there are some negative interactions between the MAC and TCP, there are important long-distance issues, the technology doesn't support QoS, and there is not a definitive solution for the *hidden node problem* [Xu and Saadawi, 2002]. Those limitations must be taken into account in the way upper levels will use wireless links in order to minimize interferences and so improve performance and stability.

The IEEE 802.11b standard describes the architecture and protocols for wireless local area networks using the spread spectrum technology at the ISM 2.4GHz band. There are basically two different operation modes which are infrastructure and ad hoc. In the infrastructure mode two types of entities are defined: access points and clients, while in ad hoc mode all nodes are identical. Obviously the ad hoc mode can serve to build ad hoc networks. It must be understood that *ad hoc* here means peer-to-peer, that is, two systems that see to each other and communicate directly. Many systems having the same SSID (service set identifier) and keys can connect among them as far as each one see all the other systems. Thus, using the ad hoc mode each node see only its neighbours.

3. The IP level in wireless ad hoc networks

As seen at the IP level, an ad hoc network, also called *mesh network*, is a set of nodes that can all act as clients, servers or routers in different communications and that constitutes a multi-hop network dynamically build and configured. Thus, the objective of a mesh network is that several independent IP nodes constitute a single IP network where any node can communicate with any other one and even with other networks if any of them act as a gateway. The mechanisms that make this possible are mainly two: address auto-configuration and multi-hop ad hoc routing. There are several theoretical proposals for address auto-configuration, but the most important is the IETF's zeroconf's model [Cheshire et al., 2005]. Unfortunately, most of the real implementations of ad hoc networks don't use this solution and prefer to solve the addressing in a different way. After studying the different proposals, zeroconf's seems to be the best, which made us decide to adopt it. There is a software implementation of it for Linux called zcip that has been chosen to perform address auto-configuration. However, we must say that we have ceased using it after the tests presented in this paper since the authors have announced a conflict of patents. Nowadays we are looking for a definitive solution, but in the meantime we produce unique IP addresses using the method used in MIT's RoofNet testbed [Aguayo et al., 2003]. When using zeroconf's system, each node was able to find a unique 169.254.X.Y IP address. A DHCP server is also installed in the node for which configuration changes each time the node is rebooted, so that it proposes addresses of the form 192.168.X.Y to clients. The node will perform network address translation (NAT) to its clients.

There are many multi-hop ad hoc dynamic routing protocols designed and simulated, some of which have been implemented and tested in the real world. AODV is the best known protocol of this type, and at least two well tested software implementations of it can be used in Linux. Other implemented protocols are DSR and OLSR. It has been established that proactive protocols are not well suited for ad hoc networks where the throughput is considered a critical resource because routing table broadcasts may starve all available resources, a consideration that is specially true when nodes are mobile. But even reactive protocols whose metrics is the number of hops have some important limitations in wireless networks [De Couto et al., 2002]. A wireless link in a 802.11b network may have a speed as of 1,2,5.5 and 11 Mbps, but the real throughput is much lower because it depends on the quality of the signal, which may vary with the distance and the presence of interferences. The routing protocol must take this into consideration because the shortest path may not be the best route. The available protocols implemented and having a metrics well suited for wireless networks are scarce. In fact, at the moment of our study we were not able to identify any available implementation of a multi-hop ad hoc routing protocol meeting these requirements. Some QoS-aware ad hoc routing protocols as QOLSR and ETX are being implemented, but those implementations were still not usable.

We have tested some implementations of standard AODV and OLSR looking for good node discovery, stability, low impact in performance and good gateway discovery. After testing several implementations, we found that both UU-AODV and Qolyester (OLSR implementation aiming to become QOLSR, but still without QoS support) are good enough for now. However, we don't give any more details as this is a temporary solution for our testbed until implementations of QoS-aware protocols well suited to wireless ad hoc networks become available. As the Linux kernel is going to be used in nodes, we assure that we have all the elements needed for IP packet switching [Radhakrishnan, 1999; Hubert, 2003].

4.   The QoS in IP routers

The QoS (Quality of Service) can be defined as a guarantee assured by the network of respecting certain maximal or minimal values to certain parameters when switching a packet throughout the network. The main problem associated to the QoS in a protocol stack is that all protocols must be QoS-aware., which is not the case of 802.11b as it has been said above; any wireless network using this technology will never support QoS completely. However, the use of certain technical procedures at the IP level will permit at least that different kinds of traffic could be differentiated and treated as needed.

Typical IP QoS architectures are IntServ and DiffServ. Both are standardized by the IETF [Blake et al., 1998; Nichols et al., 1998; Heinanen et al., 1999; Jacobson et al., 1999] but the second one is preferred generally because it scales better. None of them can be directly applied to ad hoc networks because they make some important functional differences between edge nodes and core nodes while in ad hoc networks all nodes have the same functionality; so any of these solutions will have to be adapted.

The QoS at the IP level implies that different communications (in IntServ) or different traffic classes (in DiffServ) can be identified in each router and be treated separately, with different priorities. An important handicap will be that the throughput of wireless links must be estimated in order to perform bandwidth sharing in a fair way, though the throughput may be variable due to the distance between nodes or to the presence of interferences [Mukhtar et al., 2003]. We have also mentioned that the WiFi technology is not QoS-aware [Xu and Saadawi, 2002]. However, a partial support for QoS may be obtained at the IP level applying QoS-aware IP switching, what permits to give different priorities to different traffic classes. The parameters that can be adjusted for each traffic class are mainly the following ones: throughput, delay and packet-dropping probability. Additionally, traffic shaping functions give us a way to avoid network overload, what permits us to guarantee that the network performance will approach what is expected.

We will be interested in differentiating six types of traffic which are voice (EF), control and interactive terminal sessions (AF1), video (AF2), navigation (AF3), file downloading (AF4), and the rest (BE). Linux kernel 2.4.20 or newer incorporate several queue disciplines, filters and other facilities that permit to implement a simplified version of DiffServ just by configuring the kernel with the tc utility [Radhakrishnan, 1999; Hubert, 2003; Almesberger et al., 1999]. Using dsmark, tc_index, gred, htb, red and pfifo in the linux kernel we can implement the following procedure:

1 Packets coming into the network (identified by their source IP address) are marked with a DSCP value corresponding their type. Packet classification will be performed in order to distinguish the six different traffic classes mentioned above. In order to achieve this, several packet fields will be evaluated: transport protocol, IP address, ports, size and even the payload. The main difficulty is to separate voice and small video packets but even if we make some errors considering an small percentage of them as voice packets, the bandwidth will be shared in a way that avoids those errors to be critical. UDP packets smaller than 160 bytes are identified as VoIP. We could get better results analyzing the payload in order to identify packets containing RTP/RTCP with something having a well known audio codec, but the increment in the CPU load of nodes is more significant than the one in the amount of successful identifications. The rest of UDP packages will be considered video, which is obviously a very simplistic approach (traffics as common as DNS or NFS use to be UDP) but useful for us.

2 Once all packets circulating in the network have been marked with a DSCP, all routers will be able to easily separate them as belonging to different traffic classes. Egress queues in all routers will put each type of traffic in a different subqueue. Each of them will have a share of bandwidth, an appropriated queue length, an appropriated queue dropping probability and other parameters like maximum bust traffic, etc. Voice is given priority over all other traffic classes and so the other classes have relative priorities as listed above.

3 When a packet is going to quit the ad hoc network through an Internet gateway, its DSCP will be given an acceptable value for the Internet.

The implementation of this QoS architecture will use a DSMARK queuing discipline with six subclasses. The EF will be managed by a HTB queue with a guaranteed bandwidth equal to 30% of the total (to be measured in the laboratory). AF classes will be implemented with GRED queues and share 45% of available bandwidth. The rest of the bandwidth (25%) would be given to best effort traffics, managed with a FIFO or eventually an SFQ queue. The DS-MARK queuing discipline is used as a container of all other classes because it lets subclasses handle the DSCP. The specific configuration of the traffic control block will depend on the results of experiments presented below.

The ingress queue of each node is programmed to switch transparently every packet with the DS field marked with values 0xa0 or 0x60, or coming from another ad hoc node. Other packets coming from client terminals will be analysed in order to mark audio packets with 0xa0 and video packets as 0xa0. Any other packet will be given a DS value of 0x00 and distinguished with their port field in the egress queue.

5. Building the system

This work consists of building a node of the wireless ad hoc network. A number of identical systems should permit to deploy a network for voice and data switching.

These systems will be installed in isolated rural areas where there is no power source, so nodes need to have a solar power subsystem which means that the cost and the size of a system will be proportional to its power consumption. On the other hand, ultra-low consuming embedded computers are extremely expensive and software development for those platforms can be difficult. Each system will be constituted by three main parts: the power subsystem, the computer subsystem and the radio subsystem.

The first one will consist of a 22 Wp solar panel, a 3A regulator and a 17Ah battery, calculated for powering a system consuming about 3W 24 hours a day in the worst weather conditions that we can find in EHAS networks, which are deployed in tropical regions. Obviously, solar radiation in Spain is much lower, so during our experiments in Spain we had to recharge the batteries from time to time.

For the computer subsystem, Soekris net4521 embedded computers have been chosen because they meet all the requirements: low power consumption, three expansion slots where we can insert WiFi cards and hardware watchdog. However, less consuming boards like StrongARM platforms will be evaluated in future developments. The hardware is completed with a 32MB SanDisk CompactFlash that will contain the operating system.

Finally, the radio subsystem will include one or two PCMCIA Engenius Senao SL-2511-CD Ext2 200mW WiFi cards which may be connected to pigtails and external antennas if needed. See Fig. 1.

The operating system is built using a cross-compiling toolchain, following Karim Yaghmour's guidelines. We could simplify this just by compiling the software in a x86 platform, but this way of software development permits to migrate easily to other hardware platforms. A basic Linux filesystem has been created, with basic devices and directories. Additionally, an appropriated kernel has been cross-compiled, as well as glibc, busybox, hostap, wireless-tools, pcmcia-cs, iproute2, iptables, tinylogin, pump, kernel-aodv, openssl, zlib, openssh, sysklogd, zcip and MobileMesh. Besides configuration files, starting scripts and so forth are manually created. Although the filesystem obtained has a size of 13MB, it can be compressed in less than 5MB. With GRUB as the bootloader and the filesystem configured to be decompressed in RAM, we have obtained an operating system that can live in a small Compact Flash while having all the power of a QoS-aware wireless IP router.

6.   Performance evaluation

A solar-powered wireless ad hoc node has been fully designed. A prototype has been developed with its hardware, operating system, auto-configuration procedures and traffic control politics. Now it is time to find out if the design serves for deploying auto-configurable ad hoc networks that enable transport VoIP and other data with acceptable quality.

There are three main tests that must be run in order to validate this work:

1 Nodes must detect each other automatically and adapt their routing table to any changes in the topology. In particular, the presence of a gateway node must be recognized as such by the others, which must add a default route through it.

2 Any WiFi or Ethernet client terminal correctly configured and having a DHCP client must be provided with a private IP address from any of the nodes to be able to access the other nodes and eventually the Internet.

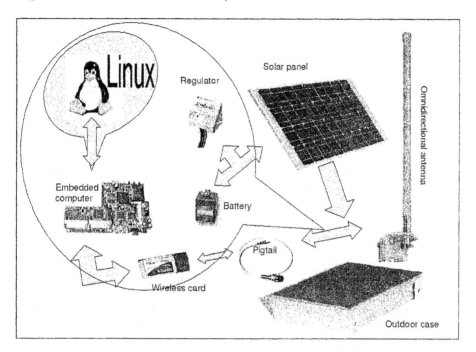

Figure 1.   Parts of a node

3 When several connections are overloading the network, voice traffic must be protected from the others.

We deployed our testbed in the laboratory with four nodes in cascade. Our testbed can operate in a reduced space because the WiFi cards chosen lack of any kind of internal dipole antennas. If we don't connect external antennas to them, their range of communication is kept below one meter. We configured the first card of each node in WiFi channel 1 and the second in channel 6 or superior so that both cards will not interfere. The first WiFi card is used to access the ad hoc network while the second and the Ethernet ports are for client terminals.

The first test was straight forward once we chose the UU-AODV, developed by the University of Upsala. It is well understood that this routing protocol is not QoS aware, so it is specially important that two nodes associate only if they can maintain a high quality wireless link between them. That can be assured by fixing a high association threshold (i.e. -70 dBm or superior) to the first wireless card of each node.

The second test was also simple and the success was almost assured, as the configuration of DHCP and NAT is just a matter of system administration.

Once we had four nodes forming an ad hoc network, one of which was connected to the Internet through its first Ethernet port, and all of them detecting

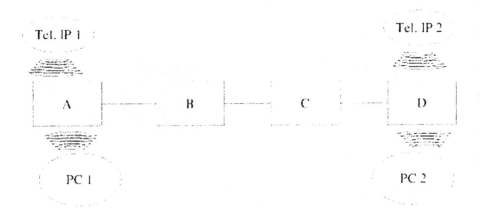

Figure 2.   Network topology for test 3

the network topology properly and being able to give access to client terminals, we associated a computer to node D and connected two IP telephones to nodes A and D through their second Ethernet port, as seen in Fig. 2.

The IP phones are configured to use the value 0xa0 for the DS field.

We will conduct the following tests:

1 Measure of the total available bandwidth.

2 Objective tests: by using a traffic generator as iperf, we simulate a continuous TCP-BE traffic flow between A and D. This tool permits us to measure bandwidth, delay and jitter at arrival. 20 seconds later a new traffic flow simulating a voice conversation is injected. 20 seconds later traffic simulating video is introduced, and finally other UDP traffic flows follow. These tests are performed with and without traffic control.

3 Subjective tests: the same tests are run but voice traffic is not simulated. A real voice communication happens between the two IP phones that is perturbed with different concurrent traffic flows.

7.   Results

The first test shows a total throughput of about 590 Kbps in absence of traffic control. That is completely normal because the links have been fixed to 1 Mbps in order to simulate the worst real conditions. Based on this first result and after evaluating different alternatives, the traffic will be controlled according to the following simplified configuration (we distinguish only among voice, video and the rest in this case):

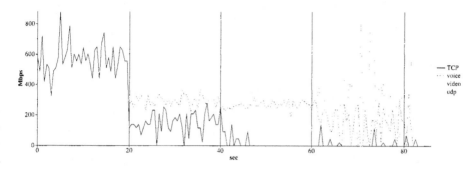

Figure 3.   Bandwidth without traffic control

tc qdisc add dev wlan0 handle 1:0 root dsmark indices 64 set_tc_index default_index 1
tc filter add dev wlan0 parent 1:0 protocol ip prio 4 tcindex mask 0xfc shift 2
tc qdisc add dev wlan0 handle 2: parent 1:1 htb
tc class add dev wlan0 parent 2: classid 2:1 htb rate 500Kbit ceil 550Kbit
tc class add dev wlan0 parent 2:1 classid 2:10 htb rate 300Kbit ceil 500Kbit prio 1
tc class add dev wlan0 parent 2:1 classid 2:20 htb rate 150Kbit prio 2
tc class add dev wlan0 parent 2:1 classid 2:40 htb rate 64Kbit prio 3
tc qdisc add dev wlan0 parent 2:10 sfq perturb 10
tc qdisc add dev wlan0 parent 2:20 sfq perturb 10
tc qdisc add dev wlan0 parent 2:40 red limit 64KB min 5KB max 15KB burst 8 avpkt 1000 \
    bandwidth 64Kbit probability 0.1
tc filter add dev wlan0 parent 2: protocol ip prio 1 handle 0x28 tcindex classid 2:10 pass_on
tc filter add dev wlan0 parent 2: protocol ip prio 1 handle 0x18 tcindex classid 2:20 pass_on
tc filter add dev wlan0 parent 2: protocol ip prio 2 u32 match ip tos 0x00 0x00 flowid 2:40

It is important to observe that although other possible configurations have
been evaluated (with PRIO instead of HTB, etc.) this configuration has resulted to be the best for our needs. The DSMARK queuing discipline is used
only for giving subclasses access to the DSCP but actually all traffic goes to a
HTB queuing discipline, whose main mission is to manage bandwidth sharing.
Here in there are two possible approaches: HTB subclasses might share their
dedicated bandwidth in excess of what they need, or they can keep their dedicated bandwidth empty when they don't use it. HTB main class is supposed
to manage bandwidth sharing so that each traffic class always finds its dedicated bandwidth when necessary but lends it when idle. We have tested both
possibilities. The configuration for bandwidth among classes is similar to the
previous one but giving a *ceiling* of 500 kbps to classes 2:20 and 2:40, and a
limit of 500 kbps to the RED qdisc.

The objective tests without traffic control show that traffic flows perturb
enormously to each other, as we can see in Fig. 3 and Fig. 4.

We can see how the bandwidth utilization of the BE flow drops immediately
when the voice appears. That is expected, as TCP uses its congestion avoidance

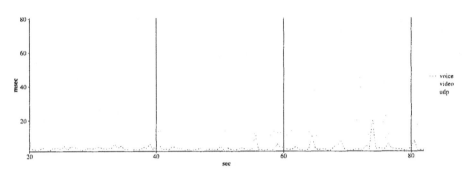

Figure 4.   Jitter without traffic control

mechanism for adapting itself to available resources. When video appears, the voice keeps using the same bandwidth just because the network is not yet saturated and because UDP has no congestion avoidance. At the same time, we can see that both UDP flows have starved the bandwidth and the TCP traffic has almost disappeared. As the forth traffic flow appears, all the flows are perturbed, with a very important visible impact on the quality of service.

When applying traffic control, the result of the same tests is as shown in Fig. 5 and Fig. 6. We can see that each traffic flow is preserved. The TCP flows are more sensitive than the UDP flows as expected. We can also see that voice is not perturbed by TCP traffic, but video perturbs voice a little bit. However, we have achieved a situation where different traffic flows are somehow preserved from each other's influence.

When the traffic control block permits sharing of available bandwidth among classes, we can see that the result is much worse for the bandwidth (Fig. 7) and similar for the jitter (Fig. 8). This result shows that, at least for the voice traffic, we must avoid other classes to borrow its available bandwidth. Even more: when dedicated bandwidth is restricted but adjusted to the exact needs of voice traffic, the result is similar to the case of bandwidth sharing. We get the result showed in Fig. 7 only if we limit the total bandwidth to at most 85% of the the maximum throughput obtained in the first test. This way we are wasting bandwidth significantly, but the sacrifice is necessary in order to assure the best QoS for telephony.

In both Fig. 4 and Fig. 6, and also in Fig. 8, we can see that the jitter is strongly modified in voice communications independently we have or not applied traffic control. That means that voice quality can be maintained by applying traffic control, but packet delay will augment significantly in both cases when the network is overloaded.

Subjective tests run without traffic control showed that VoIP:

- has a very good quality when the network is dedicated,

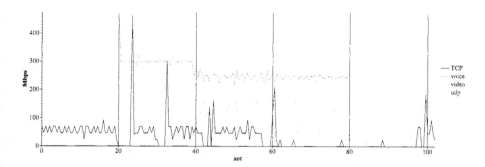

Figure 5.   Bandwidth with traffic control

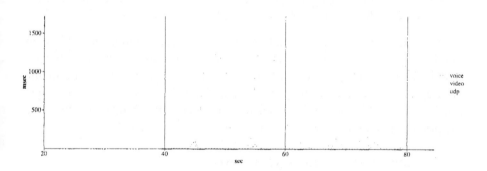

Figure 6.   Jitter with traffic control

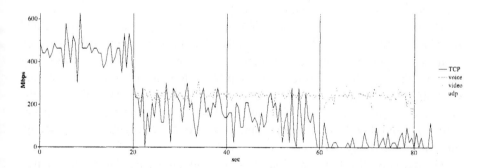

Figure 7.   Bandwidth with traffic control (BW shared)

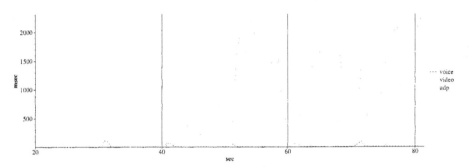

Figure 8.   Jitter with traffic control (BW shared)

- is good enough but with some audible *clicks* whenever sharing the network with TCP flows, and

- is bad, with long delays (seconds) but it offers almost acceptable audio
  quality when the network is overloaded.

When applying traffic control, the quality of voice communications remains
good and stable in presence of TCP or intense UDP traffic. Only real network
overload causes longer delays of voice packets, but with good audio quality
anyways. Actually this result is end-system dependent: VoIP terminals that do
much less buffering would have much lower delays in overloaded networks at
the price of perceiving a worse audio quality due to packets lost.

8.   Discussion and conclusions

The aim of this research was to develop and evaluate a real wireless ad hoc
network with address and route auto configuration, and partial QoS support.
The network developed should be easy to deploy in isolated rural areas and be
able to switch voice and data traffic taking into account the quality of service
required for each differentiated service.

The process of evaluation itself has been presented above. All software and
hardware products needed have been verified and routing protocols have been
compared. The performance evaluation test showed that our network deals
well with differentiated services, giving priority to real-time traffic classes and
specially protecting voice flows from data traffic load. However, these results
don't mean that voice communications can be of the same quality in any in-
stallation, and therefore, it is important to consider the limitations imposed by
the WiFi technology, which is not QoS-aware.

The network developed will permit to do some real installations in isolated
rural areas of developing countries, and will serve at the same time for a deeper
evaluation of all software and hardware technologies that are being used and
the interactions among them. Nevertheless, there are several aspects in the pro-

totype that must be optimized: power consumption may be much lower using a more efficient computer architecture, the IP auto-configuration procedure must be consolidated, a QoS-aware ad hoc routing protocol must be used, and traffic control architecture should be optimized in order to avoid bandwidth waste and extremely high delays and jitters when the network is overloaded.

In the next future we intend to develop a second version of the hardware, based on the StrongARM architecture, with IPv6 for an easier auto configuration and more appropriated routing protocols as ETX or future QoS-aware versions of Qolyester. Additionally, traffic control will be studied more in depth in order to obtain a more efficient model.

References

Aguayo, D., Bicket, J., Biswas, S., de Couto, D.S.J., and Morris, R. (2003). MIT's RoofNET implementation. http://pdos.csail.mit.edu/roofnet/design/. PDOS-LCS. MIT.

Almesberger, W., Salim, J., Kuznetsov, A., and Knuth, D. (1999). Differentiated services on linux. Internet Draft: draft-almesberger-wajhak-diffserv-linux-01.txt.

Blake, S., Black, D., Carlson, M., Davies, E., Wang, Zh., and Weiss, W. (1998). An architecture for differentiated services. RFC 2475.

Cheshire, S., Aboba, B., and Guttman, E. (2005). Dynamic configuration of link-local ipv4 addresses. RFC 3927.

De Couto, Douglas S. J., Aguayo, Daniel, Bicket, John, and Morris, Robert (2003). A high-throughput path metric for multi-hop wireless routing. In *Proceedings of the 9th ACM International Conference on Mobile Computing and Networking (MobiCom '03)*, San Diego, California.

De Couto, Douglas S. J., Aguayo, Daniel, Chambers, Benjamin A., and Morris, Robert (2002). Performance of multihop wireless networks: Shortest path is not enough. In *Proceedings of the First Workshop on Hot Topics in Networks (HotNets-I)*, Princeton, New Jersey. ACM SIGCOMM.

EHAS Foundation (2003). EHAS: Enlace hispanoamericano de salud. http://www.ehas.org. Website created in November 2003.

Ge, Ying, Kunz, Thomas, and Lamont, Louise (2003). Quality of service routing in ad-hoc networks using OLSR. In *HICSS*, page 300.

Heinanen, J., Baker, F., Weiss, W., and Wroclawski, J. (1999). Assured forwarding PHB group. RFC 2597.

Hubert, B. (2003). Linux advanced routing and traffic control. http://www.lartc.org.

Jacobson, V., Nichols, K., and Poduri, K. (1999). An expedited forwarding PHB. RFC 2598.

Martínez, A., Villarroel, V., Seoane, J., and del Pozo, F. (2004a). Rural telemedicine for primary healthcare in developing countries. *IEEE Technology and Society Magazine*, 23(2).

Martínez, A., Villarroel, V., Seoane, J., and del Pozo, F. (2004b). A study of a rural telemedicine system in the Amazon region of Peru. *Journal of Telemedicine and Telecare*, 10(4).

Mohapatra, Prasant, Li, Jian, and Gui, Chao (2003). QoS in mobile ad hoc networks. *IEEE Wireless Communications*.

Mukhtar, Rami G., Hanly, Stephen V., and Andrew, Lachlan L. H. (2003). Efficient internet traffic delivery over wireless networks. *IEEE Commun. Mag.*

Nichols, K., Blake, S., Baker, F., and Black, D. (1998). Definition of the differentiated services field (DS field) in the IPv4 and IPv6 headers. RFC 2474.

Radhakrishnan, S. (1999). Linux - advanced networking overview. http://qos.ittc.ukans.edu/howto.pdf. ITTC, Univ. Kansas.

Xu, Shugong and Saadawi, Tarek (2002). Revealing the problems with 802.11 medium access control protocol in multi-hop wireless ad hoc networks. *Comput. Networks*, 38(4):531–548.

ENERGY EFFICIENCY IN WIRELESS SENSOR NETWORKS USING MOBILE BASE STATION

Dorottya Vass*, Zoltán Vincze, Rolland Vida and Attila Vidács[†]
Dept. of Telecommunications and Media Informatics
Budapest University of Technology and Economics
Magyar tudósok krt. 2, 1117 Budapest, Hungary
{vass,vinczez,vida,vidacs}@tmit.bme.hu

Abstract   A sensor network consists of a large number of small, low-cost devices with sensing, processing and transmitting capabilities. The sensor nodes have limited battery power; therefore energy efficiency is a critical design issue. In this paper we propose to move the sink node, called Base Station (BS) so as to decrease the energy consumption of the whole network. We present two possible strategies to move the BS: the first one minimizes the average consumed energy, while the other one minimizes the maximum transmission energy for every active sensor. To evaluate the performance of the two strategies, we compare these with the case, when the BS is deployed in a fixed position. Simulation results show that the proposed processes can reduce energy consumption, thereby significantly extending the lifetime of the entire sensor network.

Keywords: sensor network, mobility, mobile base station, energy efficiency

1.   Introduction

A sensor network consists of a large number of small, low-cost devices with sensing, processing, and transmitting capabilities. The main goal of the operation is to observe a region and gather and relay information to a sink node or set of sink nodes, called Base Station (BS). Forwarding the data to the BS is possible in two ways: using direct or multihop communication. In the first case every sensor transmits its data directly to the sink; in the second case, the sensors are communicating with the neighbors that forward the information in the direction of the sink.

*This work has been partly supported by the European Union under the E-Next Project FP6-506869 and by the Inter-University Centre for Telecommunications and Informatics.
[†]A. Vidács is with the Research Group for Informatics and Electronics of the Hungarian Academy of Sciences, grantee of the János Bolyai Scholarship.

The sensor networks can be also categorized by the periodicity of data transmissions. In a time-driven network every node sends messages periodically, while in an event-driven one a node sends message only when sensing a phenomenon [Yao and Gehrke, 2002]. The third category is the query-driven approach, when the sensors send data only after receiving a query from the BS. There are also hybrid networks that combines the previous three models.

The sensors are usually deployed densely and often on-the-fly [Gandham et al., 2004]. They operate untethered and unattended, are limited in power, computational capacities and memory. Because of these constraints the sensor network must have efficient self-organizing capabilities, while optimising energy consumption.

A primary design issue in sensor networks is energy efficiency. The sensors are small-sized, cheap, and usually deployed in inaccessible regions; therefore they are supplied only by a small battery which is impossible (or very costly) to recharge. The main goal is to prolong the lifetime of the network, which can be defined in several ways:

- the time when the first node depletes its battery,

- the time till a given percentage of the sensors has enough energy to operate,

- the time till a given percentage of the region is covered by alive sensors.

Communicating 1 bit over a wireless medium at short ranges consumes far more energy than processing that bit. With the current technology, the energy consumption for communication is several magnitude higher, than the energy required for computation; and wireless communication is foreseen to continue to dominate energy consumption in the near future [Doherty et al., 2001]. There are two possible ways to decrease the energy used for communication in a sensor network: minimize the amount of the transmitted data, or shorten the communication range. The transmission energy is proportional to d^{α}, where d is the transmission distance, while α is the attenuation exponent. Due to multipath and other interference effects, α is typically in the range of 2 to 5 [Zhao and Gubias, 2004]. Thus, minimizing the amount and the range of communication as much as possible can significantly prolong the life of a sensor network.

In order to decrease the transmission distance in sensor networks, we propose an approach where the BS is capable to change its position. The BS tries to find the optimal location as far as energy consumption concerned, using two optimization strategies: the first one minimizes the average consumed energy, while the other one minimizes the maximum transmission energy for every active sensor. We evaluated the strategies using simulation, the results showing, that they significantly prolong the lifetime of the network.

The rest of the paper is organized as follows: Section 2 summarizes the related work. Section 3 introduces the concept of the mobile BS and the two strategies to locate the optimal location of the BS. The results of the simulations evaluating the performance of the strategies are presented in Section 4. Finally, Section 5 sketches the conclusions and presents some tasks for the future work.

2. Related Work

Recently, energy efficiency has been one of the focus points of research in the field of sensor networks. There have been a lot of proposals to minimize energy consumption in sensor networks [Intanagonwiwat et al., 2000] [Gan et al., 2004] [Ganesan et al., 2001] [Schurgers and Srivastava, 2001] [Rahul and Rabaey, 2002] . These proposals are common in the fact that they all assume the BS and the sensor nodes to be static.

The majority of the research papers that appeared until now consider sensor networks to be entirely static. However, some consider that these networks should be able to cope with the mobility of either the BS or the sensor node themselves [Al-Karaki and Kamal, 2004]. This new approach raises the possibility of developing new methods to spare energy.

There are some papers which consider only the sensors to be mobile. On the one hand, Howard *et al.* present an incremental deployment algorithm for mobile sensor networks [Howard et al., 2002]. On the other hand, Rahimi *et al.* study the feasibility of extending the lifetime of a wireless sensor network by exploiting mobility [Rahimi et al., 2003]. They assume that a small percentage of network nodes are autonomously mobile, allowing them to move in search of energy, recharge, and deliver energy to immobile, energy-depleted nodes.

The idea of mobile BS is also considered by some papers. Ye *et al.* propose to build an overlay network in the sensor network for data dissemination to mobile sinks [Ye et al., 2002]. Kim *et al.* are examining the same problem, they suggest a technique to build dissemination tree for disseminating data to mobile sinks [Kim et al., 2003]. The mobility of the BS is unpredictable in these works (e.g. sinks move according to the random waypoint model).

Other papers are dealing with the task of moving the BS in the sensor network in order to elongate the lifetime of the network. Wang *et al.* suggest a linear programming method to determine the optimal movement of the BS and the sojourn time at different points in the network to maximize the network lifetime [Wang et al., 2005]. The authors assume the sensors are deployed in the crossing points of a bi-dimensional square grid and the BS can move only on the grid from one node to another. Gandham *et al.* propose to decrease energy consumption, thus increasing the network lifetime using multiple mobile Base Stations [Rao et al., 2003]. The number of the base stations is known *a priori* and they can be located only at *a priori* given sites on the border of the sensor network. The goal is to find the optimal place of the base stations regarding to energy consumption in order to prolong network lifetime. The common in the previous works is that the authors consider only proactive (time-driven) sensor networks where each node generates equal amount of data per time unit.

In our work we also consider the mobility of the base station. However, as opposed to the previous assumptions, we consider the BS can move anywhere inside the sensor network (for example the BS is mounted on a robot plane). The type of the network we considered is also different, hence we assumed event-driven network where the sensor sends data only when sensing an event.

3.   Strategies for Moving Mobile Base Station

In this work, we consider a typical sensor network, where the nodes have no mobility after the deployment, and operate in an event-driven way. The network is divided into small clusters, in which we assume the sensors are distributed uniformly. Each cluster has a clusterhead, this is the BS. The small size of the clusters makes it possible for sensors in the cluster to communicate with the BS directly. We assume that every sensor knows its distance from the BS.

Although sensing also requires energy, this is far less, than the energy used for communication. Therefore in this paper we deal only with the transmission energy. The energy used for the communication is proportional to d^α, where d is the transmission distance and α is the attenuation parameter. Sensors are able to change the level of the transmission energy depending on their distance d.

We consider that the BS is mobile and is able to reach every point in the area of the cluster. It has relatively sufficient energy, because it has access to power supply. We assume that the BS moves fast enough to reach the optimal location very rapidly (practically 'immediately' after calculating the location).

In this paper we examine two strategies for moving the BS, and compare their performance with the case when the BS is fixed.

3.1   Minimizing the average energy consumption

This strategy minimizes the energy consumed by the active sensors in the network at every moment once an event happens. Let (x_0, y_0) denote the co-ordinates of the BS, and (x_i, y_i) the coordinates of the ith ($i = 1 \ldots n$) sensor. The distance d_i between the BS and the ith sensor is

$$d_i = \sqrt{(x_0 - x_i)^2 + (y_0 - y_i)^2}. \tag{1}$$

Let E_{ti} be the energy used by the ith sensor for the communication with the BS and let E_0 be the energy needed to transmit one unit of data. Then if the ith sensor transmits one unit of data

$$E_{t_i} = E_0 d_i^\alpha, \quad \alpha \in [2,5]. \tag{2}$$

If V is the set of sensors, and $A \subset V$ is the set of active nodes, then the energy consumed by the active sensors is

$$E_t = E_0 \sum_{i \in A} d_i^\alpha. \tag{3}$$

The method places the BS where this sum reaches its minimum:

$$(x_0, y_0) = \arg \min_{x,y} E_t. \tag{4}$$

In the rest of the paper we will refer to this strategy as 'minavg'. The idea here is that using this strategy causes the network to always spend the minimal energy for the communication between the active sensors and the BS. Therefore the total energy of the network will remain the highest compared to other strategies.

The used total energy is minimal when

$$\left. \frac{\partial E}{\partial x} \right|_{x=x_0} = 0 \quad \text{and} \quad \left. \frac{\partial E}{\partial y} \right|_{y=y_0} = 0. \tag{5}$$

The partial derivatives are

$$
\begin{aligned}
\frac{\partial E}{\partial x} &= \frac{\partial}{\partial x} \left(E_0 \sum_{i \in A} d^\alpha \right) \\
&= E_0 \sum_{i \in A} \frac{\partial}{\partial x} \left(\sqrt{(x_0 - x_i)^2 + (y_0 - y_i)^2}^\alpha \right) \\
&= E_0 \sum_{i \in A} \alpha [(x_0 - x_i)^2 + (y_0 - y_i)^2]^{\frac{\alpha-1}{2}} \\
&\quad \times \frac{\partial}{\partial x} \left(\sqrt{(x_0 - x_i)^2 + (y_0 - y_i)^2} \right) \\
&= E_0 \alpha \sum_{i \in A} (x_0 - x_i)[(x_0 - x_i)^2 + (y_0 - y_i)^2]^{\frac{\alpha-2}{2}}
\end{aligned}
\tag{6}
$$

and similarly,

$$\frac{\partial E}{\partial y} = E_0 \alpha \sum_{i \in A} (y_0 - y_i)[(x_0 - x_i)^2 + (y_0 - y_i)^2]^{\frac{\alpha-2}{2}}. \tag{7}$$

Unfortunately there is no closed formula solution to find the optimal (x_0, y_0) coordinates, thus it has to be determined using optimisation methods (for example some kind of gradient-based search [Carson and Maria, 1997]).

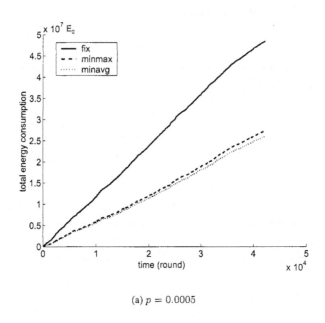

(a) $p = 0.0005$

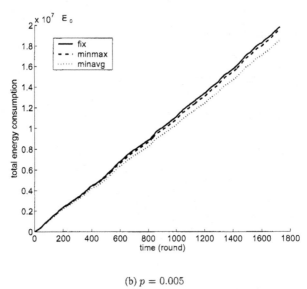

(b) $p = 0.005$

Figure 1.   The total energy consumption of the network

3.2   Minimizing the maximum energy consumed by an active sensor

The drawback of the *minavg* approach is that it does not take into account the interests of the individual sensors. For example, it may happen that most of the active sensors are close to the BS, while one or more nodes are far from it. Therefore these sensors use much more energy than the others and deplete their battery sooner, so they have less lifetime.

The strategy introduced in this subsection is able to avoid this problem. In order to do so, it minimizes the maximum transmission energy for the sensors in the network; i.e.,

$$\max_{i \in A} E_{t_i} \to min . \tag{8}$$

hence, energy consumption will be more balanced.

As the transmission energy depends on the distance between the sensor and the BS, this strategy is equivalent with minimizing the maximum distance between the BS and every active sensor in the network. The location of the BS is given by the coordinates minimizing the next expression:

$$(x_0, y_0) = \arg \min_{x,y} \left[\max_{i \in A} \sqrt{(x_0 - x_i)^2 + (y_0 - y_i)^2} \right] . \tag{9}$$

In the rest of the paper we will refer to this strategy as 'minmax'.

The optimisation task is equivalent to the problem of finding the minimal enclosing circle, where we have a set of points and the task is to find the minimum radius circle that encloses all of them. There are several algorithms to solve this problem. The simplest one considers every circle being defined by two or three of the n points, and finds the smallest of these circles that contains every point. This solution has a total running time of $O(n^4)$. On the other hand it has been shown that the minimal enclosing circle problem can be solved in $O(n)$ time using the prune-and-search techniques for linear programming [Megiddo, 1983].

4.   Simulation Results

In the simulations we considered the sensor network introduced in Section 3. Recall that we assumed a network divided into small clusters, every cluster having a BS. Inside the cluster we assumed that the sensors are distributed uniformly; therefore, we used a 20 size grid topology for the simulations, where the sensors were situated in the points of the grid. During the simulations we examined the performance of the BS placement strategies in one cluster.

Recall that the transmission energy is $E_t \sim \sum d_i^\alpha$, where we chose α to be 3 in the simulations. The time was split into equal periods and we assumed that

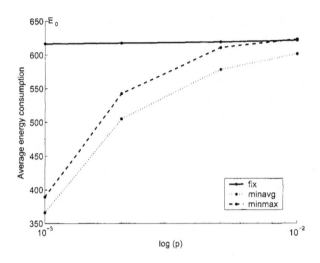

Figure 2.   The average energy consumption of one active sensor in one round

an event can occur or end only at the beginning of the time period. Every active sensor sends the same amount of data in a round. The BS can be relocated also at the start of a round.

We simulated an event-driven network, hence a sensor sends data only when sensing an event. We considered that an event can occur in a uniformly distributed manner in the area of the cluster and it is sensed only by one sensor. During a round, an event appeared in the region of a sensor with probability p. The duration of event is geometrically distributed, i.e., an existing event persisted in the next round with probability q. Therefore, every sensor became active independently with probability p; after becoming active, the sensor stayed in active state in every following round with the probability q. In the simulations p was in the range of 0.0005 to 0.01, while q was 0.9. During the simulations the initial energy of every sensor was 300 kJ, the distance of the points of the grid was 5 m, every active sensor sent one unit of data in every round, and E_0 was 0.25 mJ.

For the simulation we used the MATLAB environment. To evaluate the performance of the two mobile BS strategies, we compare these with the case when the BS is deployed in a fix position. Since in our considerations every node becomes active with the same probability, the best place for the fixed BS is the center of the network.

Figure 1 presents the total energy consumption of the whole network, in the case when sensors became active with the probability of $p = 0.0005$ and $p = 0.005$, respectively. In both cases q is 0.9. In the first case two sensors are

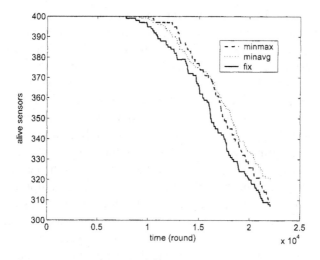

Figure 3.   The alive sensors in the network

active in one round on the average, while in the second case that number is 20 nodes.

As shown in Figure 1, if the number of active nodes is low, both mobile BS strategies are significantly more energy-saving than the fixed BS solution. If the ratio of the active sensors is higher, then there is no major difference regarding the energy consumption.

Figure 2 shows the average energy consumption of one active sensor in one round, as a function of p.

When p is low, the number of active sensors is also low. Therefore the two mobile BS strategies are significantly better than the fixed solution. For the individual sensors, both the *minmax* and the *minavg* strategies result in the energy consumption being decreased; therefore, the network lifetime is extended.

Figure 3 compares the number of alive sensors as a function of time in the case of the three strategies. The results show, that the first node dies first in the case of the fixed BS, at last in the case of *minmax* strategy. On the other hand with the *minmax* strategy the total energy of the network decreases more rapidly than with *minavg*; therefore, on the long run the *minavg* strategy proves to be a better choice. Depending on our goals, there are two possibilities to choose from. *Minmax* can be used if the main goal is to have the first node die at the latest possible moment in time. Meanwhile *minavg* can be used when we want to maximize the lifetime of the majority of the nodes.

We examined the performance of the strategies based on the time while the network operates as a function of the event intensity (p) for different network lifetime definitions. Figure 4 shows the results of these simulations. We can see that, as the number of simultaneous events decreases (fewer active nodes), the *minmax* and *minavg* strategies outperform the fix placed BS more and more. This can be explained by the fact that if the number of active sensors is high, then it is more probable that there is an active sensor in every part of the cluster; hence, the optimal BS location is near the center of the network in case of both BS moving strategies. In contrast with that, having fewer active sensors results in a higher probability of having active sensors only in a smaller part of the cluster; thus, the optimal BS location is not in the center of the network.

The time elapsed till the depletion of the first node in the network is shown by Figure 4(a). It can be seen that the *minmax* strategy outperforms the *minavg* strategy for every value of p, except the lowest one. This is because, as mentioned earlier, the *minmax* strategy minimizes the maximum energy spent by a sensor in every round; this leads to a more balanced energy usage of the sensors, compared to the two other strategies. At the lowest event intensity the performance of the two mobile strategies is similar. The reason is that at this intensity the number of simultaneous events is about 2; therefore in most of the cases the optimal place is the same for both strategies. The results also show that the usage of the mobile BS prolongs the network lifetime more than 100% if the number of simultaneous events is low. Figure 4(b) shows the lifetime of the network for all the three strategies, supposing that the network is operable till 90% of the sensors are still alive. In this case both mobile strategies have approximately the same performance. However, if the lifetime of the network is defined as the time till 20% of the nodes die (Figure 4(c)), then the *minavg* strategy outperforms the other solutions. This is because the *minavg* strategy is places the BS always to the spot where the total energy required for the communication of the active sensors in the network is minimal, without taking into account the interests of individual sensors, as in *minmax*. Therefore, it can happen that some of them uses much more energy than the others, hence, some sensors may die sooner, while at the same time the majority of the sensors live longer compared to the *minmax* strategy. This operational difference leads to the effect that, as the operation of the network can tolerate more and more depleted sensors, the *minavg* strategy outperforms the *minmax* solution even more. Figure 4(d) shows the results that prove this statement.

In the next step of the performance evaluation we examined the effect of the two strategies on the distribution of the BS placement in the area of the cluster. We used long ran simulations, where the sensors had infinite energy; therefore, the depletion of the nodes did not bias the results. Figure 5 shows the distributions in the case of an event intensity of 0.0025. The results show that the BS moves more often to the center of the cluster when the *minmax* strategy is used, while in the *minavg* strategy the of the BS is more evenly distributed in the cluster. It can be also seen that the peak of the distribution is in the center

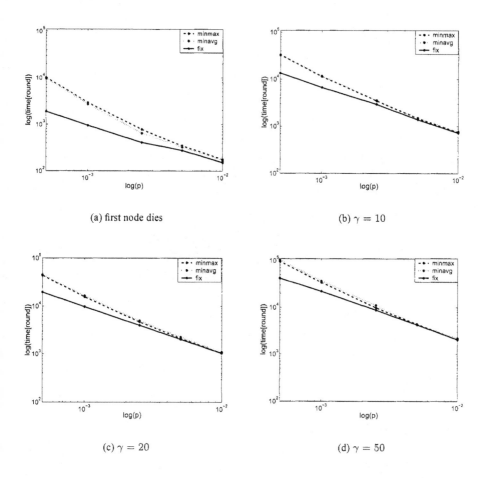

(a) first node dies   (b) $\gamma = 10$

(c) $\gamma = 20$ (d) $\gamma = 50$

Figure 4.   Time till the γ percent of sensors die, in function of the event intensity(p)

of the field in both cases. This is because the events appear independently in the area of the cluster; thus, it often happens that there is an active sensor in every part of the network.

For the explanation of the more balanced BS placement of the *minavg* strategy imagine the following. There are some active sensors close to each other in one part of the network. Meanwhile, there is one active sensor approximately equally far from the center, but on the opposite side of the network. If the optimal place of the BS is determined by the *minavg* strategy, then it is near to the group of the active sensors. If using the *minmax* strategy, the BS will be moved into the center area, minimizing the maximum distance.

Further results (not presented here), also suggest that decreasing the number of simultaneous events leads to a more balanced BS placement in the cluster.

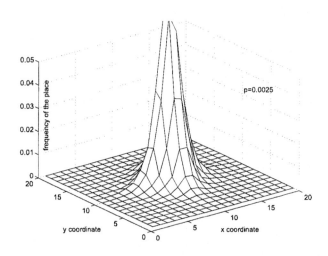

(a) *minmax* strategy

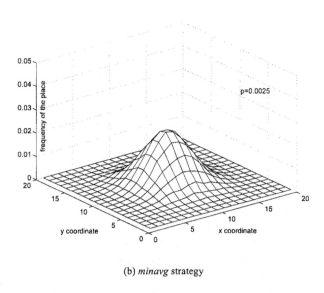

(b) *minavg* strategy

Figure 5.   The distribution of the place of the BS

5.   Conclusions and Future Work

In this paper we presented the idea of moving the BS of a sensor network, in order to decrease the amount of energy required for communication, and hence prolong the lifetime of the network. We introduced two different strategies for moving the BS: *minmax* and *minavg*. The first one minimizes the maximum energy consumption of one active sensor, while the other one minimizes the average energy required for the communication between the BS and the active sensors.

After the introduction of the strategies we presented simulation results evaluating their performance. The results have shown that if the number of simultaneous events is low, then the *minmax* and the *minavg* strategies outperform the fix placed BS and significantly prolong the lifetime of the network. From the results it can be established also that the *minmax* strategy has the better performance if the network is operable only while every sensor is alive. On the contrary, the *minavg* strategy performs better if the operation of the network is able to tolerate the depletion of some sensors.

In this work we considered only direct communication in the network. One of our future goals is to examine the applicability and the performance of the two mobile BS strategies in sensor networks where multihop communication is also present. As future work other BS moving strategies will be examined, which also consider the depletion of sensors. Another possible future direction is to examine the case when the event in the sensor network is sensed not only by one sensor, but by a larger number of neighboring sensors.

References

Al-Karaki, J. and Kamal, A. (2004). *A Taxonomy of Routing Techniques in Wireless Sensor Networks*. Sensor Networks Handbook. CRC Publishers.

Carson, Y. and Maria, A. (1997). Simulation optimization: Methods and applications. In *Proc. 9th conference on Winter Simulation*, pages 118–126, Atlanta, USA.

Doherty, L., Warneke, B. A., Boser, B. E., and Pister, K. (2001). Energy and performance considerations for smart dust. *International Journal of parallel Distributed Systems and Networks*, 4(3):121–133.

Gan, L., Liu, J., and Jin, X. (2004). Agent-based, energy efficient routing in sensor networks. In *Proc. 3rd International Joint Conference on Autonomous Agents and Multiagent Systems (AAMAS'04)*, volume 1, pages 472–479, New York, USA.

Gandham, S., Dawande, M., and Prakash, R. (2004). An integral flow-based energy-efficient routing algorithm for wireless sensor networks. In *Proc. IEEE Wireless Communications and Networking Conference (WCNC'04)*, volume 5, pages 2344–2349, Atlanta, USA.

Ganesan, D., Govindan, R., Shenker, S., and Estrin, D. (2001). Highly-resilient, energy-efficient multipath routing in wireless sensor networks. *ACM SIGMOBILE Mobile Computing and Communications Review*, 5(4):11–25.

Howard, A., Mataric, M., and Sukhatme, G. (2002). Mobile sensor network deployment using potential fields: A distributed, scalable solution to the area coverage problem. In *Proc. Distributed Autonomous Robotic Systems (DARS'02)*, pages 299–308, Fukuoka, Japan.

Intanagonwiwat, C., Govindan, R., and Estrin, D. (2000). A scalable and robust communication paradigm for sensor networks. In *Proc. 6th Annual International Conference on Mobile Computing and Networks (MobiCOM 2000)*, pages 56–67, Boston, USA.

Kim, Hyung Seok, Abdelzaher, Tarek F., and Kwon, Wook Hyun (2003). Minimum-energy asynchronous dissemination to mobile sinks in wireless sensor networks. In *SenSys '03: Proceedings of the 1st international conference on Embedded networked sensor systems*, pages 193–204, New York, USA.

Megiddo, N. (1983). The weighted euclidean 1-center problem. *Mathematics of Operations Research*, 8(4):498–504.

Rahimi, M., Shah, H., Sukhatme, G., Heidemann, J., and Estrin, D. (2003). Studying the feasibility of energy harvesting in a mobile sensor network. In *Proc. IEEE International Conference on Robotics and Automation*, pages 19–24, Taipai.

Rahul, C. and Rabaey, J. (2002). Energy aware routing for low energy ad hoc sensor networks. In *Proc. IEEE Wireless Communications and Networking Conference (WCNC'02)*, volume 1, pages 350–355, Orlando, USA.

Rao, S., Gandham, S., Dawande, M., Prakash, R., and Venkatesan, S. (2003). Energy efficient schemes for wireless sensor networks with multiple mobile base stations. In *Proc. IEEE Globecom*, volume 22, pages 377–381, San Francisco, USA.

Schurgers, C. and Srivastava, M. B. (2001). Energy efficient routing in wireless sensor networks. In *MILCOM Proc. on Communications for Network-Centric Operations: Creating the Information Force*, pages 28–31, McLean.

Wang, Z. Maria, Basagni, Stefano, Melachrinoudis, Emanuel, and Petrioli, Chiara (2005). Exploiting sink mobility for maximizing sensor networks lifetime. In *HICSS '05: Proceedings of the Proceedings of the 38th Annual Hawaii International Conference on System Sciences (HICSS'05) - Track 9*, page 287.1, Washington, USA.

Yao, Y. and Gehrke, J. (2002). The cougar approach to in-network query processing in sensor networks. *SIGMOD Record*, 31(3):9–18.

Ye, Fan, Luo, Haiyun, Cheng, Jerry, Lu, Songwu, and Zhang, Lixia (2002). A two-tier data dissemination model for large-scale wireless sensor networks. In *MobiCom '02: Proceedings of the 8th annual international conference on Mobile computing and networking*, pages 148–159, New York, USA.

Zhao, F. and Gubias, L. (2004). *Wireless Sensor Networks: An Information Processing Approach*. Elsevier.

A SURVEY ON MAC PROTOCOLS FOR AD HOC NETWORKS WITH DIRECTIONAL ANTENNAS

Robert Vilzmann
Technische Universität München, Institute of Communication Networks
Munich, Germany

Christian Bettstetter
DoCoMo Euro-Labs, Future Networking Lab
Munich, Germany

Abstract   The application of directional antennas in the mobile devices of wireless ad hoc networks has the potential to increase the network connectivity and capacity. However, new solutions for medium access control (MAC) are needed. This paper provides a survey and overview of recently proposed MAC protocols for this scenario. We summarize problems specific to this setup and categorize proposed protocols.

Keywords: Ad hoc networking, medium access, directional antennas, beamforming

1.   Introduction and Motivation

AD HOC networking promises to provide the technical concepts for a variety of future wireless systems and services, such as short-range data transfer, vehicular communication, robust emergency services, and multihop access to infrastructure. An ad hoc network connects mobile devices, referred to as *nodes*, which act as relays to provide a communication between remote nodes in a multi-hop fashion.

Recently, interest in the application of directional (or *beamforming*) antennas in ad hoc networks has arisen [Ramanathan, 2001]. Due to high antenna gains, directional antennas are expected to provide increased coverage and connectivity among nodes. Limiting the area in which the transmission signal is radiated can reduce high-frequency emissions and prolong the battery lifetime. Furthermore, directional antennas can increase the network capacity by allowing for higher spatial reuse of radio resources. The latter advantage is particularly alluring since, for omnidirectional antennas, it has been shown in [Gupta and Kumar, 2000] that, under certain models defining successful transmissions, the capacity per node diminishes to zero with an increasing node density. These benefits from the networking layer — in conjunction with increased data rates achieved on the physical layer — may facilitate the provision of quality of service (QoS) in wireless ad hoc networks. For instance, increased transmission ranges may reduce the hop distance between two nodes, and thus reduce the end-to-end delay.

A challenging task in ad hoc networks is the problem of medium access control (MAC). Since sharing the medium has to be controlled in a distributed fashion, centralized MAC approaches, which may easily manage guaranteed (scheduled) access in a typically time slotted manner, are not feasible. Mastering data streams with imposed QoS constraints is thus tough. Moreover, the wireless environment imposes restrictions and impairments that complicate the design of appropriate MAC protocols as compared to fixed (wireline) networks, most notably the half-duplex operation of transceivers, the time-varying, unpredictable and unreliable wireless channel, frequent and bursty channel errors, and location dependent carrier sensing [Gummalla and Limb, 2000]. The problem of location dependent carrier sensing inhibits collision detection mechanisms, at least if only one transceiver unit per node is available.

All above-mentioned MAC issues in wireless networks also apply to the case of directional antennas. Interestingly, when trying to exploit the benefits of directional antennas, additional challenges in the design of MAC protocols arise, especially in mobile ad hoc networks where nodes may move and rotate.

This paper provides a survey and overview of recently proposed MAC protocols for this scenario. We summarize problems specific to this setup and categorize proposed protocols that deal with these problems. The paper is organized as follows. First, Section 2 expands on MAC issues with directional antennas. Next, Section 3 surveys a considerable number of MAC protocols addressing these issues. Section 4 gives a summary and comparison of the proposed approaches. Finally, Section 5 concludes.

2. Medium Access Problems using Directional Antennas

The capabilities of directional antennas are typically not fully exploited when using conventional MAC protocols, such as IEEE 802.11. In fact, the network performance may even *deteriorate* due to issues specific to directional antennas. In the following sections, we summarize the major problems.

2.1 Neighbor location and main lobe direction

With omnidirectional antennas, the angular direction of a neighbor (a node that can be reached via a direct link) is not relevant. In the case of directional antennas, however, the relative angular position of the neighbors is indeed critical. First, when using beamforming at the transmitter, the node must know where the main lobe of the antenna gain pattern should be directed to maximize the link quality. Second, when increasing the spatial reuse by allowing for simultaneous transmissions in the vicinity of a receiver, it is important to know whether beamforming ensures that no or limited interference is caused at other neighbors.

At least two basic methods for determining the angular position of neighbors exist. The first possibility is to use GPS information. This requires a GPS unit at each node and the exchange of GPS information for the computation of neighbor directions. The dependence on an auxiliary positioning system is generally precarious, and GPS usually does not work indoors. The second possibility is direction-of-arrival (DOA) estimation in the receive path. Besides the complexity of the algorithm and the accuracy of the results, the time to estimate the direction of incoming signals is an important aspect. A comprehensive review of DOA estimation methods can be found in [Godara, 1997]. It is important to note that the topographical position of a node may not be the optimal beamforming direction. This is due to the real signal propagation path, where reflection, diffraction and scattering may occur. Consequently, this is a strong argument for preferring DOA estimation over GPS-based approaches.

In summary, the problem of neighbor discovery is augmented with location or angle of arrival discovery when using. Many MAC protocols for directional antennas assume known node locations.

2.2 Extended transmission range

By exploiting the beamforming capabilities of directional antennas, increased transmission ranges can be achieved. For instance, when using a phased array antenna with isotropic antenna elements, the maximum antenna gain roughly equals the number of antenna elements. The high antenna gain corresponds to longer transmission ranges, helping the network to reduce the number of hops between the source and the sink of a packet and increasing the network connectivity by bridging between otherwise disconnected network clusters.

A question relevant in medium access is whether increased ranges can be exploited, and how links ranging beyond the omnidirectional range can be set up. If two nodes can only communicate if they point their main beam toward each other, they are called DD (Directional-Directional)-neighbors. The MMAC protocol [Choudhury et al., 2002], for example, suggests the setup of DD-links through short-range control packets exchanged via multiple hops.

Besides the problem of facilitating longer links, transmission beyond the reserved transmission floor is a MAC-layer issue caused by high antenna gains.

Problems occur when directionally transmitted data packets cause interference at nodes outside the area which was reserved by exchanging omnidirectional control messages. A possible solution to this problem is to apply means for power control. In this case however the extended transmission range of beam-forming antennas is not exploited.

2.3   Side lobe pattern

Multi-element array (MEA) antennas are often considered in research on directional antennas in ad hoc networks. An MEA antenna comprising N antenna elements provides N degrees of freedom for beamforming. When a receiving node points a main lobe toward a transmitter, $N - 1$ degrees of freedom remain for maximizing the signal-to-interference (SIR) ratio. This can be done by placing antenna gain nulls in the direction of interferers ("null beam forming" or "null steering"). While the angular direction of the main beam and the nulls may be governed by the MAC-layer, the exact antenna gain pattern cannot be assumed to be known to the MAC layer. When steering the main beam around the node, the entire side lobe pattern may change drastically, and even the maximum gain and beamwidth of the main lobe is not constant.

For the MAC-layer, this raises the problem that the exact amount of interference caused through side lobes at (for transmitting nodes) or by (for receiving nodes) neighboring nodes cannot not be known a priori medium access. For a known main beam direction relative to the array orientation the entire beam-forming pattern can, in theory, be calculated for a given antenna array configuration (number of antenna elements, symmetry and spacing), see Fig. 1. However, having this data available and eventually making use of it for medium access may be impossible due to complexity issues.

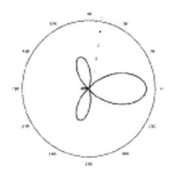

Figure 1.   Horizontal section of the antenna gain pattern of a uniform circular array antenna with $N = 4$ antenna elements and half-wavelength element spacing, main lobe direction $0°$

Many proposals for MAC-layer design published recently stick with very simplified antenna models, e.g. simple sector models. Such "areal" models may be very inappropriate.

2.4 Directional carrier sensing

In recently proposed MAC protocols for beamforming antennas, *directional* physical carrier sensing is a frequently used technique that is helpful to some extend. The goal of carrier sensing preceding channel access is to prevent from collisions by signal interference. When a signal is transmitted into a sector in space using a directional antenna, it makes some sense to also limit the carrier sensing to this sector in order to increase the spatial reuse of radio resources.

However, impairments exist: In mobile networks, there is the general problem that sensing the carrier at the transmitter does not accurately reflect the situation at the receiver. This means that the channel may be busy at the intended receiver, while it appears to be free at the transmitter. With directional carrier sensing, there are even more possible scenarios in which a parallel signal transmission may not be detected.

2.5 New hidden terminals

For a transmission from Node A to Node B, a Node C is "hidden" with respect to A if it is located outside the transmission range of Node A, but within the range of Node B. If not blocked, hidden terminals may cause corruptive interference at the receiver. Virtual carrier sensing, such as the request-to-send/clear-to-send (RTS/CTS) exchange in IEEE 802.11, seeks to avoid hidden terminals.

The application of the IEEE 802.11 RTS/CTS scheme to directional antennas can create new kinds of hidden terminals. These new problems arise due to increased directional antenna gains and due to unheard control packets (because of beamforming) [Choudhury et al., 2002].

2.6 Deafness

Deafness is another problem that may arise when using beamforming antennas. We would like to give the following definition: A node is *deaf* with respect to a second node, if it cannot receive from the second node due to its antenna gain pattern, while the node could receive from the second node, if the second node would be in omnidirectional mode. Deafness may thus occur when a receiving node stays beamformed toward its transmitter in between two successive packets (directional carrier sensing), and a third node tries to transmit to the receiving node. According to our above definition, a situation where a currently transmitting node has formed a null gain toward a second node is not deafness per se, since the transmitting node could not receive from the second node even if it was in omnidirectional mode (half-duplex operation).

Reference [Choudhury and Vaidya, 2003] contributes with an evaluation of the impact of deafness and addresses the tradeoff between maximizing the benefits of beamforming antennas and the deafness problem. An interesting aspect of the deafness problem is that chains or even deadlock situations are possible where no node can communicate. The authors argue that prolonged deafness can lead to multiple packet drops, which may mislead higher layers. Furthermore, it is emphasized that deafness affects fairness among transmitting nodes.

2.7   Antenna array rotation and changing beamforming pattern

In ad hoc networks, MAC decisions have to be made in a distributed manner. Hence, network changes typically entail the need for information exchange, leading to signaling overhead. The performance of MAC protocols thus degrades with increasing system dynamics, and malfunctions may occur in highly dynamic scenarios. Typical sources for network dynamics are time-varying traffic loads and transmission urgencies. Moreover, in wireless systems, the channel can vary rapidly over time. In mobile systems, the (translatory) mobility of all nodes is another source of dynamics.

When using beamforming antennas, antenna array *rotations* introduce dynamics that used to be unknown as long as ad hoc networks with isotropic antennas were considered. Note that, since the determination of the angular direction of neighbors is typically essential to MAC approaches for directional antennas, the angular direction of neighbors has to be re-determined frequently if mobile nodes are free to rotate.

Even more dynamics is due to the fact that nodes can change their beamforming pattern. In this case, not only the main lobe direction changes. In fact, the entire beamforming pattern (including the side lobes) changes if the main lobe direction of an antenna array is electrically steered. Adaptations of the beamforming pattern may be performed packet-wise. From the protocol and physical point of view, respectively, neighborhood relationships and interference levels may thus completely change over time in the order of one millisecond (assuming a typical packet size of 1 kByte and a transmission rate of 10 Mbit/s).

3.   MAC Protocols for Directional Antennas

This section discusses MAC protocols designed for controlling medium access if nodes are equipped with directional antennas. Most of these protocols are extensions to the distributed coordination function (DCF) of IEEE

802.11, which comprises physical and virtual carrier sensing, implemented by an RTS/CTS handshake preceding the data transmission. These protocols are surveyed in Section 3.1. For future ad hoc networks, being either fully self-organizing or an access network for fixed infrastructure networks, it may be necessary to entirely reconceive the MAC problem and develop novel, "non-802.11" MAC protocols. Characteristics that are considered to be different from 802.11 comprise in particular scheduled approaches, protocols which do not rely on virtual carrier sensing, and protocols which are not based on the notion of blocking an area by RTS/CTS messages. The rather limited literature on such protocols is discussed in Section 3.2.

3.1   802.11-type MAC protocols for directional antennas

The protocols summarized in the following are based on the IEEE 802.11 DCF protocol. They typically comprise the well-known RTS-CTS-DATA-ACK procedure, also known as virtual carrier sensing. Another concept known from 802.11 is using a so called *Network Allocation Vector* (NAV); it keeps track of the time a node has to remain in a blocked state upon overhearing a control message. With a number of directional protocols, the NAV vector is extended for maintaining direction-specific blocking information. It is commonly referred to as *Directional NAV* (DNAV).

One of the first modifications of DCF that aims at directional antennas was proposed in the *Directional MAC (D-MAC)* protocol [Ko et al., 2000]. It is a rather straightforward extension of the 802.11 protocol. Here, RTS, DATA, and ACK packets are sent directionally. Alternatively, RTS packets are sent omni-directionally if none of the directional antennas of the transmitter is blocked. This reduces the probability of control packets collisions.

Another early protocol was the *Multi-Hop RTS MAC (MMAC)* protocol [Choudhury et al., 2002]. It facilitates DD-links through multi-hop signaling. To this end, a special type of RTS packet is used, the reception of which does not affect DNAV tables.

The *Tone-based directional MAC (ToneDMAC)* protocol [Choudhury and Vaidya, 2003] seeks to indicate deafness to blocked transmitters and thus increase fairness. Using omnidirectional tones after the DATA/ACK exchange, both transmitter and receiver indicate that they were recently engaged in communication. Thus, a neighboring node can realize deafness if it overhears a tone from its intended receiver. In this case, the node reduces its contention window to the minimum value and has thus a fair chance to win the next channel contention. Multiple tones are used, and a node has to be able to identify the transmitter of a tone. It is assumed that a set of tone frequencies and durations is available. Further, the transmitter of a tone can be determined with a certain probability by means of its unique identifier and a hash function. The authors propose to exploit location information about neighboring nodes in order to reduce the probability of tone mismatching.

In [Nasipuri et al., 2000], *Nasipuri et al.* focus on interference reduction by directional transmission of data packets. This protocol requires all nodes to maintain the antenna orientation at all times. Both RTS and CTS packets are sent omnidirectionally. Hence, a transmitter does not need to know the location of the intended receiver. As compared to 802.11, the silenced region is not reduced by the proposed protocol, spatial reuse is thus not increased. The authors observe that the mobility of nodes does not affect throughput. However, they note that their mobility model only allows for position changes at discrete intervals of time.

In the protocol of *Sanchez et al.* [Sánchez et al., 2001], CTS and DATA packets are transmitted using directional antennas. The authors argue that an omnidirectional transmission of RTS packets reduces the hidden terminal problem, whereas a directional transmission reduces the exposed terminal problem. The authors propose two corresponding schemes of their protocol. By means of simulation, they conclude that a directional transmission of RTS packets generally outperforms the omnidirectional scheme. The authors further elaborate on the performance impact of the carrier sensing threshold. They conclude that without carrier detection the hidden terminal problem dominates over the exposed terminal problem.

The *Directional Virtual Carrier Sensing* (DVCS) approach [Takai et al., 2002] deploys a directional RTS/CTS exchange and a timer-controlled DNAV table. Location information is cached whenever a node overhears signals. This information is used when setting up a communication. If a node does not have up-to-date location information about its intended receiver in its cache, or if no CTS packet was received upon directional transmission of a RTS packet, the RTS packet is sent omnidirectionally. The authors refer to this mechanism as *angle of arrival* (AOA) *caching*. Power control is assumed in order to not extend the transmission range beyond the omnidirectional range. This work is one of the few studies where mobility is considered in the simulations. The authors report that in the case of mobility, physical carrier sensing brings about a dramatic performance improvement, in particular if nodes experience an accumulated interference due to numerous concurrent transmissions. In such cases, where nodes may fail to receive control packets (RTS or CTS) successfully, physical carrier sensing can effectively help to avoiding collisions.

The MAC protocol of *Lal et al.* [Lal et al., 2002] is receiver-based and allows for simultaneous receptions (receiver-SDMA). A particular aim is to increase the throughput at nodes that lie on many active nodes, so called bottleneck nodes. A receiver synchronizes a number of packet receptions from other nodes. This is done by polling neighboring nodes by means of a periodically transmitted ready-to-receive (RTR) packet. The following RTS/CTS handshake (RTS packets contain training sequences for the purpose of beam-forming) and data transmission is fully directional.

The *Dual Busy Tone Multiple Access with Directional Antennas* (DBTMA/DA) protocol [Huang et al., 2002] adapts the Dual Busy Tone Multiple Access (DBTMA) protocol to directional antennas. The idea here is to transmit tones directionally in addition to the directional transmission of control packets. This is motivated by the authors' observation that the performance of MAC protocols relying on the RTS/CTS scheme deteriorates in cases of control packet collisions. With DBTMA/DA, a 'transmit busy tone' and 'receive busy tone' is transmitted along with data transmission and reception, respectively. This provides a means for alleviating the hidden and exposed terminal problem. Numerical work showed remarkable beneficial effects on throughput and end-to-end delay. The authors also investigate the omnidirectional use of busy tones as well as hybrid schemes. The directional transmission of transmit busy tones turns out to be superior over the omnidirectional transmission, since it helps to avoid the exposed terminal problem. The performance comparison of directional and omnidirectional receive busy tones is less straight forward. In fact, a tradeoff exists. Omnidirectional receive busy tones do not result in new hidden terminal problems, but reduce spatial reuse. In contrast, directional receive busy tones provide better spatial reuse, but suffer from new hidden terminal problems. It should be noted that, by using busy tones, the maintenance of DNAV tables can be avoided.

A MAC protocol for full exploitation of directional antennas is proposed by *Korakis et al.* in [Korakis et al., 2003]. The most distinct protocol aspect is the rotational directional transmission of RTS packets. This ensures a directional communication setup without requiring knowledge about the receiver location. However, multiple RTS packets transmitted for a single data packet may degrade the MAC performance. Note that another MAC-mechanism using rotational beamforming was proposed by Roy et al. [Roy et al., 2003]. Another major aspect is the use of a location table, maintaining the identity of each detected neighbor, the beam index on which it can be reached, and the corresponding beam index used by the neighbor. The location table is updated upon each packet reception and keeps track of the angular direction of neighboring nodes. Second, it is used for blocking beam directions that are skipped in the circular RTS transmission. The method seems to be particularly vulnerable to antenna rotation. The maintenance of location tables induces overhead and may not be suitable for highly dynamic scenarios.

The *Smart-802.11b* protocol [Singh and Singh, 2004] is based on 802.11 and deploys beamforming, a direction-of-arrival algorithm and nulling. A transmitter must transmit a sender-tone and must not transmit the data packet before receiving a receiver-tone. The sender- and receiver-tones serve as a substitute for the conventional RTS/CTS exchange. Both tones are transmitted directionally. The sender-tone is used for beamforming at the receiver, i.e. both beamforming toward the transmitter and nulling toward interferers. A receiving node estimates the direction of the transmitter as the direction with the maximum received signal strength. As compared to RTS packets, no destination node can be indicated by the sender-tone. Thus, a receiver may receive a data packet that was not intended for it. Note that tones preceding control packet transmissions are also used in reference [Roy et al., 2003].

3.2   "Non-802.11"-type MAC protocols for directional antennas

The *Receiver-Oriented Multiple Access* (ROMA) protocol [Bao and Garcia-Luna-Aceves, 2002] is the only scheduled MAC protocol discussed in this survey. Relying on local two-hop topology information, ROMA splits nodes into transmitters and receivers, which are paired together for maximum throughput. This allows for transmission-SDMA and reception-SDMA. The separation into transmitters and receivers is carried out in a random fashion. The ROMA protocol comprises the steps of priority-assignment, transmission/reception mode assignment, hidden terminal avoidance and selection of simultaneous receivers (for transmitting nodes) and simultaneous transmitters (for receiving nodes). In this survey, ROMA is the only protocol having explicit means for supporting QoS. A weight associated with each link reflects the data flow demand governed by upper layers of the transmitter and is used for contention resolution.

The *Direction-of-arrival MAC (DOA-MAC)* protocol [Singh and Singh, 2003] is a time-slotted approach based on the Slotted-ALOHA protocol. With DOA-MAC, time slots are broken into three *mini slots*. During the first slot, each transmitter transmits a tone toward the intended receiver. The receiving nodes run a direction-of-arrival algorithm and lock their beam toward the strongest signal. Furthermore, the receivers form nulls toward all the other identified directions. Data packets are transmitted during the second mini slot. A packet is not acknowledged in the third mini slot if the receiving node was not the intended receiver. False packet receptions may occur since no RTS/CTS handshake is performed before data transmission. This is why this approach is considered to allow for a high amount of randomness. Besides throughput, additional performance measures would be interesting for the evaluation of DOA-MAC, in particular the probability of unintended packet receptions and the probability of deadlocks. The authors proposed a similar approach [Singh and Singh, 2004], called *Smart-Aloha*. As an enhancement of DOA-MAC the authors implemented a single-entry cache scheme. It allows a receiver to beamform toward the second strongest signal if the receiver was not the intended receiver of a packet transmitted by a node providing the strongest signal.

Table 1. Protocol comparison: Usage of omnidirectional (o), directional (d) and rotational directional (rot) antenna patterns

	phys. carrier sensing	RTR TX	RTR RX	RTS TX	RTS RX	CTS TX	CTS RX	DATA TX	DATA RX	ACK TX	ACK RX	tones t/r
IEEE 802.11 DCF	o	–	–	o	o	o	o	o	o	o	o	–
D-MAC scheme 1	d	–	–	d	o	o	o	d	o	d	o	–
D-MAC scheme 2	d	–	–	o/d	o	o	o	d	o	d	o	–
MMAC	d	–	–	d	o	d	d	d	d	d	d	–
ToneDMAC	d,o	–	–	d	o	d	o	d	o	d	o	o/o
Nasipuri et al.	o	–	–	o	o	o	o	d	d	–	–	–
Sanchez et al.	o	–	–	d(o)	o	d	d	d	d	–	–	–
DVCS	o/d	–	–	d/o	d	d	d	d	d	d	d	–
Lal et al.	o/d	o	d	d	d	d	d	d	d	d	d	–
DBTMA/DA	o	–	–	o		d		d		–	–	d(o)/d(o)
Korakis et al.	o	–	–	rot	o	d	o	d	d	d		–
Smart-802.11 b	–	–	–	–	–	–	–	d	d	d	d	d/d
ROMA	–	–	–	–	–	–	–	d	d	–	–	–
DOA-MAC/ Smart-Aloha	–	–	–	–	–	–	–	d	d	d	d	d/–

Table 2. Protocol comparison: Antenna model and assumptions

	antenna type	side lobe (interference) model	exploits adap. nulling	direct. range exten.	DO links	DD links	static antenna orient.
D-MAC	switched	omnidirect.	n/a	–	–	–	–
MMAC	steered	flat-top	n/a	yes	yes	yes	–
ToneDMAC	switched	sidelobes	n/a	yes	yes	–	–
Nasipuri et al.	switched	ideal sect.	n/a	–	–	–	yes
Sanchez et al.	switched	flat-top	n/a	–	–	–	–
DVCS	adaptive	realistic	–	–	–	–	–
Lal et al.	adaptive	realistic	yes	–	–	–	yes
DBTMA/DA	switched	omnidirect.	n/a	–	–	–	–
Korakis et al.	switched	ideal sect.	n/a	yes	yes	–	yes
Smart-802.11 b	adaptive	realistic	yes	yes	yes	–	–
ROMA	adaptive	no side lob.	ideal	–	–	–	–
DOA-MAC/ Smart-Aloha	adaptive	realistic	yes	yes	yes	–	–

Table 3. Protocol comparison: Classification, node coordination, mobility

	re-ceiver sched-uled	receiver initi-ated	requires receiver DOA-location inform.	runs DOA algo-rithm	TX/RX SDMA	amount of neigh-borhood inform.	ran-dom-ness	mobil-ity in simu-lations
D-MAC	–	–	yes	–	–/–	low	–	–
MMAC	–	–	yes, DD	yes	–/–	medium	–	–
ToneDMAC	–	–	yes	select	–/–	low	–	–
Nasipuri et al.	–	–	–	select	–/–	low	–	yes
Sanchez et al.	–	–	yes	select	–/–	low	–	–
DVCS	–	–	yes	yes	–/–	medium	–	yes
Lal et al.	–	yes	–	yes	–/yes	medium	some	–
DBTMA/DA	–	–	–	select	–/–	low	–	–
Korakis et al.	–	–	–	select	–/–	high	–	–
Smart-802.11 b	–	–	yes	yes	–/–	medium	medium	–
ROMA	yes	yes		yes	yes/yes	high	some	–
DOA-MAC/ Smart-Aloha	–	–	yes	yes	–/–	medium	high	–

4. Comparison of MAC Protocols for Directional Antennas

Tables 1–3 summarize and compare the main properties of the discussed MAC protocols. In case of absent information, entries were left blank. Table 1 indicates which message type is sent using omnidirectional (o) or directional (d) antenna mode; the usage of tones, which may serve different purposes, is indicated in the last column. Table 2 lists the used antenna type, along with the modeling assumptions of the respective papers. It shows how the authors model side lobes, whether they exploit nulling or range extension and whether they assume a static antenna orientation.

Table 3 further categorizes the protocols and summarizes the required information from and coordination with neighboring nodes. The amount of neighborhood information is considered to be low if nodes simply keep track of RTS and CTS packets. Maintaining a DNAV table or gathering information for adaptive nulling gives raise to a medium amount of neighborhood information, whereas any further need for neighborhood information is regarded as resulting in a high amount. Table 3 further indicates whether mobility is considered by the authors.

There may be different reasons why certain protocols consciously allow for *randomness*, such as "hit-or-miss" transmissions or a relaxed protection of transmission against interference. Due to the dynamics in mobile systems, the lack of network infrastructure in ad hoc networks, and the peculiarities of using directional antennas, a certain degree of randomness may be unavoidable or even beneficial for the network performance by reducing protocol overhead.

We also observe that many of the discussed protocols employ the idea of a *directional network allocation vector* (DNAV) table. While a conventional network allocation vector (NAV) indicates the resource allocation—detected e.g. by the reception of a RTS or CTS packet—irrespective of the angle of arrival, the DNAV table keeps track of the resource allocation in a direction-specific manner. To this end, the elements of the DNAV table typically represent a quantized angle of arrival. Different policies are conceivable for setting the DNAV table. In the simplest case, those directions are set, from which RTS or CTS packets were received. If a node has detailed information about its surrounding topology and ongoing transmissions, more complex policies may be considered. The use of DNAV tables adds complexity, but is helpful in managing spatial reuse. If control packets include the duration of the following communication, the problem of outdated DNAVs can be avoided.

5.   Conclusions

The application of directional antennas in ad hoc networks is expected to increase the system performance but requires appropriate MAC protocols. These should exploit the benefits of directional transmission, i.e., reduce interference, increase the link quality, and increase the spatial reuse. Although directional transmission and/or reception reduces the reserved transmission floor, a fundamental tradeoff between spatial reuse and packet collisions generally resides in the surveyed protocols.

This paper gave a survey and classification of MAC protocols in this area. Most of the protocols are extensions to IEEE 802.11, using different combinations of directional and omnidirectional messages. While most of them seem to increase the performance compared to standard 802.11, we believe that further work in this area is needed to exploit the benefits of beamforming to a further extend. From our point of view, taking an approach that goes away from the RTS/CTS paradigm of 802.11, and in particular an approach that uses outband signaling, seems to be an interesting option.

References

Bao, L. and Garcia-Luna-Aceves, J.J. (2002). Transmission scheduling in ad hoc networks with directional antennas. In *Proc. ACM MobiCom.*

Choudhury, R. R. and Vaidya, N. H. (2003). Deafness: A mac problem in ad hoc networks when using directional antennas. Technical report, University of Illinois at Urbana-Champaign.

Choudhury, R. R., Yang, X., Vaidya, N. H., and Ramanathan, R. (2002). Using directional antennas for medium access control in ad hoc networks. In *Proc. ACM MobiCom.*

Godara, L. C. (1997). Application of antenna arrays to mobile communications, part II: Beam-forming and direction-of-arrival considerations. *Proceedings of the IEEE*, 85(8):1195–1245.

Gummalla, A. C. V. and Limb, J. O. (2000). Wireless medium access control protocols. *IEEE Commun. Surveys and Tutorials*, 3(2).

Gupta, P. and Kumar, P. R. (2000). The capacity of wireless networks. *IEEE Trans. Inform. Theory*, 46(2):388–404.

Huang, Z., Shen, C.-C., Srisathapornphat, C., and Jaikaeo, C. (2002). A busy-tone based directional MAC protocol for ad hoc networks. In *Proc. IEEE Milcom*.

Ko, Y.-B., Shankarkumar, V., and Vaidya, N. H. (2000). Medium access control protocols using directional antennas in ad hoc networks. In *Proc. IEEE Infocom*.

Korakis, T., Jakllari, G., and Tassiulas, L. (2003). A MAC protocol for full exploitation of directional antennas in ad-hoc wireless networks. In *Proc. ACM MobiHoc*.

Lal, D., Toshniwal, R., Radhakrishnan, R., Agrawal, D., and Caffery, J. (2002). A novel MAC layer protocol for space division multiple access in wireless ad hoc networks. In *Proc. IC3N*.

Nasipuri, A., Ye, S., and Hiromoto, R. E. (2000). A mac protocol for mobile ad hoc networks using directional antennas. In *Proc. IEEE WCNC*.

Ramanathan, R. (2001). On the performance of ad hoc networks with beamforming antennas. In *Proc. ACM MobiHoc*.

Roy, S., Saha, D., Bandyopadhyay, S., Ueda, T., and Tanaka, S. (2003). A network-aware MAC and routing protocol for effective load balancing in ad hoc wireless networks with directional antenna. In *Proc. ACM MobiHoc*.

Singh, H. and Singh, S. (2003). A MAC protocol based on adaptive beamforming for ad hoc networks. In *Proc. IEEE PIMRC*.

Singh, H. and Singh, S. (2004). Smart-802.11b MAC protocol for use with smart antennas. In *Proc. IEEE ICC*.

Sánchez, M., Giles, T., and Zander, J. (2001). CSMA/CA with beam forming antennas in multihop packet radio. In *Proc. Swedish Workshop on Wireless Ad hoc Networks*.

Takai, M., Martin, J., Ren, A., and Bagrodia, R. (2002). Directional virtual carrier sensing for directional antennas in mobile ad hoc networks. In *Proc. ACM MobiHoc*.

PART FOUR

MIDDLEWARE AND APPLICATIONS

ADVANCED COLLABORATIVE SERVICES PROVISIONING IN NEXT GENERATION NETWORKS

Miguel Gómez[1], Tomás P. de Miguel[2], and Fermín Galán[1]

[1]*Agora Systems S. A., C/ Aravaca 12 1°A, 28040 Madrid, Spain;* [2]*Universidad Politécnica de Madrid, E.T.S.I. de Telecomunicación, Ciudad Universitaria s/n, 28040 Madrid, Spain.*

Abstract: The 3GPP IMS subsystem, adopted also by the ITU-T/ETSI NGN initiative, proves to be a powerful framework for the provision of conferencing services. Collaborative Services, although based on multipoint conferencing, present their own set of requirements and distinguishing features. This paper tries to present an overview of the conferencing framework available in IMS-based networks, in order to analyse next the requirements and necessary extensions for advanced collaborative service provisioning in this environment. Finally, an architecture proposal for an IMS-compatible collaborative server is presented, and the undertaken validation experiments and prototypes tackled.

Keywords: collaborative services; CSCW; IMS; next generation networks

1. INTRODUCTION

Collaborative Services attempt to bring people together by offering a diverse set of communication and information sharing features that enable the effective cooperation of geographically distributed teams. Advanced Collaborative Services go one step further by trying to emulate real-life cooperation environments (e.g. conferences, meetings, classes, business presentations, etc.) and make them available to a distributed audience by providing an enhanced multipoint conferencing framework. These services have been traditionally relegated to large corporations or educational institutions due to the low availability of both the network and terminal requirements necessary for their operation.

The adoption of packet-switched core networks by mobile operators and the deployment of SIP-based multimedia provisioning platforms, like the UMTS IP Multimedia Subsystem (IMS) standardised by 3GPP, promises to change this environment in the next few years. Besides, the adoption of the IMS standard by the ITU-T/ETSI NGN initiative will make this framework available also in fixed networks, extending the scope of this platform and making even more interesting to design services that can be deployed on it.

This paper tries to provide an overview at the IMS multimedia framework and multipoint conferencing model, in order to analyse how it could be extended to support the provisioning of IMS-compatible Advanced Collaborative Services.

2.   CONFERENCING IN IMS-BASED NETWORKS

One of the basic features provided by the 3GPP IMS is to allow users to create, modify and terminate SIP-based multimedia sessions [Rosenberg at al., 2002]. Although these basic mechanisms already enable users to setup multipoint conferences on their own, the IMS network architecture comprises a set of dedicated elements and functions designed to allow more advanced conferencing scenarios and to facilitate an easier and more efficient conference setup. This section will provide an overview to the IMS architecture, focusing on the nodes relevant to multipoint conferencing services, as well as to the centralised conference model adopted in NGN and the set of protocols which is currently being designed at IETF for its control and management.

2.1   Subsystem Architecture

The IMS [IMS, 2005] is a subsystem included in the UMTS Packet-Switched Core-Network since Release 5 for the provision of IP-based multimedia services.

Figure 1 summarises the IMS elements relevant to conferencing [CN, 2005], as well as the interfaces between them. As we can see, all the native IMS element groups need to be combined for advanced conferencing services provisioning. The involved nodes are:

- Serving Call Signalling Control Function (S-CSCF): The S-CSCF is the node in charge of session management in the IMS network. It behaves as a stateful SIP proxy providing registrar, authentication and session control features. The S-CSCF is always located in the operator's home network, and it constitutes the central control point for operator-provided services by applying the filter criteria for the execution of SIP-based IMS services. Filter criteria are just a set of rules defined per user which enable to trigger services upon information contained in the SIP header fields.

- SIP Application Server (SIP AS): SIP Application Servers are the key elements for the provision of native IMS services, taking the roles of SIP proxies, UAs, or B2BUAs. The S-CSCF, upon a correct match of a service filter criterion, will forward the SIP request to appropriate SIP AS, which will in turn perform the associated service logic.
- Multimedia Resource Function (MRF): The MRF is the IMS element in charge of providing the media-related functions for the provision of advanced services, comprising features such as announcement playback or media mixing for multipoint conferencing. It is divided into two logical functions:
  - Multimedia Resource Function Processor (MRFP): The MRFP is the actual media processing function, in charge of manipulating media streams in order to perform tasks like media transcoding, mixing, filtering, etc.
  - Multimedia Resource Function Controller (MRFC): This is the entity in charge of MRF control. It behaves as a SIP User Agent, accepting SIP requests coming from the S-CSCF or a dedicated SIP Application Server. It controls the MRFP via the MEGACO-based Mp interface. The border between the AS and the MRFC is quite diffuse, since services may be provided just by an AS controlling directly the MRFP, by the MRFC acting as SIP AS and receiving directly requests from the S-CSCF, and by a combination of both, with a SIP AS behaving as SIP B2BUA or proxy and the MRFC acting as SIP UA.

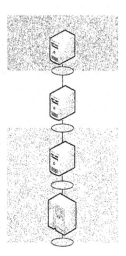

Figure 1. IMS elements for multipoint conferencing.

2.2   Conference Model

Once we have described the functional entities for conferencing in the IMS, we may take a closer look to the supported conference model [Rosenberg, 2005] [Barnes, 2005].

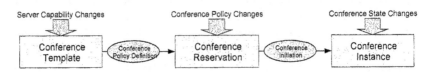

Figure 2. The Conference life cycle.

Figure 2 depicts the life cycle of a generic conference. First of all, every conferencing server (MRFC/AS + MRFP combination) must provide a set of conference templates describing the available service features, so that conferencing clients (UEs) may define a conference by filling the appropriate data or choosing from the different options provided in the template. Since conference templates are tightly coupled with the conferencing features available at the server, a change in the server capabilities must comprise a subsequent change in the set of offered templates (or the addition of a new template to the set) so that users may take advantage of these new capabilities.

Users create a conference reservation by filling the appropriate template in order to define the policy for a particular conference. We may describe Conference Policy as the set of parameters and rules that govern the conference behaviour. Conference Policy may be changed as many times as desired during the conference lifetime, even once the conference is active. A conference reservation is a policy definition for a conference that has not started yet.

Once a conference starts, the conference reservation becomes a conference instance. Conference initiation also comprises the creation a SIP signalling user agent, named conference focus, associated to the SIP URI which univocally identifies the conference instance. The SIP focus allows the exchange of call control signalling between the conferencing server and the conferencing clients. Only for the fact of being instantiated, a conference also acquires a certain Conference State, which may be defined as the set of dynamic information that describes a conference instance in progress. Conference State, due to its dynamic nature, may change many times during a conference:

- Due to 1st party call control signalling (e.g. a new participant dials into the conference).
- Due to 3rd party call control signalling (e.g. a user requests the conference focus to invite a new participant using SIP 3PCC – e.g. REFER – mechanisms).

- Due to policy changes (e.g. a conference policy update bans users belonging to domain "unwanted.com", so "user@unwanted.com" is expelled from the conference).
- Due to direct conference state changes (e.g. a user requests the conferencing server to invite a new user to the conference using the conference state control features provided).

Conference state is maintained at the conferencing server, but clients are notified periodically of conference state changes so that they can keep a consistent local copy of the conference state parameters relevant to them.

An additional optional feature that may be provided by conferencing servers is Floor Control. A Floor may be defined as a set of resources belonging to a particular conference instance to which a user is granted access or modification rights, either exclusive or not. A Floor example might be the right to speak in a full-mesh audio-conference. Floors and Floor policy are part of Conference Policy, but Floor Control provides the mechanisms for managing floor requesting, releasing, granting and revoking within an active conference [Camarillo et al., 2005].

The conference model standardised by the 3GPP in UMTS Release 6 does not consider direct conference control features, and therefore conference policy is either implicit or controlled via proprietary mechanisms and all conference state changes are triggered through call control signalling. However, conference control is currently an active research topic within the IETF Centralised Conferencing (XCON) Working Group, and the 3GPP has expressed the necessity of this kind of features and its intention to include them in future releases of the UMTS specifications.

2.3   Conference Control framework

In order to implement the conference model described in the previous section, a set of different protocols is being object of study and standardisation both by IETF and 3GPP. In this section we will try to summarise the most relevant aspects of conference control, as well as to present the set of protocols and signalling mechanisms that are being designed in order to fulfil the previously presented service picture.

2.3.1   Call Control Signalling

As explained in section 2.2, each conference is univocally represented by a SIP URI. Conference initiation comprises the creation of a SIP signalling User Agent, named the conference focus, associated with that URI. The conference focus is in charge of the SIP signalling exchange between the conferencing server and the clients in order to implement the SIP-based conferencing framework defined in [Rosenberg, 2005]. As described in the conference model, clients may influence the conference state either using SIP first-party or third-party call control, and the new conference state is notified to clients using a specific event package [Rosenberg et al., 2005] of the SIP notification framework [Roach, 2002]. These SIP-based conferencing call control features are defined in [Johnston and Levin, 2005] and, as we have previously described, they are the only conference control features offered by the IMS multipoint conferencing framework.

A key element for this SIP-based conferencing framework is the ability of Conference-Aware clients to identify that their interlocutor is a conference focus and behave in consequence. The "isfocus" feature tag defined in the SIP User Agent capabilities discovery framework [Rosenberg et al., 2004] is used to indicate that a SIP URI belongs to a focus entity and, therefore, the SIP dialog belongs to a conferencing session. The mechanism is fairly simple; it consists on appending the "isfocus" tag to the standard contact address header field contained in the SIP requests and responses sent by the focus (e.g. "Contact: <sip:3402934234@example.com>;isfocus"). A Conference-Aware user agent may be defined as a SIP User Agent which recognizes the "isfocus" feature parameter, is able to process Conference State notifications, and can perform and handle SIP third-party call control signalling.

2.3.2   Conference Policy Management

The Conference Policy Control Protocol (CPCP) [Khartabil et al., 2004] has been designed to enable conferencing clients to define and manipulate Conference Policy. It defines an XML Schema that enumerates the conference policy data elements that enable a user to define the settings and behaviour for a particular conference.

Users may create a conference reservation by placing a new conference policy document at the server. Depending on server policy and user privileges, the server may accept or reject the reservation. Once a reservation has been made, it can be modified as many times as required, even once the conference has started. A conference can be deleted permanently by removing the conference policy document from the server, which consequently frees the allocated resources.

In many cases, the creator of the conference policy will be the only user with access rights to the conference policy file. This implies that other users might take part in the conference, but only the conference creator will be able to read and manipulate the conference policy. Although this is the default behaviour, in many other cases it may be convenient to allow other users to read and/or modify different parts of the conference policy document. The Conference Policy Privileges document format defined in [Khartabil and Niemi, 2004] provides the means to set and regulate those privileges. A certain conference creator may override the default policy rules by uploading a conference policy privileges document along with the conference policy file.

The CPCP protocol specification is transport-independent; therefore the conference policy and conference policy privileges documents may be uploaded, read, modified and deleted from the server using any mechanism. However, a key feature in a conferencing framework like the one presented above is to provide an efficient and reliable mechanism for performing those actions. The protocol of choice for CPCP transport has been The XML Configuration Access Protocol (XCAP) [Rosenberg, 2005].

XCAP is a protocol intended to allow the manipulation of XML data resident on a server. By extending the XPath notation to HTTP URLs, XCAP allows to identify univocally with an URL any element from any XML file located on the server, from the whole document itself to any element or attribute on it. The invocation of standard HTTP methods allows clients to read (GET), add or modify (PUT) and delete (DELETE) any possible XML resource identified with the URL syntax presented above.

Since XCAP is a generic protocol for remote XML manipulation, each particular application requires the definition of the application-specific conventions that will apply. These conventions normally consist on the XML schema that defines the structure and constraints of the data to be managed. The XCAP usage for the manipulation of Conference Policy and Conference Policy Privileges is defined in [Khartabil, 2004].

2.3.3   Conference State Management

The Centralised Conference Control Protocol (CCCP) [Levin et al., 2005] allows conference participants or any other authorised entity to directly manipulate the state of an active conference. CCCP is based on a set of transactions issued over a reliable transport protocol. Each transaction consists of a request carrying the required information in an XML body and a corresponding response or set of responses (any number of provisional responses plus a final one) carrying an appropriate XML body. Opposed to CPCP-based Conference Policy manipulation through XCAP, CCCP-based conference state manipulation does not imply direct modifications on the conference state XML file. Clients issue CCCP requests containing the desired conference state after the change is applied, and the server will process these requests according to its own policy and the role of the requesting agent. When a request is processed, its result is notified to the requester, and all conference participants are informed of the new conference state by the notification mechanism defined in section 2.3.1.

CCCP syntax is based on the conference information schema type and its sub-types described in [Rosenberg et al., 2005], plus the necessary extensions to support the CCCP request primitives: conference state retrieval, addition, modification and removal, user retrieval, addition, modification and removal, etc.

Although no preferred transport mechanism is yet chosen for CCCP, transaction-based object-oriented approaches such as SOAP, XML-RPC, or similar are the most likely options for its implementation.

3.   MODEL EXTENSION FOR COLLABORATIVE SERVICES PROVISIONING

Computer-Supported Cooperative Work (CSCW) is a vast research field comprising disciplines as heterogeneous as computer-science, telecommunications, psychology, and sociology. Its main goal is to develop tools and techniques that enable to ease and facilitate collaboration for workgroups thanks to computer networking.

Groupware is one of the physical concretions of CSCW, as it may be defined as the software designed to enable the collaboration of physically distributed teams by means of network communications. Groupware may provide many different collaboration models, from asynchronous communication via messaging and web-based repositories to multimedia-based real-time collaboration. The cooperation facilities offered to users by the combination of groupware and networking features may be defined as Collaborative Services. Advanced Collaborative Services are usually based on multipoint videoconferencing features, but they are habitually oriented to the provision of professional or academic services such as distributed lectures or classes, business meetings or presentations, etc. Therefore, they present the following particularities:

- Media rich conferencing: The lack of face-to-face interaction is minimised through high-quality and media extensive communication.
- Complex moderation mechanisms: The lack of social mechanisms to regulate interventions needs to be overcome by moderation mechanisms such as user roles, turn management, floor control, etc.
- Information sharing features: Opposed to conferencing, Collaborative Services most of the times place the value not on the conversation itself but on the work resulting from it (e.g. a document has been produced). Additionally, the shortcomings of remote collaboration need to be compensated through additional reinforcement mechanisms such as drawings, schemas, slides, etc. Therefore, information-sharing features such as file distribution, application sharing, collaborative document edition, shared whiteboards, etc. are key components in this kind of services.

In this section we will try to outline the requirements for Collaborative Services provisioning in IMS-based networks, as well as the necessary modifications and extensions to the conferencing model previously presented in order to meet these requirements.

3.1   Requirements for Collaborative Services Provisioning in Next Generation Networks

As already described in this section's introduction, one of the key elements of Advanced Collaborative Services is media-rich interaction. If we want to substitute efficiently a face-to-face meeting we must provide the multimedia mechanisms to make communication fluent and meaningful, imitating when possible the interaction mechanisms found in real life collaboration.

In order to provide this kind of interaction, we cannot constrain media exchange to the symmetric model habitually found in conferencing environments, in which the central mixing element (MRFP) processes (i.e. mixes) media so that each participant just receives a downstream flow per each of his tributary upstreams. Advanced Collaborative Services require a more complex behaviour of the MRFP, providing different asymmetric media combinations at different moments of the session (e.g. in a lecture, participants will just receive the professor's video and audio during the presentation, but during the questions they will receive in addition the video and audio of the alumnus issuing the question).

Additionally, users should be able to provide descriptive information about themselves (e.g. name, institution, etc.) to be distributed among participants, enabling thus easier identification between people that have never met in person before.

Another key element to reflect real life interactions as close as possible is the definition of interaction modes and enabling fast interaction mode switching within the collaboration session. We may define an interaction mode as the particular combination of some of the available sub-elements of the collaborative service in order to offer the user a certain interaction experience. Example interaction modes would be the ones previously presented for the lecture scenario: the collaboration activity would be a distributed class, and the interaction modes would be the distributed presentation mode, which involves the professor giving the lecture through audio, video and maybe a whiteboard or a slides presentation, and the questions mode, which would involve the audio and video of both the professor and one alumnus at a time.

One problem naturally associated with interaction modes is the ability to deal with heterogeneous client terminals and networks. A desirable feature in Collaborative Services is the consistent interaction mode model presented above, in which all participants receive the same media and present it in a similar manner. But in an environment as NGN in which we will deal with a huge variety of terminals (mobile phones, PDAs, PCs, etc.) and networks (GPRS, xDSL, WLAN, etc.), we cannot assume that all clients will be able to deal with the same amount of media and present it in a similar way. Therefore, another necessary feature is to provide media with associated semantic information, which would enable clients to decide which media to accept or not when negotiating the session and how to render it locally. Examples of this kind of attributes would be if video/audio is principal or auxiliary; if video can be resized, suggested video sizes, etc.

Collaborative Services must also overcome the lack of natural moderation mechanisms in distributed collaboration, since the social mechanisms for regulating interventions found in face-to-face conversations are lost in this environment. Therefore, Collaborative Services must compensate this handicap with a complex moderation system. Roles are a key feature in this kind of services, and permissions should be more related to roles that to actual personal identities. Continuing our lecture example, we would have just two roles: Lecturer and Alumnus. It is clear that alumni should not be able to speak or write in the whiteboard while the lecturer is presenting. They should just request the permission to ask a question, which should be granted by the lecturer only. Instead of defining those permissions to the alumni one by one based on their SIP identity, it makes more sense to assign user roles and provide per-role permissions.

The example above shows also that Floor Control is not the only necessary moderation element in advanced collaborative systems. Mechanisms for Conference State Control moderation must also be provided, since not only is important to decide who can or cannot apply certain changes, but also when are those changes to be applied (e.g. Alumni can request to change to questions mode, but this change needs to be accepted by the professor first).

3.2   Required Model Extensions

In order to achieve the advanced media control features and the interaction mode model defined in the previous section, the media control framework for conferencing needs to be enhanced. The current proposal for media control in centralised conferencing is based on Media Policy [Jennings and Rosen, 2005]. This Media Policy framework allows conferencing servers to express their capabilities through a set of media policy templates. Conference creators can then select the media configuration for their conference by filling the desired template trough CPCP/XCAP. Conference participants can learn also the media policy trough CPCP/XCAP in order to control the media server (MRFP) within the declared limits.

This model assumes that media configuration will be maintained during all session, as it is part of the conference policy. Changing media settings on an ongoing conference would imply to upload a new conference media policy using CPCP/XCAP, which is inefficient and collision-prone if changes are going to be quite common. Besides, the CPCP/XCAP model is pull-based, and therefore clients would not be notified of changes in the media configuration.

In order to support multiple interaction modes within the same conference and fast switching between them, the Media Policy model should be enhanced to enable to define several possible media configurations for the conference, selecting also the default or initial one. These settings should also be included as part of the Conference State, enabling thus all clients to receive them and keep updated via the Conference State notification service. Interaction mode changes could then be triggered though CCCP, affecting only the conference state but not the pre-defined media policy for the conference. If the interaction mode change implies also a change in the kind or number of media involved in the session, the conference focus should be notified also in order to re-invite the participants accordingly for media re-negotiation.

In order to be able to cope with the variety of terminals and networks available in NGN environments, the conferencing model needs also to be extended in order to add semantic information to media definitions. This meta-information can then be used by clients in order to select which media accept or not when negotiating or re-negotiating collaborative sessions, and decide later how to render the available media locally in order to provide the best possible user experience. The conference media streams section of the CPCP conference policy document model could be enhanced in order to provide this kind of information, which could then be notified to the SIP conference focus upon conference activation in order to be included in the SIP/SDP session negotiation via SDP media-level attributes.

Additionally, the Conference Dial-Out and Refer lists of the CPCP conference policy document could be enhanced to include a more complex user-definition model that enables to convey additional information for well-know users invited to the conference, both of personal (e.g. name, company, etc.) and service-related (e.g. user role) nature. This information could then be mapped into the conference state, so that it gets notified to all users and spontaneous users can fill personal data through CCCP. Role assignment for non-predefined users may be controlled via the Authorisation Rules in the conference policy (e.g. all users from the "university.edu" domain are allowed to join and their role is "Alumnus"). Authorisation rules can then be defined according to user roles when necessary, instead of using individual identities.

Finally, in order to achieve the advanced moderation scheme for conference state control required for Collaborative Services provisioning, some kind of moderation protocol for CCCP needs to be implemented. A possibility for implementing this moderation framework would be to define a SIP event package for Conference State moderators, so that they can be notified when a new CCCP request arrives. Petition grating or revocation commands could be implemented over the same transaction-oriented protocol used for CCCP transport (e.g. SOAP). This framework would also need to be integrated into the conference policy framework, so that Conference Policy may regulate which parts of the conference state are moderated and which users or user roles should act as moderators.

4.   PROPOSED SYSTEM ARCHITECTURE

Figure 3 depicts the proposed architecture for a Collaboration Server suitable for the conferencing framework to be adopted in IMS networks and alike (e.g. NGN).

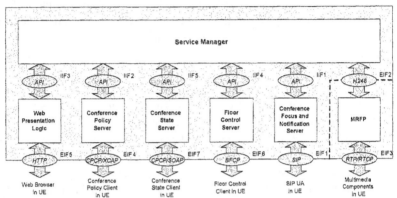

Figure 3. Collaboration Server (MRFC/AS + MRFP) Architecture.

As shown in the figure, the server presents the following sub-components:

- Multimedia Resource Function Processor (MRFP): This component performs the required media transformation and processing actions for collaboration support, such as mixing, switching, forking, transcoding, etc. It mainly exchanges RTP-based information with clients, but other formats are possible since they are highly dependant on the components being used in the collaboration session. It communicates with the Service Manager via a MEGACO (i.e. H.248) interface This architectural decomposition allows to locate this element in a separate node if desired, following thus the MFC decomposition into MRFC and MRFP suggested by 3GPP.

- Conference Focus and Notification Server: This element behaves as a SIP signalling UA, allowing to exchange call control signalling with the clients. It also behaves as SIP Notification server for the supported event packages (e.g. Conference event package, conference state moderation package, etc.), accepting subscription requests from the clients and delivering the associated notifications when an event occurs.

- Conference Policy Server: This element allows clients to manage Conference Policy through XCAP-transported CPCP transactions.

- Web Presentation Logic: This component allows clients to access to the Conference Policy, Conference State, and Floor Control features offered by the server through a web-based interface, and it also presents the information otherwise conveyed through the Notification Service. It is intended to allow standard SIP UAs to take part in the collaboration service by overcoming through this additional interaction interface the lack of capabilities of their local software or user terminals. It may interact directly with the Service Manager through a dedicated API (shown in Figure 3 as IIF3) or interface through the Conference Policy Server, Conference State Server, Floor Control Server and Notification Server by implementing the appropriate interfaces (EIF1, EIF4, EIF6 and EIF7).

- Floor Control Server: This component allows clients to manage conference floors through TCP-transported BFCP transactions.
- Conference State Server: This element allows to manage Conference State through CCCP transactions transported over an object-based transaction-oriented protocol (e.g. SOAP).
- Service Manager: This element constitutes the highest-level control logic of the server. It handles the conference data objects and ensures a consistent conference state by coordinating the different sub-components and enforcing Conference Policy.

Several types of clients are possible in this architecture, depending on their particular combination of the available framework features: standard SIP UAs, UMTS R6 clients, collaborative clients implementing one or several of the conference control protocols described in section 2.3, etc.

5. EXPERIENCES AND PROTOTYPES

Since developing an Advanced Collaborative Services provisioning framework as the one presented in the previous sections is a major task, a layered incremental approach has been undertaken in order to enable to validate individually all the required elements as soon as they are ready, and to deploy and test increasingly complex services within the available framework.

Therefore, in a first phase a MEGACO-controlled MRFP has been developed following the requirements outlined in section 3.1, implementing a plug-in based architecture that enables the incremental addition of further codecs, media types and transformation functions. In addition, a first attempt of SIP focus and Service Manager has also been developed, allowing the SIP-based conference management interactions for Conference-Unaware UAs described in [Johnston and Levin, 2005]. Several basic adaptive multipoint conferencing services have been tested within this framework, using as clients standard SIP UAs such as Microsoft's Windows Messenger or one Agora's own videophone applications.

In a second phase we plan to enhance this framework by adding CPCP-based policy control features to the server, as well as a web-based interface for non-CPCP enabled clients. The SIP logic will also be enhanced to support Conference-Aware clients, and the SIP notification service will be implemented. We intend to validate this framework with a set of heterogeneous clients, adding to the legacy ones previously described new Conference-Aware clients for PC, PDA and mobile phone.

In a third and final phase, the server will be enhanced with floor and conference state control features, developing also a compatible client implementing all the necessary reciprocal logic.

6.   CONCLUSIONS AND FURTHER WORK

Collaborative Services had until now been adopted by reduced user groups only, since their extensive requirements of bandwidth and system capabilities made them suitable just for large organisations or academic institutions with strong remote collaboration commitment. The development of the Next Generation of SIP-based Collaborative Services and the standardisation of the SIP-based IMS framework by the 3GPP is both a great opportunity for this kind of services, which will finally find widespread the networks and clients required for their operation, but also a great challenge since it is also necessary to adapt service provisioning to this new framework and the available subsystem elements.

The IMS conferencing architecture standardised by the 3GPP for UMTS Release 6 and developed at the IETF SIPPING and XCON working groups proves to be a powerful yet flexible framework for the deployment of multipoint conferencing services. However, although it composes a great base for the development of Advanced Collaborative Services, those services comprise a set of requirements that needs to be taken into consideration in the framework. The scalable and extendable nature of the IMS conferencing framework and its proximity to the Internet world allows to easily include the required enhancements, maintaining compatibility and high interoperability levels with both the set of clients available now and the ones expected in the future.

REFERENCES

Barnes, M., Boulton, C. and Levin, O. (2005). A Framework and Data Model for Centralized Conferencing, IETF draft-ietf-xcon-framework-01, July 2005, Work in progress.

Camarillo, G., Ott, J. and Drage, K. (2005). The Binary Floor Control Protocol (BFCP), IETF draft-ietf-xcon-bfcp-05, July 2005, Work in progress.

CN (2005). 3rd Generation Partnership Project, Technical Specification Group Core Network, Conferencing using the IP Multimedia (IM) Core Network (CN) subsystem, Stage 3 (Release 6), 3GPP TS 24.147 v6.3.0, June 2005.

IMS. (2005). 3rd Generation Partnership Project, Technical Specification Group Services and System Aspects, IP Multimedia Subsystem (IMS), Stage 2 (Release 6), 3GPP TS 23.228 v6.10.0, June 2005.

Jennings, C. and Rosen, B. (2005). Media Conference Server Control for XCON, IETF draft-jennings-xcon-media-control-03, July 2005, Work in progress.

Johnston, A. and Levin, O. (2005). Session Initiation Protocol Call Control - Conferencing for User Agents, IETF draft-ietf-sipping-cc-conferencing-07, June 2005, Work in progress.

Khartabil, H. (2004). An Extensible Markup Language (XML) Configuration Access Protocol (XCAP) Usages for Conference Policy Manipulation and Conference Policy Privileges Manipulation, IETF draft-ietf-xcon-cpcp-xcap-03, October 2004, Work in progress.

Khartabil, H. and Niemi, A. (2004). Privileges for Manipulating a Conference Policy, IETF draft-ietf-xcon-conference-policy-privileges-01, October 2004, Work in progress.

Khartabil, H., Koskelainen, P. and Niemi, A. (2004). The Conference Policy Control Protocol (CPCP), IETF draft-ietf-xcon-cpcp-01, October 2004, Work in progress.

Levin, O., Even, R. and Hagendorf, P. (2005). Centralized Conference Data Model, IETF draft-levin-xcon-cccp-02, February 2005, Work in progress.

Roach, A. B. (2002). "Session Initiation Protocol (SIP)-Specific Event Notification," IETF RFC 3265, June 2002.

Rosenberg, J. (2005). A Framework for Conferencing with the Session Initiation Protocol, IETF draft-ietf-sipping-conferencing-framework-05, May 2005, Work in progress.

Rosenberg, J., Schulzrinne, H. and Kyzivat, P. (2004). Indicating User Agent Capabilities in the Session Initiation Protocol (SIP), IETF RFC 3840, August 2004.

Rosenberg, J., Schulzrinne, H. and Levin, O. (2005). A Session Initiation Protocol (SIP) Event Package for Conference State, IETF draft-ietf-sipping-conference-package-12, July 2005, Work in progress.

Rosenberg, J., Schulzrinne, H. et al. (2002), SIP: Session Initiation Protocol, IETF RFC 3261, June 2002.

Rosenberg. J. (2005). The Extensible Markup Language (XML) Configuration Access Protocol (XCAP), IETF draft-ietf-simple-xcap-07, June 2005, Work in progress.

THE IMPACT OF CONTENT DISTRIBUTION ON STRUCTURED P2P NETWORKS IN MOBILE SCENARIOS

S. Zöls, R. Schollmeier, Q. Hofstätter
Lehrstuhl für Kommunikationsnetze, Technische Universität München
Arcisstr. 21, D-80333 München, Germany
stefan.zoels@tum.de, ruediger.schollmeier@tum.de, q@mytum.de

A. Tarlano, W. Kellerer

Future Networking Lab, DoCoMo Communications Laboratories Europe

Landsberger Str. 312, D-80687 München, Germany

tarlano@docomolab-euro.com, kellerer@docomolab-euro.com

Abstract: Structured Peer-to-Peer (P2P) networks are promising approaches for the use of P2P technologies in resource constrained environments such as mobile communication scenarios. The signaling overhead can be reduced significantly by using a hash function to map the nodes as well as the shared objects onto the same identifier space. Queries need not be flooded through the network but can be routed directly to the responsible node. This node stores references to all peers in the network providing the requested object. The mapping algorithm of the used protocol and the actual content distribution determine the number of object references one node is responsible for. This responsibility affects the maintenance traffic in structured P2P networks, as references (responsibilities) have to be shifted among nodes when a node joins or leaves the overlay. Especially in mobile scenarios a high amount of maintenance traffic heavily influences the system performance. Therefore the content distribution has great impact on the applicability of structured P2P approaches. In this paper, we present the results of our experimental analysis of content distribution in an existing large P2P network and its consequences for the structured P2P system Chord. Based on these results we evaluate the applicability of structured P2P networks in mobile scenarios.

Keywords: content distribution, mobile scenarios, peer-to-peer, structured P2P networks

1.   INTRODUCTION

To apply Peer-to-Peer (P2P) technologies for mobile communications, the implemented P2P protocol has to be able to deal with the special challenges of such scenarios, i.e.
- the mobility of the users,
- the limited storage capacity of mobile devices,
- the low access data rate of mobile devices,
- the high failure probability of mobile users (due to wireless link breaks or limited battery resources),
- the high churn rates due to the high costs of mobile data transfer.

Promising approaches addressing such requirements are structured P2P protocols like Chord [Stoica, 2001] or CAN [Ratnasamy et al., 2001]. By using hash keys for every node and also for all content in the network they allow direct localization of content. Therefore, flooding of QUERY messages can be avoided, which can reduce the signaling overhead in comparison to unstructured P2P protocols like Gnutella 0.6 [Gnutella] or Freenet [Freenet].

Depending on the mapping algorithm of the used protocol as well as the actual content that is distributed in a structured P2P network, the responsibility for storing object references is shared between the participating nodes. In the worst case, one node would be responsible for storing all object references. As stated above, mobile environments are characterized by limited resources. Therefore it is crucial to have well balanced responsibilities among the nodes. As a result it is of major interest to find out the impact of real world content distributions on the applicability of structured P2P networks in mobile scenarios.

In this work, we use the Chord protocol as an example for structured P2P protocols. Chord assigns a unique ID to every node and every shared object in the network, e.g. by hashing a node's IP address or a file name. (Within this work, we will use the term "key" for the ID of a shared object.) All nodes are ordered in a one-dimensional ring that covers an ID range from 0 to 2^m-1, where m is the length of the IDs in bit. A reference to a shared object with key k is assigned to the first node whose ID is equal to or follows k. This node is therefore called the successor of k. A detailed description of the Chord protocol is given in [Stoica et al., 2001].

Assuming that the used hash function spreads all keys evenly over the nodes, every node in the Chord ring is responsible for

$$f = \frac{K}{n} \quad \forall n$$

keys, where K is the total number of keys and n the total number of nodes in the network. Although all keys are equally distributed in the network, the number of shared objects mapped onto a key can vary significantly. For example, the successor of the hash value of "Madonna" stores significantly more object references than the successor of the hash value of "Diamond Dog", a relatively unknown German rock band. In unfavorable cases, this may lead to storage capacity problems. Furthermore, all object references have to be transferred from or to the succeeding node when a node joins or leaves the network, in order to maintain the hash key mapping rules. As we must assume high churn rates in mobile scenarios due to the movement and the short online times of mobile nodes, this can result in a heavy traffic load for the involved peers.

The goal of this paper is to evaluate the impact of content distribution on the applicability of structured P2P concepts in mobile scenarios. As there currently exists no large structured P2P network, we evaluate the content distribution of a large unstructured P2P network (Gnutella 0.6 [Gnutella]) and derive the consequences of this distribution for a Chord network in mobile scenarios. In particular we have performed the following steps:

1. Find as many shared objects as possible that are provided in the Gnutella 0.6 network.
2. Determine the distribution of the discovered content in a Chord network with a given number of nodes.
3. Investigate the consequences of the determined distribution for a mobile P2P scenario.

The remainder of this paper is structured as follows. In section 2 we give an overview about our methodology for the content analysis in Gnutella. One basic criterion is to determine the optimal measurement period for a query, which is explained in detail in section 3. In section 4 we analyze the results of our measurements. In section 5 we draw conclusions for the applicability of structured P2P protocols in mobile scenarios. Finally, in section 6 we conclude our results and provide an outlook to future work.

2. PREREQUISITES FOR THE CONTENT DISCOVERY

To discover the availability and distribution of shared objects in a real world P2P network, we create a list with 578,627 different keywords, as described below. Additionally, we modify the Gnutella client application "Mutella" [Mutella] to automatically start a query for every keyword and to log the number of QUERY HIT messages for every query.

2.1   Creation of the keyword list

To create a list with a high number of different keywords we combine the contents of different, free accessible dictionaries:
- the German-English-Dictionary of the Technical University of Chemnitz with more than 170,000 entries [TU Chemnitz]
- the "National Puzzlers' League" 2nd unabridged dictionary [Unabridged] (235,544 entries)
- the "Official Scrabble Player's Dictionary" [Scrabble] (172,823 entries)

In addition we take into account that today's content of P2P networks mainly consists of compressed audio files. As the names of most song writers and artists can not be found in a normal dictionary, we also add the content of FreeDB [FreeDB] (1,486,728 entries) to our list. FreeDB is a free music data base that contains information about artists and CDs. Combining the data of all databases mentioned above and removing duplicated entries, we finally can generate a list with 578,627 different keywords.

2.2   Modification of the Mutella client

As Gnutella 0.6 is one of today's most popular P2P protocols with an open protocol specification and open source clients, we use the Gnutella 0.6 network for our content measurements. An appropriate open source client is "Mutella", a command line based Linux client implemented in C++. To use it for our measurements the "Mutella" client is modified so that it can automatically perform the following tasks:
- Read a given number of keywords from the list.
- Start a query for every keyword.
- Collect and count the received QUERY HIT messages separately for every keyword.
- After a given measurement period t_q, write every keyword together with the number of QUERY HIT messages into a log file.

To eliminate statistical aberrations, we conduct the measurements five times within several weeks and build the average values of all results.

3.   DETERMINATION OF THE OPTIMAL MEASUREMENT PERIOD

When querying an unstructured P2P network like Gnutella 0.6, every QUERY message is flooded through the network. All peers that receive a QUERY message and share objects that match the keyword stated in the QUERY message, respond with a QUERY HIT message. Due to this search mechanism, the time between initializing a query and receiving the according QUERY HIT messages can vary significantly, according to the number of hops between the querying node and the replying node and also according to the replication rate of the requested content.

As already mentioned in section II, the time to collect the according QUERY HIT messages for one QUERY is restricted to t_q. To keep the overall time for the measurements short, the measurement period t_q for one query should be as small as possible. On the other hand, t_q must be long enough to find the majority of the peers in the network that share objects that match the keyword stated in the initial QUERY message.

To determine the optimal value for t_q, we use five common keywords and trigger the Gnutella 0.6 network with a QUERY message for every keyword. We log every five seconds the number of received QUERY HIT messages. In Figure 1, the cumulative number of received QUERY HIT messages for the keywords "easy", "madonna", "music", "contact" and "value" is plotted against the duration of the measurement period.

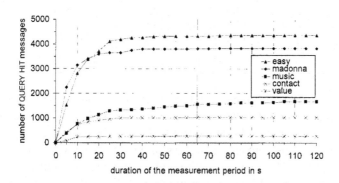

Fig.1.   Number of received QUERY HIT messages against the duration of the measurement period

As we can observe from the diagram the number of QUERY HIT messages increases significantly at the beginning of the measurement period and reaches a level of saturation after approximately 65 seconds. Afterwards, the growth in the number of received QUERY HIT messages can nearly be neglected.

Resulting, we use in all our following measurements a measurement period of t_q = 65 s for every keyword. Thus we can keep the overall time for the measurements short and at the same time can guarantee that we can find a majority of the peers that share objects matching the used keyword.

4.　　ANALYSIS OF THE MEASUREMENT RESULTS

We conduct our measurements five times to eliminate statistical aberrations. Table 1 shows the results of all five measurements and the average number of QUERY HIT messages. Our first measurement results in 4,183,027 QUERY HIT messages for 578,627 different keywords. The next measurements lead to 4,058,265, 4,486,803, 3,991,511 and 4,111,175 QUERY HIT messages, respectively. This yields an average number of QUERY HIT messages of 4,166,156. Throughout the rest of this paper we will use the average values of all five measurements.

Table 1. Results of all five measurements and average number of query hit messages

number of keywords	578,627
total number of QUERY HIT msg., 1st try	4,183,027
total number of QUERY HIT msg., 2nd try	4,058,265
total number of QUERY HIT msg., 3rd try	4,486,803
total number of QUERY HIT msg., 4th try	3,991,511
total number of QUERY HIT msg., 5th try	4,111,175
average number of QUERY HIT msg.	4,166,156

One result from our measurements is that 495,648 or 85.7 % of all keywords result in zero QUERY HIT messages. For the remaining keywords, we receive between one and 4,595 QUERY HIT messages for each keyword.

In Figure 2, the percentage of successful queries (= keywords that lead to at least one QUERY HIT message) with a given maximum number of QUERY HIT messages is plotted against the number of QUERY HIT messages. For example, 29.2 % of all successful queries produce just one QUERY HIT message, while 40.5 % result in one or two QUERY HIT messages. As expected, there are many keywords that result in only a few QUERY HIT messages, while only a minority of the used keywords leads to a high number of QUERY HIT messages.

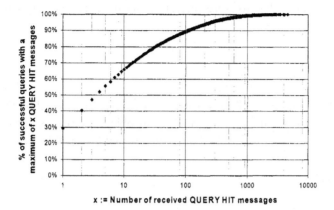

Fig. 2. Percentage of successful queries with a given maximum number of QUERY HIT
    messages against the number of QUERY HIT messages

Based on our measurement results in the Gnutella network, we calculate
the resulting load balance for nodes in a structured P2P network containing
the discovered content. As stated above, we use the Chord protocol as an
example for a structured P2P network. Chord is a DHT-based protocol that
uses a hash function like SHA-1 [FIPS, 1995] to derive the keys of all shared
objects. For example, the SHA-1 key of "Madonna" is
"e4ddaa79edcafaacb559c5731edaa55455f2b069". All shared objects that
match the keyword "Madonna" are therefore mapped onto that node that is
responsible for this key, i.e. with a minimum positive difference between the
node's hash value and the hash value of the keyword.

Assuming that all nodes are distributed uniformly over the whole ring
(this is guaranteed by the use of an appropriate hash function) all nodes are
responsible for an equally sized ID section of the Chord ring. With regard to
this consideration, we set up a fictive Chord ring, split up the ID space of
this ring into n equally sized sections and assign every section to one node (n
again is the total number of nodes in the Chord network). Thus the ID
section of node j is given by

$$I_j = \left((j-1) \cdot \frac{2^m}{n}, j \cdot \frac{2^m}{n} \right] \quad \forall j \in [1, n]$$

where m is the length of the IDs in bit. Now all QUERY HIT messages
received for a certain keyword are assigned to that node that is responsible
for the keyword.

Therefore node j has to store references to all shared objects with key k that satisfy

$$k \in I_j$$

Although the number of keys per node is equally distributed by the use of an appropriate hash function, the number of object references per node can vary significantly. Figure 3 shows the load balance that results for our fictive Chord ring ($m = 160$).

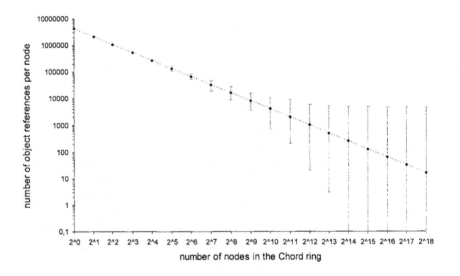

Fig. 3. Number of object references per node against the total number of nodes in the Chord ring

In the diagram, the number of object references per node is plotted against the total number of nodes participating in the Chord ring. Assuming an equal number of object references per key, any node j would store the same number of object references

$$e_j = \frac{o}{n} \quad \forall j \in [1; n]$$

where o denotes the total number of shared objects and n the total number of nodes in the network. e_j refers to the average value for the number of object references per node in our scenario. As Figure 3 uses a double-logarithmic scale, e_j is depicted as a straight line. For every simulated number of nodes between 2^0 and 2^{18}, the deviation from e_j is plotted. The deviation is given by the node with the highest load and the node with the smallest load. For example, when spreading all object references over 2^{12} nodes, the average load per node is given by

$$e_j = \frac{o}{n} = \frac{4,166,156}{2^{12}} = 1,017$$

However, as we can see from the diagram, there are nodes whose load deviates considerably from this value. The node with the highest load is responsible for 5,870 object references, while the node with the lowest load has to store only 20 object references. Another appealing result is the fact that for a number of nodes larger than 2^{14} the highest load of a node is not decreasing any more with an increasing number of nodes in the network. This follows directly from Figure 2, as the keyword with the highest number of QUERY HIT messages (4,595) is mapped onto one node and therefore this node has to store all references to the 4,595 shared objects that match this keyword.

5. APPLICABILITY OF CHORD IN MOBILE SCENARIOS

From the results of our measurements, we are now able to evaluate the applicability of the Chord protocol in mobile scenarios. We separate mobile communication networks into two main categories: Cellular networks and Mobile Ad Hoc Networks (MANETs).

5.1 Applicability in cellular networks

Cellular wireless networks are one-hop wireless networks. Mobile P2P nodes are thus connected to the fixed Internet only via a single wireless link. Resulting we can state that even if nodes move, the physical path to a node alters not much. Further on we can assume that most problems resulting from the mobility of the cellular wireless node are already managed by lower layers of the cellular network. We therefore have to evaluate the applicability of the Chord system in a cellular network based on the following aspects:
- storage capacity
- access data rate

– content availability

As derived from above, the minimum number of object references that one node always has to store is 4,595. Assuming that an object reference consists of a keyword with 20 Bytes, a hash value with 160 bit (20 Bytes), an IP address with 32 bit (4 Bytes) and a port number with 16 bit (2 Bytes), the total load of this node is given by

$$\ell = 4,595 \cdot 46 \; Bytes = 206.41 \, kB$$

This load is acceptable for the storage capacity of today's mobile devices. Even if the load of a node exceeds this value (e.g. due to a very low number of nodes in the ring) we can assume enough storage capacity on the mobile device to handle the load.

However, regarding the available access data rate of mobile devices, we have to take into account the higher churn rates of mobile nodes in cellular networks. Every time a node joins the network, all object references the node is responsible for have to be transmitted from the node's successor to the new node, in order to maintain the hash key mapping rules. In the above example, more than 200 kB have to be transferred. (On a mobile phone running GPRS with a data rate of 100 kbit/s, this would take more than 16 s!) As online time in cellular networks is expensive, the user will usually not stay in the Chord ring for a long period of time. Thus the same amount of data has to be retransferred to the node's successor after a short period of time when the node leaves the network again. For this reason, the limited access data rate of mobile devices can be a significant challenge for structured P2P protocols like Chord. It becomes even more critical when the protocol has to deal with high churn rates as they usually appear in mobile scenarios. In this case, a high amount of the available data rate is consumed by network maintenance traffic. (As we have seen above, a joining or leaving node may be blocked for 16 seconds from any further communication.)

Another critical aspect when using structured P2P protocols in a cellular network is the comparatively high probability for a connection loss. As mobile devices have commonly a wireless connection to the Internet and only a limited power supply, the probability that a mobile Chord node fails is notably higher than in a fixed environment. When a Chord node fails, all its object references are lost, if they are not replicated on other nodes. A failed node has no possibility to transfer its object references to the node's successor. This results in the unavailability of all content that is mapped onto the failed node, until the content is republished by the sharing nodes and therefore available again. The high variance of content distribution, as depicted above, makes this problem even more evident.

Concluding, we can state that structured P2P networks are, generally speaking, a suitable solution for cellular networks, because the signaling traffic in structured P2P networks is lower than in unstructured approaches. However, the two main challenges we still have to bear in mind are the low transmission data rate of mobile devices and the high probability of a connection loss.

5.2   Applicability in MANETs

If we want to operate a structured Peer-to-Peer network on top of a MANET, we have to take into account the mobility of the nodes. The reason therefore is that MANETs are self configuring, wireless multi-hop networks, within which we have to assume the possibility that the physical path between two nodes changes frequently, due to the movement of the nodes [Gruber and Li, 2003]. Besides the challenges mentioned above, i.e. low transmission data rates and high failure probability, further problems can occur in MANETs:

If the overlay structure is established completely independent from the underlying MANET topology, this results in a significant number of long and unstable zigzag routes in the MANET layer. The connections between the overlay nodes can not be mapped onto the physical topology of the MANET [Eberspächer et al. 2004]. This leads to significantly higher traffic volumes, which might not be bearable by the MANET [Klemm et al. 2003]. Further on we have to take into account the significant overhead to keep alive overlay connections via more than 5 physical hops. According to [Gruber and Li, 2003] paths longer than 5 hops hardly survive more than a few seconds.

However, if we assign IDs to the participating overlay nodes which reflect the current position of a node in the MANET, an overlay network is established that solves the problems mentioned above, i.e. zigzag routes and long physical paths. As the IDs reflect the current position of a node, as proposed in [Zhuang and Zhou, 2003], the connection between two overlay nodes with a small distance in the ID space also results in a small distance in the physical space of the MANET. However, as the nodes are assumed to move, the IDs of the nodes have to change constantly, to reflect the changing physical network. This results in a continuous transfer of object references between the nodes, as the IDs and therefore the responsibility of the nodes changes constantly. Concluding, this results in high network maintenance traffic, especially when the content distribution has such a high variance as pointed out in section IV.

With regard to the above conclusions we can state that structured P2P networks are hardly applicable in MANETs. For the use of P2P technologies in such networks, other promising protocols that are based on an unstructured overlay architecture, like the Mobile Peer-to-Peer protocol [Schollmeier et al., 2003] are more suitable.

6.   CONCLUSION AND FUTURE WORK

In this paper, we presented the results of our experimental analysis of content distribution in an existing Gnutella 0.6 network and derived the consequences this distribution would have for the structured P2P system Chord. Based on these results we evaluated the applicability of structured P2P networks in mobile scenarios.

To find approximately all content that is shared in the Gnutella network, we created a list with a high number of keywords. Then we queried the network for every keyword and logged the number of QUERY HIT messages after a given measurement period t_q. As illustrated in section III, the optimal measurement period in the Gnutella network is 65 s. The results of our measurements show that many keywords result in no or only a few QUERY HIT messages and only several keywords lead to a high number of QUERY HIT messages.

In a second step, we apply our measurement results on a fictive Chord system with a given number of nodes. For this case we determine the load balance that results in the Chord ring. With an increasing number of nodes, the deviation from the average number of object references per node e_j increases significantly.

Based on these results, we can evaluate the applicability of structured P2P protocols like Chord in mobile scenarios, where we differentiate between cellular networks and Mobile Ad Hoc Networks. In cellular networks, structured P2P networks can be applicable, although the low transmission data rate of mobile devices and the high probability of a connection loss are challenges that have to be met. In MANETs, structured P2P networks are hardly useable. For MANETS, other promising P2P protocols, based on an unstructured architecture, have been proposed.

Currently we are working on a modification of the Chord protocol that aims to reduce the necessity of re-transmission of object references between low performance nodes [Zöls et al., 2005]. Thus the necessary maintenance traffic can be reduced significantly and adaptations to the physical network are possible. Our approach defines a two-tier architecture with two different classes of nodes participating in the Chord network. Firstly, we have a class of static, highly available nodes with higher capabilities, like a broadband connection. These nodes store the references to all objects that are provided in the Chord ring. Secondly, we have temporary nodes like mobile subscribers that do not store object references but forward all requests to their next static successor. Thus we can employ the advantages of structured P2P networks even in mobile scenarios.

REFERENCES

Eberspächer, J., Schollmeier, R., Zöls, S. and Kunzmann, G. (2004). Structured Peer-to-Peer Networks in Heterogeneous Environments. In Second International Conference on Heterogeneous Networks (Hetnets'04).

FIPS (1995). "Secure Hash Standard" Federal Information Processing Standards Publication FIPS PUB 180-1.

FreeDB, Database to Look Up CD Information Using the Internet, http://www.freedb.org

Freenet, Freenet Homepage, http://freenetproject.org/cgi-bin/twiki/view/Main/WebHome

Gnutella 0.6, RFC-Gnutella 0.6, http://rfc-gnutella.sourceforge.net/developer/testing/

Gruber, I. and Li, H. (2003). Path Expiration Times in Mobile Ad Hoc Networks. Presented at European Personal Mobile Communications Conference (EPMCC'03), 2003.

Klemm, A., Lindemann, C. and Waldhorst, O. P. (2003). A Special-Purpose Peer-to-Peer File Sharing System for Mobile Ad Hoc Networks. Presented at Workshop on Mobile Ad Hoc Networking and Computing (MADNET 2003).

Mutella, Mutella Homepage, http://mutella.sourceforge.net

Ratnasamy, S., Francis, P., Handley, M., Karp, R. and Shenker, S. (2001). A Scalable Content-Addressable Network, presented at ACM SIGCOMM Conference.

Schollmeier, R. Gruber, I. and Niethammer, F. (2003). Protocol for Peer-to-Peer Networking in Mobile Environments in International Conference on Computer Communications (ICCCN03).

Scrabble. The National Puzzlers' League, "The Word Lists: The Official Scrab-ble™ Player's Dictionary", ftp://puzzlers.org/pub/wordlists/enable1.txt

Stoica, I., Morris, R., Karger, D., Kaashoek, M. and Balakrishnan, H. (2001). Chord: A Scalable Peer-to-Peer Lookup Service for Internet Applications. In ACM SIG-COMM Conference.

TU Chemnitz, "Deutsch-Englisches Wörterbuch", http://dict.tu-chemnitz.de

Unabridged. The National Puzzlers' League, "The Word Lists: 2nd Unabridged Dictionary", ftp://puzzlers.org/pub/wordlists/unabr2.txt

Zhuang, L. and Zhou, F. (2003). Understanding Chord Performance. Technical Report CS268.

Zöls, S., Schollmeier, R., Kellerer, W. and Tarlano, A. (2005). The Hybrid Chord Protocol: A Peer-to-Peer Lookup Service for Context-Aware Mobile Applications, Internat. Conf. on Networking (ICN'05).

PERFORMANCE MANAGEMENT OF PEER-TO-PEER DISTRIBUTED HASH TABLES

Guillaume Doyen[1]
LORIA - University Henry Poincaré
Guillaume.Doyen@loria.fr

Emmanuel Nataf[1]
LORIA - University of Nancy 2
Emmanuel.Nataf@loria.fr

Olivier Festor[1]
LORIA - INRIA Lorraine
Olivier.Festor@loria.fr

[1] *The Madynes research team*
LORIA, 615 rue du Jardin Botanique
54602 Villers-lès-Nancy, France

Abstract   P2P networking is a distributed model where entities play both the client and server role. One major problem addressed in this model is the discovery, searching and routing in a dynamic distributed environment. Among the different envisaged solutions, Distributed Hash Tables (DHT) are very promising. They allow the build of robust content addressable networks. Despite good theoretical performance properties, infrastructures which implement the model need a performance management framework able to monitor them in case of a concrete deployment. In this article we propose a generic performance management information model for DHTs. Our contribution uses a standard management approach based on the Common Information Model (CIM) Metric model.

Keywords: Peer-to-peer, network management, performance, information model, Common Information Model (CIM), distributed hash tables.

1.   Introduction

Nowadays, P2P networking is an emerging model that extends the limits of the client/server one. Indeed, applications built over it present a better scalability, load balancing and fault tolerance. Although "wild" P2P applications, like that of illegal files sharing, don't want any management infrastructure at all, enterprise ones, used for critical applications, need a management infrastructure. For example, enterprises, administrations or universities may want to deploy P2P applications for several purposes like the distribution of networked file systems, including the replication of data, or the use of distributed collaboration tools for project that count remote participants. In this context, the need for a management framework is obvious in order to ensure services level agreements in value-added applications.

One of the major problems P2P infrastructures have to face concerns the discovery of resources and the routing of messages. The main cause is that P2P applications are composed of versatile entities that form a dynamic environment and may not use any central server for resource location. Among the different solutions envisaged to address the discovery and routing problem, the use of Distributed Hash Tables (DHT) proves to be a very efficient solution which enables the construction of robust content addressable networks [Fraigniaud and Gauron, 2003].

These frameworks offer interesting theoretical performances in terms of average path length, load balancing and consistency. Nevertheless, there is actually no way to monitor the performance they announce in case of real deployments. In this paper, we propose a performance management instrumentation model for DHTs. It extends a CIM generic model for P2P networks and services [Doyen et al., 2004a] that encompasses the functional, organizational and topological aspects of this networking model. Our performance model is generic and can be applied to any existing DHT infrastructure in order to monitor its performance.

This paper is organized as follows: Section 2 presents the generic P2P information model we have designed. Section 3 focuses on the DHT model and the existing theoretical performance evaluation studies. The contribution of this paper is exposed in section 4. It consists in a performance management information model based on an instrumentation approach. Finally, section 5 draws some conclusions and deals with future works.

2.   P2P Networking

Peer-to-peer (P2P) networking is built on a distributed model where peers are software entities which play both the role of client and server. Today, the most popular application domain of this model is file sharing with applications like E-mule, Napster, Gnutella and Kazaa among others[1]. However, the P2P model also covers many additional domains [Oram, 2001] like dis-

---

[1]www.zeropaid.com

tributed computing (Seti@Home [Anderson, 2001], the Globus Project [Foster and Kesselman, 1999]), collaborative work (Groove[2], Magi[3]) and instant messaging (Jabber[4], JIM [Doyen et al., 2003]). To provide common grounds to all these applications, some middleware infrastructures propose generic frameworks for the development of P2P services (Jxta [Oaks et al., 2002], Anthill [Babaoglu et al., 2002]).

The P2P model enables valuable service usage by aggregating and orchestrating individual shared resources [Milojicic et al., 2002]. The use of existing infrastructures that belong to different owners reduces the costs of maintenance and ownership. The decentralized topology increases fault tolerance by suppressing any central point of failure, and improves both load balancing and scalability. At last, the distributed nature of algorithms and some embedded mechanisms allow participating peers to maintain a great level of anonymity.

2.1 Management of P2P Applications

While some applications use built-in incentives as a minimal self management feature [Mischke and Stiller, 2003], advanced management services are required for enterprise-oriented P2P environments. The latter are the focus of our attention and deserve the availability of a generic management framework.

The first step toward this objective has consisted in designing a generic management information model for P2P networks and services that can be used by any management application as a primary abstraction. The work we have done in this direction has led to a model [Doyen et al., 2004a] that aims at providing a general management information model, that addresses the functional, topological and organizational aspects for such a type of application. We have chosen CIM [Bumpus et al., 2000; Distributed Management Task Force, Inc., 2005] as the framework for the design of our model because of its richness in terms of classes covering several domains of computing that can be easily reused and extended. This way, CIM allows any P2P application to subclass our model in order to provide dedicated classes that will represent the specific application features at best. Instances of these classes will provide a distributed Management Information Base (MIB) that a management application will use to administrate the application.

As shown on Figure 1, the model we have designed covers the various aspects of the P2P domain. First, it deals with the notion of peer and its belonging to one or several communities. A particular association class allows the link of peers together in order to establish a virtual topology. One may note that, according to the context, different criteria can be considered to link two peers;

---

[2]www.groove.net
[3]www.endtech.com
[4]www.jabber.org

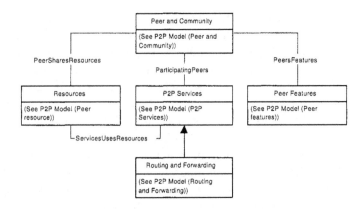

Figure 1. An overview of the CIM extension for P2P networks and services

for example, it can be based on knowledge, routing, interest or technological considerations. Then, our model features the available resources in a community and especially the ones shared by its composing peers. We particularly address the fact that a resource can be spread in a community and thus (1) we differentiate owners and hosts of shared resources and (2) we split resources into physical (e.g. the chunk of a file on a file system) and logical ones (the aggregation of the different chunks). Moreover, the latter are consumed or provided in the context of services that constitutes the fourth aspect of our model. Indeed, a P2P service is a basic functionality that is distributed among a set of participating peers; thus our model enables the global view of a service as well as the local one. Finally, we have identified particular basic services offered by any P2P framework; it concerns, for example, the way packets are routed in a P2P environment that is one of an overlay type. Therefore, we have modeled routing and forwarding services together with the routing tables they generate or use.

In this way, our CIM extension for P2P networks and services provides an abstract view of a P2P network as well as the deployed services located in a manageable environment.

In order to validate our P2P model, we have instantiated it on existing P2P applications. First, we did it on the Chord P2P framework [Doyen et al., 2004b]. Our information model allows the global monitoring of a Chord ring, its participating peers as well as the discovery and stabilization services. Moreover, we have oriented our model toward the performance management and defined metrics dedicated to the particular Chord architecture. The latter concerns the performance of the discovery service, the nodes equity and the ring consistency and dynamics. Stating from this Chord model, we built an abstraction usable for every DHT-based system and we present it in the next section.

3. The Distributed Hash Tables

The principle of a DHT consists in associating a unique key, resulting from a known hash function, to any resource in a P2P community. The collection of all the keys associated to resources represents a hash table that is scattered around nodes by using a common naming scheme for keys and nodes. Finally the use of a particular topology (De Bruijn graphs [De Bruijn, 1946], Plaxton [Plaxton et al., 1997], d-torus [Ratnasamy et al., 2001], ...) that exhibits good properties enables an efficient routing of messages. Famous DHTs are Chord [Stoica et al., 2001] that builds a ring topology, CAN [Ratnasamy et al., 2001] that uses a d-torus[5] and D2B that is built over De Bruijn graphs, among others. These infrastructures are mainly deployed in large scale data storage [Kubiatowicz et al., 2000; Dabek et al., 2001; Druschel and Rowstron, 2001].

3.1 Existing Performance Evaluations of DHTs

The need of a performance evaluation for DHTs has been established in [Rhea et al., 2003]. Performance evaluation works for P2P architectures and especially DHTs are numerous and of different nature. First, a theoretical model for P2P networks has been established in [Kant, 2003] and the proposal of an analytic model for the performance evaluation of P2P file sharing system is given in [Kant et al., 2002]. Then, a simulation approach has been used in [Tsoumakos and Roussopoulos, 2003] to compare the different P2P search methods. If these works provide a very precise evaluation of DHTs in static cases, their theoretical nature prevents them from dealing with all the phenomena that can appear in case of a real deployment. This is why [Rhea et al., 2003] proposes a benchmarking evaluation approach for Chord [Stoica et al., 2001] and Tapestry [Zhao et al., 2001] with a real implementation under test in the PlanetLab [Peterson et al., 2000] testbed.

Given all these works, the motivation of the design of an information model for the performance evaluation of DHTs are:

- **Integration of a management framework:** In case of a real deployment, performance of DHTs may collapse, due to phenomena of a different nature, like a strong join or leave movement of nodes or the heterogeneousness of the links between peers. This context clearly shows the need for a management approach which can monitor a DHT, evaluate its current performance and act consequently.

- **Standardization:** current works use different metrics for evaluating DHTs which makes the comparison of infrastructures hardly possible.

[5]An circular Euclidean space of dimension d

Of course, such a comparison doesn't aim at establishing that a particular DHT is performing better or worse than another one, but it can show differences that can be improved in future development.

4.   A performance model for DHTs

In order to provide a generic model that can feature the performance of any DHT, we have identified the aspects common to all the DHTs and deduced a consistent way to evaluate them. As described on Figure 2, the different criteria we have selected are related to the lookup mechanism, the maintenance of routing tables as well as metadata and finally the insertion and removal of nodes in the DHT.

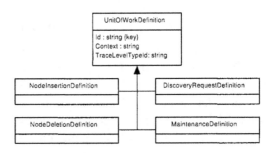

Figure 2.   The units of works definitions

4.1   Global Featuring of Distributed Hash Tables

Before characterizing the performance of DHTs, we need to model their components. Figure 3 represents the model we propose to represent, in the management plane, the elements of a DHT. This model is an extension of our general model for P2P networks and services. First, we represent participating nodes through the *DHTNode* class. The *NodeDegree* property represents the number of connections with direct neighbors a node owns. Then, we represent a DHT community (e.g. a chord ring, a CAN torus, ...) with the *DHTcommunity* class. This class provides general information about the grouping of nodes (e.g. *HashMethod, NumberOfNodes, ...*) as well as metrics that feature the community behavior (*NodesJoinFrequency, KeysMigrationFrequency,* ...). Detailed information about the way we compute these metrics is given in [Doyen et al., 2004b]. Finally, the *PeerResource* represents a resource stored in a DHT. We have chosen to represent it as an abstract class to let the application built over a DHT inherit from it and thus represent any concrete resource.

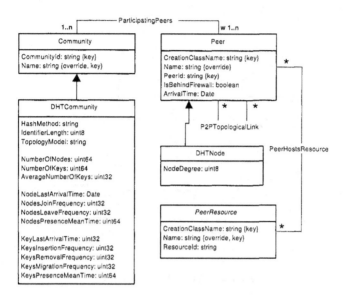

Figure 3.   The model for DHT nodes and communities

4.2   The CIM Metrics Model

The CIM metrics model [Distributed Management Task Force, 2003] aims at allowing the management of availability, fault and performance of distributed applications as well as local ones. It provides a set of classes for gathering and managing metrics information. The two concepts introduced in the CIM metric model are the *unit of work* and *metric* ones. According to Figure 4, a unit of work represents a piece of code, currently executed, (a batch job, a network transaction, an end-user command, . . .) that has to be characterized. A unit of work can be composed of several sub-units of work that allow different granularity levels. A unit of work is related to a definition that provides informational data about it. Then, the characterization of a unit of work is achieved through metrics. A metric is an assessable criterion that characterizes an aspect of a unit of work. For example, it can be the response time for a web transaction or the amount of used memory for an application. In the same way as the unit of work, metrics are associated to a definition.

4.3   Instrumentation of Discovery Requests

The main goal of DHTs is to allow a user to discover and access resources in a P2P environment. The lookup function provided by the DHT has to remain efficient whatever the number of participants, the network dynamic or the routing distance between resources and requesters. Figure 5 shows the general way

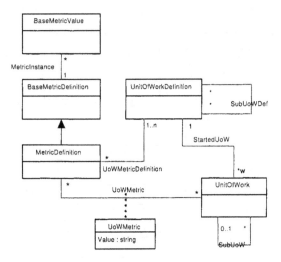

Figure 4.   The CIM metrics model

nodes participating to DHTs treat discovery requests. When a request arrives, the receiving node checks in its local cache for the required resource. If the resource is not cached, the node goes through its routing table to find a remote node that can help to satisfy the request. If such a node is found, the request is forwarded. Otherwise, an error message is sent back. This general scenario applies to all existing DHTs.

Based on this general scheme, we have represented the different measurements we propose to feature the discovery service.

The first measurement consists in evaluating the time a node needs to process a request. For a requester node it will represent the time spent to respond to an end-user request and for an intermediate node it will represent to total time spent to process it. Then, we estimated that the local computation time[6] could be interesting to measure. Indeed, in case of too large caches or routing tables size, the amount of time for local processing may be high and such a piece of information is useful to address scalability problems, in particular in environments like the ones described in [Kubiatowicz et al., 2000]. Finally, for all remote calls, we take a snapshot of several parameters in order to evaluate the network load.

The way we model the discovery request operation is shown on Figure 6. As described previously we have distinguished three different units of works. The first one, named *DiscoveryRequest* represents a particular discovery request

---

[6]it consists in checking the local cache and skim the routing table

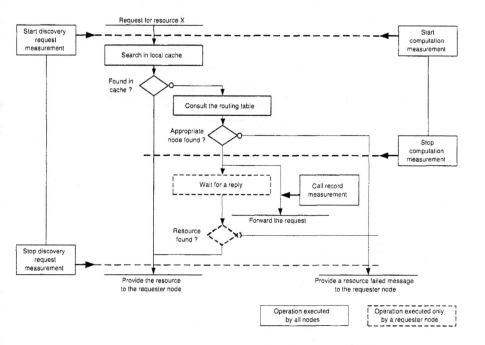

Figure 5.   The general scenario for resource discovery

seen by an end user or processed by a forwarding node. The second unit of work is *LocalRequestComputation* and it aims at featuring the local processing operated by nodes. Finally, the *RemoteNodeCall* features the call to a remote node.

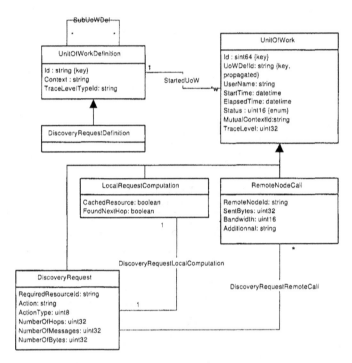

Figure 6.   The discovery model

Now, given the preceding context of measurement, we have defined a set of metrics that can feature the discovery requests at best. These are:

- **the average number of hops:** Most existing DHTs theoretically route requests in $O(\log n)$ hops. Nonetheless, in case of strong dynamic of nodes or resources, this value can grow up to $O(n)$ for some of them. This variation needs to be monitored.

- **the global response time:** It corresponds to the time spent to complete a request, from an end-user perspective.

- **the success of the request:** Due to overload or dynamic phenomena, the success rate of discovery requests may collapse; existing resources may become unavailable. This is why we measure the success rate of requests, and consider that this indicator informs about the health of a DHT.

- **the request cost:** Discovery requests have a cost that can be expressed in terms of number of messages, number of bytes and bandwidth that we characterize through this metric.

- **the local computation time:** As described above, we want a node to inform about the time spent processing requests. This time includes both the local cache search and the routing process.

4.4 Performance Evaluation of Other Operations

Existing DHTs exhibit theoretical performances that apply in the context of a stable environment. Nevertheless, in case of a concrete deployment, nodes can come and go in an unpredictable way inducing a dynamic presence and location of resources and routing paths. Such a behavior mandates the presence of a process that can update metadata maintained by nodes so that they will reflect the reality at best. This process is called maintenance process and is executed regularly by all the nodes participating in a DHT.

Moreover, when a node joins a DHT, it becomes responsible for a new set of resources. As a consequence, some metadata have to migrate and involved nodes have to update their routing tables. The same set of changes is done in case of a node departure.

In our performance management oriented information model, we addressed these three operations and we designed dedicated unit of work classes for them. In addition, we have defined standard metrics that feature the global cost of such operations.

4.5 Correlation of the Distributed Measurements

The performance measurements we propose in our model are related to distributed transactions. Indeed, a user request initiated on a particular node may imply the launch of several transactions on different nodes. In this context we need a way to correlate each transaction measurement to a particular context. To do that, we have used the method proposed by CIM in the metrics model. It consists in creating a correlator object that will be attached to each request so that a manager can link it to a particular initial transaction.

Figure 7 displays the correlator class. Among all the properties, the *InitiatorNodeId* provides the identifier of the node that has initiated a transaction; the latter is represented through the *InitiatorTransactionId* attribute. The *previousNode* attribute refers to the last node the transaction has crossed. Finally, the *hopNumber* counts the number of hops crossed by the correlator. This way, we are able to bind each transaction to a context.

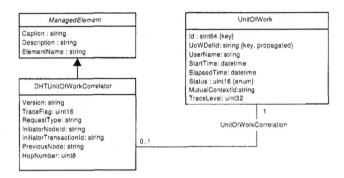

Figure 7.   The correlation CIM class

5.   Conclusion and Future Work

To propose an efficient alternative to the client/server model, P2P applications need a management framework that ensures service levels without altering the main advantage of these systems: their high distribution. The core of most P2P applications contains a DHT that ensures the discovery and routing aspects with guaranteed theoretical performances. This is why DHTs seem to be unavoidable for the P2P management.

In this paper, we have proposed a performance management information model based on CIM. It enables the monitoring of main DHT operations such as the discovery and the maintenance processes as well as the cost of join and departure of nodes. To do that, we have defined performance metrics and added measurement points within nodes participating to DHTs. This work is generic enough so that any existing DHT implementation can implement it.

Concerning the validation of this model, we plan to achieve it through its deployment. We have instrumented the FreePastry[7] implementation of the Pastry DHT [Rowstron and Druschel, 2001] and Jxta[8]. At this time, all the classes defined in the context of our generic P2P model have been integrated in these two frameworks. The remaining part concerns the performance aspect and we plan to do that by integrating ARM[9] agents into nodes and by exporting collected measurements through a JMX[10] agent.

The work presented in this paper in conjunction with the one presented in [Doyen et al., 2004b] allows us to completely monitor DHTs and to deduce global performance estimators. The current work consists in establishing a

---

[7]freepastry.rice.edu
[8]www.jxta.org
[9]Application Response Measurement
[10]Java Management eXtension

reactive management behavior from these estimators. Another direction focuses on the management architecture itself and especially the way we could distribute the manager role among managed peers.

References

Anderson, D. (2001). *Peer to peer: Harnessing the Power of Disruptive Technologies*, chapter SETI@Home, pages 67–76. O'Reilly & Associates, Inc.

Babaoglu, O., Meling, H., and Montresor, A. (2002). Anthill: A framework for the development of agent-based peer-to-peer systems. In *Proceedings of the 22th International Conference on Distributed Computing Systems*. IEEE Computer Society.

Bumpus, W., Sweitzer, J. W., Thompson, P., R., Westerinen; A., and Williams, R. C. (2000). *Common Information Model*. Wiley.

Dabek, F., Kaashoek, M.F., Karger, D., Morris, R., and Stoica, I. (2001). Wide-area cooperative storage with CFS. In *Proceedings of the 18th ACM Symposium on Operating Systems Principles - SOSP'01*, pages 202–215. ACM Press.

De Bruijn, N. (1946). *Koninklijke Nederlanse Academie van Wetenschappen Proc.*, volume 49, chapter A combinatorial problem, pages 758–764. Indagationes Math.

Distributed Management Task Force (2003). Common Information Model (CIM) Metrics Model, version 2.7. www.dmtf.org.

Distributed Management Task Force, Inc. (2005). Common information model v2.7. www.dmtf.org.

Doyen, G., Festor, O., and Nataf, E. (2003). Management of peer-to-peer services applied to instant messaging. In Marshall, A. and Agoulmine, N., editors, *Management of Multimedia Networks and Services*, number 2839 in LNCS, pages 449–461. Springer-Verlag. End-to-End Monitoring Workshop - E2EMON'03.

Doyen, G., Festor, O., and Nataf, E. (2004a). A cim extension for peer-to-peer network and service management. In De Souza, J. and Dini, P., editors, *Proceedings of the 11th International Conference on Telecommunication - ICT'04*, number 3124 in LNCS, pages 801–810. Springer-Verlag.

Doyen, G., Nataf, E., and Festor, O. (2004b). A performance-oriented management information model for the chord p2p framework. In Vicente, J. and Hutchison, D., editors, *Management of Multimedia Networks and Services - MMNS'04*, number 3271 in LNCS, pages 200–212. Springer-Verlag.

Druschel, P. and Rowstron, A. (2001). Past: A large-scale, persistent peer-to-peer storage utility. In *Proceedings of the 8th IEEE workshop on Hot Topics in Operating Systems - HotOS VIII*, pages 75–80. IEEE Computer Society.

Foster, I. and Kesselman, C. (1999). The Globus project: a status report. *Future Generation Computer Systems*, 15(5-6):607–621.

Fraigniaud, P. and Gauron, P. (2003). An overview of the content-addressable network D2B. In *Proceedings of the 22nd ACM Symposium on Principles of Distributed Computing - PODC'03*, pages 151–151. ACM Press.

Kant, K. (2003). An analytic model for peer to peer file sharing networks. In *Proc. of International Communications Conference, Anchorage, AL*.

Kant, K., Iyer, R., and Tewari, V. (2002). A performance model for peer to peer file-sharing services. In *Accepted for WWW-11 poster session*.

Kubiatowicz, J., Bindel, D., Chen, Y., Eaton, P., Geels, D., Gummadi, R., Rhea, S., Weatherspoon, H., Weimer, W., Wells, C., and Zhao, B. (2000). Oceanstore: An architecture for global-scale persistent storage. *SIGARCH Computer Architecture News*, 28(5):190–201.

Milojicic, D., Kalogeraki, V., Lukose, R., Nagaraja, K., Pruyne, J., Richard, B., Rollins, S., and Xu, Z. (2002). Peer-to-peer computing. Technical Report HPL-2002-57, HP Laboratories.

Mischke, J. and Stiller, B. (2003). Peer-to-peer overlay network management through Agile. In Goldszmidt, G. and Schenwalder, J., editors, *Proceedings of the 8th symposium on Integrated Network Management - IM'03*, pages 337–350. Kluwer Academic Publisher.

Oaks, S., Traversat, B., and Gong, L. (2002). *Jxta in a nutshell*. O'Reilly.

Oram, A., editor (2001). *Peer-to-peer: Harnessing the Power of Disruptive Technologies.* O'Reilly & Associates, Inc.

Peterson, L., A., Anderson;, Culler, D., and Roscoe, T. (2000). Planetlab: A blueprint for introducing disruptive technology into the internet. In *Proceedings of the First ACM Workshop on Hot Topics in Networks (HotNets-I)*, Princeton, NJ.

Plaxton, C. G., Rajaraman, R., and W., Richa A. (1997). Accessing nearby copies of replicated objects in a distributed environment. In *Proceedings the 9th annual ACM Symposium on Parallel Algorithms and Architectures*, pages 311–320. ACM Press.

Ratnasamy, S., Francis, P., Handley, M., Karp, R., and Shenker, S. (2001). A scalable content addressable network. In *Proceedings of the ACM Conference on Applications, Technologies, Architectures and Protocols for Computer Communication - SIGCOMM'01*, pages 161–172. ACM Press.

Rhea, S., Roscoe, T., and Kubiatowicz, J. (2003). Structured peer to peer overlays need application driven benchmarks. In Kaashoek, F. and Stoica, I., editors, *Proceedings of the 2nd International Peer-to-Peer Systems Workshop (IPTPS'03), Berkeley, CA*, volume 2735 of *LNCS*. Springer-Verlag.

Rowstron, A. and Druschel, P. (2001). Pastry: Scalable, decentralized object location, and routing for large-scale peer-to-peer systems. In *Proceedings of the IFIP/ACM International Conference on Distributed Systems Platforms - Middleware'01*, number 2218 in LNCS, pages 329–350. Springer-Verlag.

Stoica, I., Morris, R., Karger, D., Kaashoek, M. F., and Balakrishnan, H. (2001). Chord: A scalable peer-to-peer lookup service for internet applications. In *Proceedings of the ACM Conference on Applications, Technologies, Architectures and Protocols for Computer Communication - SIGCOMM'01*, pages 149–160. ACM Press.

Tsoumakos, D. and Roussopoulos, N. (2003). A comparison of peer-to-peer search methods. In *Sixth International Workshop on the Web and Databases, San Diego, USA*.

Zhao, B., Kubiatowicz, J., and Joseph, A. (2001). Tapestry: An infrastructure for fault-tolerant wide-area location and routing. Technical Report UCB/CSD-01-1141, Computer Science Division, U. C. Berkeley.

EXPLOITING THE OVERHEAD IN A DHT TO IMPROVE LOOKUP LATENCY

Gerald Kunzmann, Rüdiger Schollmeier
Institute of Communication Networks, University of Technology, 80333 Munich, Germany

Abstract: Third generation Peer-to-Peer (P2P) networks are characterized by the fact, that they are based on Distributed Hash Tables (DHT). Thus, it is intended to reduce the high signaling overhead observed in unstructured P2P networks like in Gnutella. However especially if the churn rate in the considered approach is high, i.e. nodes leaving and joining the network frequently (small session duration) the signaling traffic needed to maintain the DHT structure increases considerably. In the Chord protocol, which is investigated in this work, so called fingers are used to establish shortcuts though the DHT structure to achieve a scalable routing performance. To keep these fingers up to date in regular Chord, a significant amount of signaling traffic is necessary, especially in high churn scenarios. Therefore we propose a new scheme which provides additional finger update methods without causing additional traffic.

Keywords: chord, finger update, P2P, proactive routing

1.INTRODUCTION

In today's networks the majority of traffic is caused by P2P applications like Gnutella, BitTorrent and Kazaa [Gnutella, 2002][BitTorrent, 2004][Kazaa, 2003]. However, a large amount of this P2P traffic is not caused by the transmission of user data, but by signaling traffic. The reason is that in unstructured P2P networks a large amount of the messages is flooded through the overlay network. Additionally, upon each request a route to the requested object has to be determined in unstructured P2P networks. Therefore, such an approach is classified as a reactive routing protocol. It is especially advantageous in frequently changing environments as in Mobile ad hoc scenarios and even in file sharing applications where the session duration is comparably small [Kazaa, 2003].

However, in more stable scenarios, e.g. in a Voice over P2P applications like Skype [Skype, 2004], such a high signaling overhead, like the one in unstructured P2P networks, seems to be unnecessary. Further on, in voice applications it is necessary to receive an answer from the network whether a certain object is available or not. Therefore proactive routing protocols like Chord or CAN present a promising approach to provide dedicated answers with an additionally comparably low signaling overhead [Stoica et al., 2001][Ratnasamy et al., 2001]. These networks are also referred to as structured P2P networks, because the topology of the overlay network is determined by the protocol.

In this work we concentrate on the routing performance and possibilities to reduce the signaling traffic of the Chord protocol. In a Chord network a ring structure is established upon which nodes and content are arranged in the same identifier space. Thus nodes as well as content become routable. To provide a scalable routing approach, concerning the number of participants, additional routing shortcuts through the ring structure are established by any node in the network. These shortcuts are called *fingers*. We propose a new scheme which provides Chord with additional fingers at no additional cost. We therefore call these fingers *freebie fingers*. Using these freebie fingers together with a symmetrical routing algorithm can reduce the average path length by 25%. Further related work can be found in S-Chord where a symmetrical routing algorithm is presented [Mesaros et al., 2003]. F-Chord proposes a routing scheme based on Fibonacci numbers [Cordasco et al., 2004]. Both papers try to improve the maximum and average number of hops for lookups.

The remainder of this work is organized as follows. In chapter 2 we begin with a short introduction to the basic Chord finger and routing algorithms. We continue by presenting our *freebie finger* concept followed by an analysis of its applicability and advantages. Chapter 5 concludes this paper with some discussion and further research interest.

2.   CHORD FINGERS

To provide scalable routing within the Chord ring each Chord node maintains connections to m nodes, called *fingers*, whereas $0...2^m$ is the identifier space for the unique IDs of the nodes. Each finger entry is updated periodically by the *fix_finger* procedure to avoid storing links to nodes that are no longer part of the Chord network. Content items stored in the Chord network are assigned and transferred to the nodes that succeed the IDs of the content items. Upon receiving a query for a certain id each node first checks whether it hosts the content or not. In the first case it answers the query directly. Otherwise, it forwards the query to the neighbor, with the largest ID in its *finger table* that does not exceed (using modulo function) the ID of the queried content.

In basic Chord a node's k^{th} finger points to the first node succeeding the node id by at least 2^{k-1} (mod 2^m). Fingers are initialized by running a *find_successor* query for the theoretical finger position $(n.id + 2^{k-1}) \bmod 2^m$, resulting in the first node succeeding it. Due to this routing and key assignment algorithm any content available in the network is found in at most m hops, with high probability.

Improved finger algorithms do not stick to such a completely determined finger selection but offer the possibility to chose fingers based on different criteria. In our point of view, the most promising idea is to select fingers on proximity criteria (*i.e.*, latencies) from a set of nodes next to the theoretical finger positions.

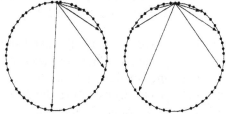

Figure 1. Sample finger distribution in a Chord ring (left image) and in S-Chord (right image) for the node on top of the ring.

The Chord finger geometry provides the nodes with a lot of routing information in close neighborhood and with little information about farther nodes (see Figure 1 left). As can be seen in the figure, the right part of the Chord ring (from the node in top's point of view) is well covered with fingers, whereas the left part is blank. Therefore, the idea of extending the *finger table* to the complete ring comes to mind. S-CHORD [Mesaros, 2003] for example proposes to keep the same number of fingers to be comparable in performance with Chord, but organizes the *finger table* in two approximately symmetric sides (Figure 1 right).

3. FREEBIE FINGERS

We propose extending the routing information each Chord node stores by a list of all nodes that have a finger table entry pointing to the node. This *freebie_finger_list* can be built-up by caching the originators of all *fix_finger* requests a node receives. The nodes in the resulting list are distributed counterclockwise in approximately the same way as the nodes in the finger table are distributed clockwise, i.e. more nodes in close neighborhood and only a few farther away. Figure 2 shows the finger distribution for a node in a sample Chord network (solid lines) and the finger table entries from other nodes that point to the node.

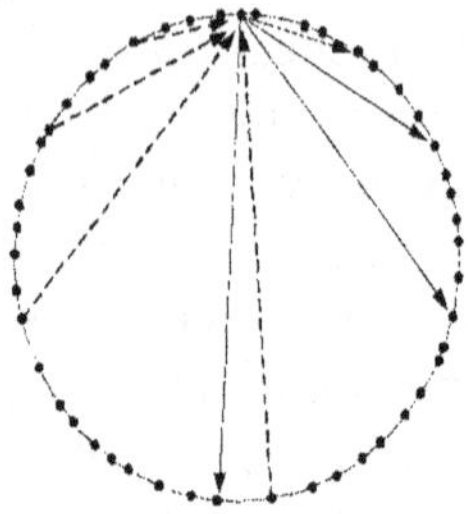

Figure 2. Sample finger distribution in a Chord ring (solid lines) and additional routing information from nodes that store a finger table entry pointing to the node (dashed lines).

Unlike S-Chord we do not have to reduce the number of fingers in the first half of the ring to be comparable to Chord in means of overhead traffic needed for updating the finger information, but can stick to m fingers and up to approximately m freebie fingers. Considering the fact that in a Chord network with N nodes each node knows only about $log_2(N)$ different fingers (Figure 3) [Binzenhöfer et al., 2004], a list with freebie fingers also consists of only about $log_2(N)$ entries (Figure 4). To avoid storing nodes in the *freebie_finger_list* that are no longer pointing to the node or even worse are no longer participating in the network, each entry is marked with a timestamp and is removed from the list if the entry has not been updated within a certain time interval, e.g. 1,5 * *fix_finger* period.

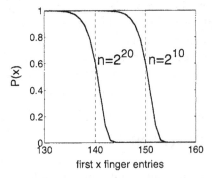

Figure 3. The distribution shows the probability P(x) of the first x finger entries being identical in a Chord network with 210 and 220 participating nodes.

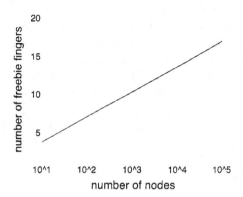

Figure 4. The chart shows the average number of freebie fingers for different network sizes as well as the 90% confidence interval.

Storing this additional routing information does not require any additional network traffic and hardly any processing power and storage. Additionally, using the freebie fingers is useful for routing queries through the network especially if symmetrical routing as proposed in S-Chord is applied. In the following chapter we describe how to use the freebie fingers to provide faster and more efficient routing through the network.

4. USING FREEBIE FINGERS

Since the basic Chord *find_successor* algorithm already searches through the finger table for the closest finger preceding the queried id, beginning with the most distant finger, extending the algorithm for using the freebie fingers is very simple. Both, expanding the existing finger table with the freebie fingers or modifying the algorithm so that it searches through both lists, is possible. In the first case you have to pay attention that *fix_fingers* still only updates the first m fingers.

Even faster routing can be achieved by using symmetrical routing that is naturally predestined for a symmetrical finger concept. As a symmetrical routing algorithm is described in detail in [Mesaros, 2003], we try to focus on analyzing the benefits such an algorithm provides.

Doubling the number of fingers (by using the freebie fingers) as well as using symmetric routing algorithms reduces the average number of hops needed for querying ids. Figure 5 shows the correlation between the number of nodes participating in a Chord network (N) and the resulting average path length (number of hops) for the three different mentioned routing algorithms basic Chord, S-Chord and Chord using Freebie Fingers. To simplify matters we assume a fully populated network, i.e. the size of the ID space equals the network's size. For the basic Chord algorithm the maximum number of hops is limited to $log_2(N)$ in an error-free environment and the average path length is $\frac{1}{2}\ log_2(N)$ hops. Using S-Chord already reduces both maximum and average path length by about 25% and 10% respectively. An additional gain of about 20% with respect to average path lengths can be achieved by additionally using our *freebie finger* concept. That is an improvement of 25% compared to basic Chord fingers. The maximum path length using freebie fingers is $\frac{1}{4}\ log_2(N)$.

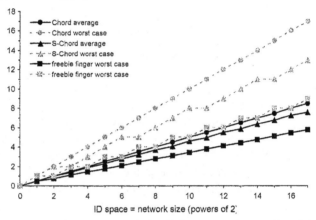

Figure 5. Correlation between the network size (fully populated network) and the resulting average path length (number of hops).

The authors of SChord claim that "the denser the network, the longer the lookup path length", and therefore, they compare only fully populated networks. We argue that this is not true and that the lookup path is longer in poorly populated networks than in fully populated networks with the same number of participating nodes. The maximum number of required hops may be more than Chord's $log(N)$ hops in networks with an ID space greater than the network size. Anyway, most lookups could be resolved within less than $log(N)$ hops.

Figure 6 shows the results from our simulations for Chord, S-Chord and our freebie finger approach. We ran all simulations in Matlab, assuming a 128bit ID space and up to 65.536 nodes participating in the network. For each network size and each Chord variant we ran 100.000 simulations. We plotted the average lookup path length and the 99%-quantile for each variant. Compared to a fully populated network (Figure 5), we come to the following conclusions: Both average and maximum path lengths in basic Chord increase, because the IDs are not evenly distributed in the ID space. S-Chord and our freebie fingers improve their average path length compared to a fully populated network, as they can route in both directions, but the maximum path lengths increase, too. Still, more than 99% of all lookups can be answered in less than *log(N)* hops. Regarding average values, S-Chord achieves 20% shorter lookup paths compared to Chord, and our freebie finger approach can reduce lookup times by about 40%.

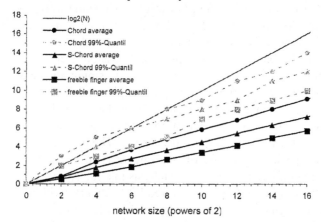

Figure 6. Correlation between the network size (poorly populated network, 128 bit ID space) and the resulting average path length (number of hops).

Reducing the average hop count similarly reduces the required traffic for lookups. It also results in shorter average query times for two reasons. First, in the ideal case where all finger entries are up-to-date and no absent nodes disturb the lookup path, the lookup time is only reduced by the transmission time the additional hops would have required. Second and more importantly, the probability of running into timeouts due to wrong finger entries that point to absent nodes is reduced with every avoided hop. As timer values are set to clearly higher values than the average transmission time, the average lookup time can be reduced clearly if fewer timeouts occur.

Another advantage of holding more fingers is a higher flexibility in choosing the next hop [Gummadi et al., 2003]. Especially under high churn rates, *i.e.* nodes joining and leaving the network frequently and therefore fingers pointing to absent nodes with high probability having more alternatives may be very valuable.

5. CONCLUSION

Unstructured P2P networks try to resolve their lookups by flooding the network, but it is not guaranteed that the queried content can be found. Due to TTL counters in the query messages queries can only be resolved in close neighborhood. That is why content has to be replicated evenly over the network to achieve a high query hit rate. The bigger the network, the more often content has to be replicated. The main advantage is that unstructured P2P networks require no higher signaling traffic in scenarios with high churn rates. Structured P2P networks on the other hand can always tell whether a certain object is available or not, but a lot of signaling traffic is required to keep the network structure stable. This is why high churn rates lead to an increase of overhead traffic in structured P2P networks.

Using our freebie finger concept is one possible step towards reducing signaling traffic and lookup latencies. In our simulation and testbed we additionally update our finger tables by exploiting existing traffic in the network. Each time a packet from a node in the finger list is received we know that this node is still participating in the network and we can skip this finger entry in the next *fix_finger()* invocation. The more traffic per node the more often a packet from one of our fingers is received. Concerning this matter we are going to present some analysis in a future paper.

In our point of view, future structured P2P networks will be applicable in scenarios with high churn rates, e.g. ad hoc and file-sharing applications.

6.   REFERENCES

Binzenhöfer, A., Staehle, D., and Henjes, R. (2004)."On the Stability of Chord-based P2P Systems," University of Würzburg 347, Nov 2004.
BitTorrent (2004). Incentives to Build Robustness in BitTorrent, bitconjurer.org/BitTorrent/bittorrentecon.pdf, 2004
Cordasco, G., Gargano, L., Hammar, M., Negro, A., and Scarano, V. (2004). "F-Chord: Improved Uniform Routing on Chord," presented at Structural Information and Communication Complexity: 11th International Colloquium, SIROCCO 2004.
Gnutella (2002) Gnutella 0.6 RFC, http://rfc-gnutella.sourceforge.net/draft.txt, 2002
Gummadi, K. et al. (2003). "The Impact of DHT Routing Geometry on Resilience and Proximity," presented at ACM SIGCOMM 2003.
Kazaa (2003) Kazaa homepage, http://www.kazaa.com/us/index.htm
Mesaros, V.A., Carton, B., and Roy P.V. (2003). "S-Chord: Using Symmetry to Improve Lookup Efficiency in Chord," presented at 2003 International Conference on Parallel and Distributed Processing Techniques and Applications (PDPTA'03).
Ratnasamy, S., Francis, P., Handley, M., Karp, R., and Shenker, S., (2001). "A Scalable Content-Addressable Network," presented at ACM SIGCOMM Conference.
Schollmeier, R. and Dumanois, A. (2003)."Peer-to-Peer Traffic Characteristics" UNICE2003
Skype (2004) homepage, http://www.skype.com/. 2004
Stoica, I., Morris, R. , Karger, D., Kaashoek, M. and Balakrishnan, H. (2001). "Chord: A Scalable Peer-to-Peer Lookup Service for Internet Applications," presented at ACM SIG-COMM Conference.

DNS: A STATISTICAL ANALYSIS OF NAME SERVER TRAFFIC AT LOCAL NETWORK-TO-INTERNET CONNECTIONS

Chris Brandhorst[1] and Aiko Pras[2]

[1]*Faculty of Electrical Engineering, Mathematics and Computer Science, University of Twente, Enschede, 7522 NK, The Netherlands*
c.j.brandhorst@cs.utwente.nl
[2]*Faculty of Electrical Engineering, Mathematics and Computer Science, University of Twente, Enschede, P.O. BOX 217, 7500 AE Enschede, The Netherlands*
pras@cs.utwente.nl

Abstract: This paper puts forward a purely statistical analysis of name server traffic captured at four different locations: two links to residential networks, and two to the Dutch academic and research institute. Analysis of the system can give insight in the use and performance of the protocol, which is helpful for future improvement. Multiple analyses can show the development of the performance over time and help create quality models. The analysis shows that a little more than 12% of all queries are not answered upon. Three quarters of the lookups are successful: they give the client the correct IP address mapping for the requested hostname. 90% is answered within 275 ms, with an average of 152 ms. In 9% of all cases, clients ask for a hostname which does not exist. At one of the locations, a client is discovered which sends queries to two DNS servers at a remarkable rate: one each 11 to 22 ms.

Keywords: DNS, Internet, measurement, performance

1.INTRODUCTION

The Domain Name System is one of the most vital protocols of the modern Internet. This protocol is responsible for translating Internet addresses (e.g. www.server.com) to network locations; also called IP addresses (e.g. 125.114.163.15). This translation occurs at DNS servers to which a client must send its queries, asking for the IP address of a specific Internet address. The DNS is vital, because virtually all applications that connect to the Internet (e.g. mail programs, web browsers and FTP utilities) make use of the protocol for their operation. Therefore, it is necessary that the system must be operable virtually 100% and have a high degree of efficiency, to provide the clients with low response times to there queries.

Analysis of the DNS traffic will give insight in the use of the protocol and may assist in improving it in the future or designing a new version. Multiple analyses can show the development of the use of the protocol over time and "studies involving certain DNS performance measures would be greatly strengthened by data from many locations"[Liston et al., 2002]. This, in turn, can address performance issues. Furthermore, when these statistics are known, quality models can be created for evaluating new protocols, algorithms and architectures [ACM, 2004].

1.1   Related Work

Past work is available on this subject. The most quoted of them was done by [Danzig et al., 1992]. Others are [Brownlee et al., 2001], [Jung et al., 2002] and [Liston et al., 2002]. This work will differ from the above in three aspects.

The first is that it will take measurements from at least four local network-to-Internet connections, all with a varying number of users, types of users and bandwidth. Jung et al. use data gathered at just two networks, both of which belong to research institutes and Liston et al. gather their data at 75 client locations, which is far less than the number of clients connected to the networks used in this study.

The second difference is the topographical network location at which the measurements have taken place. The data used for this research was captured at the switches which connect the local networks to the Internet. Danzig et al. and Brownlee et al. have concentrated on measurements at a DNS root server, where the first also takes three domain servers into account. Liston et al. have taken a different approach by measuring the DNS performance at client computers. One can say that this research can be placed closer to Liston's, because of the proximity of the clients to the switch.

Thirdly, only Jung et al. include (limited) basic trace statistics in their research. In this research an extensive breakdown of all DNS responses will be given.

1.2   Research Questions

There are a number of statistics that can be extracted from DNS traffic data. This analysis will include a breakdown of DNS queries into those that: are erroneous, are refused, ask for non-existing domains, are omitted because of a server failure, are not replied to at all, are of a type which is not implemented by the receiving DNS server and those that are answered normally. Besides this, information can be gathered about the delay between the sending and receiving of DNS queries, also called *latency*, how many queries are to be processed recursively and which fraction of the total traffic can be accounted for by the DNS.

This results in the following research questions, by which the performance of the DNS, as perceived by the client, can be analyzed:

1. What is the fraction of total traffic that can be accounted for by the DNS, measured in packets as well as bytes?
2. What fraction of the received DNS queries is to be processed recursively by the DNS servers?
3. Given a collection of DNS queries, which fractions of these queries are answered normally and which fraction results in some kind of error? We will determine the fractions of the following error conditions: queries that 1) are erroneous, 2) are refused by the DNS servers, 3) ask for non-existing domains, 4) are omitted because of a server failure, 5) are not replied to at all, and 6) are of a type which is not implemented by the receiving DNS servers.
4. What is the average delay between the time that the query is sent and the answer is received? (the measured delay is the time measured at the place in the network where the DNS data is collected, not the latency the client observes)
5. What are the differences between these results and prior research on DNS traffic, mostly focused on that of [Jung et al., 2002]?

In order to answer the above research questions, the repository set up by the M2C-project (Measuring, Modeling and Cost Allocation) at the University of Twente will be used [M2C]. This collection includes data captured at four locations, at different times. The locations include Ethernet links which connect 1) a residential network of a university to the core network of this university, 2) a research institute to the Dutch academic and research network, 3) a large college to that same research network and 4) a couple of hundred ADSL customers, mostly student dorms to an aggregated uplink of an ADSL access network.

In the following chapter a general overview of the Domain Name System is given. After this, the method of research is laid out in chapter three and in chapter four the results will be presented out of which conclusions will be drawn in the final chapter.

2.   THE DOMAIN NAME SYSTEM

The Domain Name System is a standard and is defined in RFCs 1034 [Mockapetris, 2004] and 1035 [Mockapetris, 2004]. Here, only an overview of the most important basic functionality is given.

The Internet's DNS function is to translate human-readable hostnames (e.g. www.server.com) to IP addresses (e.g. 125.114.163.15), which are used by network-hardware to identify client computers. This translation can be done for all kinds of servers, from web- and mail- to FTP-servers and is employed by the corresponding application-layer protocols (HTTP, POP/SMTP and FTP respectively), which are in turn used by computer applications. The application will ask the DNS for the IP address of the host of which the client entered the hostname by sending a DNS *query* onto the network. After a delay, the client will receive a *response* stating the hostname or possibly an error message.

The DNS can be used on top of both the UDP and TCP protocol.

2.1   Name Servers

To achieve its functionality, the DNS consists of a large number of *name servers* which are scattered around the world and ordered hierarchical. There is not one server that has *DNS records* for *all* hostname to IP-mappings for the Internet. Instead, a certain DNS server has records for a specific domain (like .nl or utwente.nl) or local network. Besides this, it can route DNS queries for mappings that that server does not contain to a DNS server which does. Therefore, there are two kinds of name servers [Jung et al., 2002]:

- **Root name servers.** If the name server in the local network of the client does not have a mapping for the requested hostname, the local name server sends a query to one of the 13 root name servers [root-servers, 2004]. These servers contain DNS records of *authoritative name servers*, one of which is returned to the local name server.
- **Authoritative name servers.** A name server is authoritative for a certain host or domain if it contains DNS records for that host or domain or has a record for another DNS server that does has these records. This layering of DNS servers can be repeated more than once.

2.2   Recursive Queries

An example of a *recursive query* is shown in Figure 1. The query and its response together often are called a *lookup*. The host 192.168.1.203 here requests the IP address of www.utwente.nl. It sends this query to its local name server, 192.168.1.1. The local server does not have the correct mapping, so it sends a query to the root server (b.root-servers.net). This root server knows the address of the authoritative name server for the.nl *top-level-domain* (ns.domain-registry.nl), which is returned to the local name server. This server in turn, when asked by the local name server, returns the address of the authoritative name server for the utwente.nl domain (ns1.utwente.nl). Finally, after querying this server, the IP-address of www.utwente.nl is obtained and returned to the client. This query is called recursive, because the client only sends one query and receives one answer. The local name server handles all the other queries in favor of the client. When a query is *iterative*, it means that the name server to which the query is sent will always send a response to the requesting host instead of to an other name server, whether it does have a DNS record for the requested hostname (it will send the requested IP address) or it does not (it will send the IP address of an authoritative name server). Not all name servers support recursive querying. Note that the local name server in the example only sends iterative queries.

2.3   Response Types

When a query is answered by a name server, this response is of one of the following types [Mockapetris, 2004]:

- **OK**. Everything went correctly and embedded in this response packet is the IP address belonging to the hostname the requesting host supplied.
- **Format error**. The name server was unable to interpret the query.
- **Server failure**. The name server was unable to process this query due to a problem with the name server.
- **No such name**. The domain name referenced in the query does not exist.
- **Not implemented**. The name server does not support the requested kind of query.
- **Refused**. The name server refuses to perform the specified operation for policy reasons. For example, a name server may not wish to provide the information to the particular requester, or a name server may not wish to perform a particular operation for particular data.

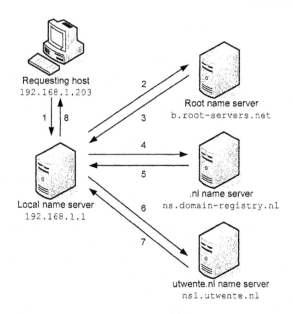

Figure 1. An example of a recursive query [Wanrooij, 2005].

2.4   Latency

The time between the sending of a DNS query and the receiving of a response is called the *latency* of that query. The latency can vary between milliseconds and tens of seconds [Kurose and Ross, 2003].

3.   RESEARCH METHODOLOGY

3.1   Used Data

In order to analyze the DNS traffic, this study makes use of the Internet data repository set up by the M2C project (*Measuring, Modeling and Cost Allocation*) [M2C, 2004]. This repository consists of 555 traces (in December 2004), each of which contains 15 minutes of packet data. The measurements were taken at four different locations, all in the Netherlands, on different days and times [M2C, 2004].

"On location #1 the 300 Mbit/s (a trunk of 3 x 100 Mbit/s) Ethernet link has been measured, which connects a residential network of a university to the core network of this university. On the residential network, about 2000 students are connected, each having a 100 Mbit/s Ethernet access link. The residential network itself consists of 100 and 300 Mbit/s links to the various switches, depending on the aggregation level. The measured link has an average load of about 60%. Measurements have taken place in July 2002" and are spread over 15 traces.

1. "On location #2, the 1 Gbit/s Ethernet link connecting a research institute to the Dutch academic and research network has been measured. There are about 200 researchers and support staff working at this institute. They all have a 100 Mbit/s access link, and the core network of the institute consists of 1 Gbit/s links. The measured link is only mildly loaded, usually around 1%. The measurements are from May to August 2003" and are spread over 183 traces.

2. "Location #3 is a large college. Their 1 Gbit/s link (i.e., the link that has been measured) to the Dutch academic and research network carries traffic for over 1000 students and staff concurrently, during busy hours. The access link speed on this network is, in general, 100 Mbit/s. The average load on the 1 Gbit/s link usually is around 10-15%. These measurements have been done from September - December 2003" and are spread over 255 traces.

3. "On location #4, the 1 Gbit/s aggregated uplink of an ADSL access network has been monitored. A couple of hundred ADSL customers, mostly student dorms, are connected to this access network. Access link speeds vary from 256 kbit/s (down and up) to 8 Mbit/s (down) and 1 Mbit/s (up). The average load on the aggregated uplink is around 150 Mbit/s. These measurements are from February - July 2004" and are spread over 102 traces.

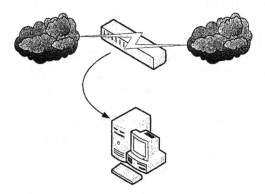

Figure 2. The setup for the collection of the packet data [Van de Meent, 2003].

3.2   Method of Collection

For every location, the method of collection was identical. "The measurements are performed by capturing the headers of all packets that are transmitted over the (Ethernet) 'uplink' of an access network to the Internet." [Van de Meent, 2003], see also Figure 2. To the switch (can also be a router), a measurement PC was connected. To capture the 15 minutes of packets into binary files, the utility *tcpdump* [TCPDUMP, 2004] was used. These traces were anonymized, compressed and published on the Internet [M2C, 2004][Van de Meent, 2003].

The *anonymization* is done for privacy reasons, which means 1) that only the packet headers are captured, so it is unknown *what* data is sent from the network to the Internet and 2) that the source and destination IP addresses of the packets are scrambled *consequently*, so that is unknown from and to which host the packets are sent. But within a trace, a single IP address is each time scrambled to the same anonymized IP address and two IP addresses that are within the same network, will have anonymized counterparts that also can be placed within the same network. For a more detailed explanation of this method, see [Van de Meent, 2003].

In section II it was said that the DNS protocol can be used on top of both TCP and UDP, but a few samples from each location revealed zero DNS packets that made use of the TCP protocol. Therefore it is assumed in this paper that the use of this protocol for the Internet is negligible.

3.3   Method of Analysis

For the analysis of the data, a self-built Java application called *ReadDump* was developed. This application opens a packet-trace file and analyses the packets within to retrieve the data necessary to answer the above research questions. When it is done, it writes a report to a log file. Because there are 555 traces, another program was developed to send the data files to the Java so it could analyze all data autonomously. *Runner* was written in VB.NET and for each packet trace file, it would decompress it and send it to ReadDump for processing.

4.   RESULTS

In Table 1 and 2, the statistical results of the analysis are presented.

4.1   Location #1: Server Failures

What immediately came to attention is the enormous amount of returned server failures at location #1 (see Table 1). 60.99% of all sent queries get this response. The first thought was that a broken DNS server was the cause of these high amounts of server failures. After further research [Van de Meent, 2004], it seemed that not a DNS server but (most probably) one single client was the cause. This will be discussed further in section 4.1. Because this abnormal behavior was observed in 7 of the 15 traces at location #1, only the remaining 8 traces were used to calculate new statistics which are laid out in Table 2. Important to note here is that retransmissions of DNS queries are taken into account as a 'new' query. The retransmissions cannot be measured because of the anonymized nature of the repository; it cannot be shown when a query is retransmitted, because of the lack of the real data of the packets.

Table 1. Trace statistics*

	Location #1		All	
Date	2002/05/23 – 06/26			
Total Gigabytes	263.3		2,487.5	
DNS Megabytes (1)	139.8	(0.05%)	1,220.3	(0.05%)
Total packets	429,846,054		4,085,445,051	
DNS packets (2)	1,556,032	(0.36%)	10,450,329	(0.26%)
Queries (3)	780,538	(50.16%)	5,527,878	(52.90%)
Recursive (4)	670,425	(85.89%)	1,011,762	(18.30%)
Iterative (4)	110,113	(14.11%)	4,516,116	(81.70%)
Unanswered (4)	5,044	(0.65%)	605,427	(10.95%)
OK (4)	233,965	(29.97%)	3,715,741	(67.22%)
Format error (4)	667	(0.09%)	167,726	(3.03%)
Server failure (4)	476,055	(60.99%)	536,729	(9.71%)
No such name (4)	64,171	(8.22%)	450,601	(8.15%)
Not implemented (4)	274	(0.04%)	4,145	(0.07%)
Refused (4)	362	(0.05%)	47,509	(0.86%)
Average latency (ms)	687, $\sigma = 364$		156, $\sigma = 206$	

* Trace statistics including 7 traces in which a client with abnormal behavior is detected. Percentages are with respect to: (1) Total bytes; (2) Total # of packets; (3) # of DNS packets; (4) # of Queries.

Table 2. Corrected trace statistics*

	Location #1	Location 2	Location 3	Location 4	All
Date	2002/05/23 – 06/26	2003/05/13 – 08/28	2003/09/02 – 11/25	2004/02/04 – 05/07	
Total Gigabytes	130.7	107.9	885.6	1,230.7	2,354.9
DNS Megabytes (1)	29.8 (0.02%)	285.4 (0.26%)	719.7 (0.08%)	75.4 (0.01%)	1,110.2 (0.05%)
Total packets	220,314,110	167,772,874	1,346,774,765	2,141,051,358	3,875,913,107
DNS packets (2)	228,883 (0.10%)	2,365,875 (1.41%)	5,885,995 (0.44%)	642,427 (0.03%)	9,123,180 (0.24%)
Queries (3)	115,679 (50.54%)	1,280,706 (54.13%)	3,130,427 (53.18%)	336,207 (52.33%)	4,863,019 (53.30%)
Recursive (4)	112,825 (97.53%)	11,011 (0.86%)	149,367 (4.77%)	180,959 (53.82%)	454,162 (9.34%)
Iterative (4)	2,854 (2.47%)	1,269,695 (99.14%)	2,981,060 (95.23%)	155,248 (46.18%)	4,408,857 (90.66%)
Unanswered (4)	2,475 (2.14%)	195,537 (15.27%)	374,859 (11.97%)	29,987 (8.92%)	602,858 (12.40%)
OK (4)	72,308 (62.51%)	868,755 (67.83%)	2,404,557 (76.81%)	208,464 (62.00%)	3,554,084 (73.08%)
Format error (4)	291 (0.25%)	58,050 (4.53%)	90,234 (2.88%)	18,775 (5.58%)	167,350 (3.44%)
Server error (4)	1,761 (1.52%)	28,619 (2.23%)	28,181 (0.90%)	3,874 (1.15%)	62,435 (1.28%)
No such name (4)	38,534 (33.31%)	127,214 (9.93%)	225,566 (7.21%)	33,650 (10.01%)	424,964 (8.74%)
Not implemented (4)	118 (0.10%)	75 (0.01%)	2,348 (0.08%)	1,448 (0.43%)	3,989 (0.08%)
Refused (4)	192 (0.17%)	2,456 (0.19%)	4,682 (0.15%)	40,009 (11.90%)	47,339 (0.97%)
Average latency (ms)	919, σ = 399	114, σ = 64	85, σ = 38	332, σ = 344	152, σ = 205

*Corrected trace statistics. Percentages are with respect to: (1) Total bytes; (2) Total # of packets; (3) # of DNS packets; (4) # of Queries.

4.2 Statistics

Several years have passed between the measurements which are used for this research and the results of the mentioned previous work, therefore adaptations to the DNS protocol may have been made too improve the performance. From the existing DNS RFCs, however, it followed that no adaptations were made in these years. The results can thus be properly compared.

4.2.1 DNS Fraction of Total Traffic

The percentage of total bytes which are DNS traffic varies little; between 0.01% and 0.26%, on average 0.05%. A little more variation is observed for the percentage of total packets which are DNS packets; between 0.03% and 1.41%, on average 0.23%. The data shows that there are two locations which in both cases have (by far) the least percentage of DNS traffic: locations #1 and #4.

4.2.2 Recursive or Iterative

Whether the queries are sent recursive, varies a great deal; between 0.86% and 97.53%. Locations #1 and #4 have high values for recursive queries, #2 and #3 show many iterative queries. This difference most probably comes from the fact that at locations #2 and #3, a DNS server that can receive recursive queries is present *inside* the local network. It can be assumed that the clients of those networks use those recursive DNS servers as a standard. This implies that virtually all DNS queries that are directed outside the local networks (the queries that are observed) will be iterative, because that traffic travels from the local DNS servers to a root server (see section II.B).

In contrast, at locations #1 and #4, the local DNS servers are placed *outside* the network. If we assume the same as for locations #2 and #3, this implies that *all* queries will be directed out of the network and measured, and because of the standard setup of the clients, these queries will be recursive. Still, at location #4, the amount of recursive and iterative queries is almost equal. The reason for this may be a privately setup DNS server inside the network.

Jung reports similar variation in the number of recursive or iterative queries in the observed networks [Jung et al., 2002].

4.2.3   Answering rates

All locations show that a little more than 50% of all DNS packets consist of queries, implying that there are few queries that are not answered. Location #2 tops with 15.27% of all queries not being answered, location #1 has the least; 2.14%. On average this is 12.40%. Compared to the results of Jung et al., these DNSs perform far better; Jung reported 20.1-23.5% unanswered [Jung et al. 2002].

4.2.4   Return types

Of the queries that *were* answered, on average 73.08% were queries for hostname mappings that could be correctly retrieved by the DNS server(s). Jung et al. found similar values (twice 64% for two locations) and one far worse (36% for the third location). As can be classified as logical, the percentage of no such name responses is not negligible. On average 8.74% of all requests are for hostnames that doesn't exist. Location #1 tops here with 33.31%. Jung also reports a large variation (10% to 42%)[5]. Their explanation lies in "inverse lookups for IP addresses with no inverse mappings" and "particular invalid names such as loopback, and [...] records that point to names that do not exist." Because of the anonymized nature of the traces, it cannot be confirmed that the same causes for these rates are applicable here.

Not implemented and refused are returned rarely, with an exception at location #4, which has a high refused rate of 11.90%. The reason for this cannot be uncovered. Format error is returned a little more, with tops of 4.53% and 5.58%. The amount of server failure responses also is quite low.

4.2.5   Latency

The observed latency times are mostly low; on average 152 ms. Location #1 tops with 919 ms. Compared to some prior studies, this is far better. Wills and Shang [as quoted [Liston, 2002]] "report lookup times exceeding 2.0 seconds for as many as 29% of lookups to random servers, and Cohen and Kaplan report lookup times exceeding 3.0 seconds for as many as 10% of lookups." Jung reports that 90% of all lookups on the MIT network had a latency of 447 ms in January 2000 and 11 months later, this number was about 2.5 times greater [Jung et al. 2002]. In our study merely 7 traces had an average latency of over 1 second and only one over than 2 seconds. Also, 90% of the traces have an average latency of 275 ms or less. 32% of all traces time between 75 and 100 ms. See Figure 3.

It can be seen that at locations #1 and #4, the average latency is far greater compared to the other locations. If the assumptions made in 4.2.2 are correct, this difference can be addressed to the fact that the fraction of observed DNS recursive queries at locations #1 and #4 is far greater. A client that sends a recursive query gets a response only after all iterative queries that are needed to resolve the client's query are resolved by the recursive DNS server. So the total latency for a recursive query is higher than for an iterative query. This high latency can be seen at location #1 and (to a lesser degree, because of the higher fraction of iterative queries) at location #4, where the recursive queries from the clients to the DNS servers are observed. This in contrast to locations #2 and #3, where the observed queries are (virtually all) the iterative queries sent from the local DNS servers to the root servers.

The higher standard deviation of the latency at locations #1 and #4 can be explained by noting that when sending a recursive query, a number of iterative queries are performed by the receiving DNS server. In the case of an iterative query, only one query is performed. Thus, the more iterative queries are performed which all have a deviation from the average, the higher the total standard deviation will be.

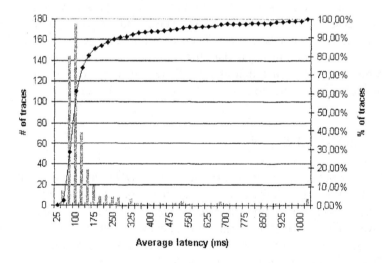

Figure 3. Cumulative latency distribution.

4.3   Client with abnormal DNS behavior

It seemed that virtually 100% of the server failure responses within the 7 discarded location #1 packets (see section IV.A) were directed to one single client. This cannot be said with full certainty, because in every trace the IP addresses were scrambled differently, but it is very reasonable to assume this.

This client was in each trace receiving DNS server failures from two different name servers. This receiving furthermore occurred at an exceptionally high rate: one received packet per 22 to 11 ms. This rate of reception implies that the client should also have approximately the same rate of sending DNS queries.

So all 'evidence' points to a client that was either deliberately sending all these queries to the name server for some reason, or who's computer was misconfigured, which caused the continuing sending of queries. It was revealed that the name servers on the university network are specifically configured to answer queries for certain zones only when these queries come from specific clients [Van de Meent, 2004]. If any other client asks for an IP from one of these zones, a server failure is returned. This complies to a certain extent with RFC 2308 [Andrews, 2004], which declares that server failures fall in two classes, one of which states that "This may be where it (the name server, red.) has been listed as a server, but not configured to be a server for the zone, or where it has been configured to be a server for the zone, but cannot obtain the zone data for some reason." This 'some reason', most probably, is the fact that the DNS servers may not return the IP mappings for certain zones to any clients but the specified ones.

5.   CONCLUSION

This paper put forward a statistical analysis of DNS data captured at four different locations: two links to residential networks, and two to the Dutch academic and research institute. The performance of the DNS, as seen by the client, was analyzed by measuring the latency and a breakdown of the various response types of the protocol. The networks analyzed here show a better DNS performance than prior research.

The percentage of queries that never receives a response is far lower than the 20+% that [Jung et al., 2002] measured. This study reports an average of a little more than 12%, which can be called acceptable, because of the non-retransmissive nature of the UDP protocol.

Three quarters of all queries are responded to with a correct IP mapping with on average a latency of 152 ms. 90% of these lookups take 275 ms or less, which is at least twice as fast as earlier research showed.

Clients ask in 9% of all cases for an IP address for a hostname that does not exist. The amount of queries that are responded to by one of the other return types is very small. Only the amount of format errors is names worthy: a little less than 3.5%. This can be accounted to bugs in client software and transmission errors.

Further research is suggested on DNS data that is not anonymized, so the reasons for the observed format and no such name errors can be analyzed. Location #4 may look into their network in order to find the reason for the large amount of refused responses.

The strange behavior of the client observed in the traces of location #1 could be worth to investigate further. Do these actions occur more often and do they bring down the performance of the DNS, or more broad, of the entire network link? Besides this, one might think of changing the settings of the DNS servers in question, so that it responds with a refused message in these situations, which is more logical than a server error response.

ACKNOWLEDGEMENT

We would like to thank Remco van de Meent for pointing us to and making available the M2C repository and collecting the data. We also thank Remco van de Meent for his extra information on the DNS system at location #1. Furthermore, thanks go out to the reviewers for useful comments on the draft version of the paper.

REFERENCES

ACM SIGCOMM, (2004). Call for papers: Measuring the Internet's Vital Statistics, http://www.acm.org/sigs/sigcomm/ccr/ivs/IVS-CFP.pdf, available: September 5, 2004

Andrews, M. (2004). Negative Caching of DNS Queries (NCACHE), RFC 2308, available at: http://www.rfc-editor.org/rfc.html, November 28, 2004

Brownlee, N., Claffy, K., Nemeth, E., (2001).DNS measurements at a root server, Global Internet 2001, November 2001

Danzig, P.B., Obraczka, K., Kumar, A., (1992).An analysis of wide-area name server traffic: a study of the Internet Domain Name System, ACM SIGCOMM Computer Communication Review, Conference proceedings on Communications architectures & protocols, Volume 22 Issue 4, October 1992, Pages 281-292

Jung, J., Sit, E., Balakrishnan, H., Robert Morris (2002). DNS Performance and the Effectiveness of Caching, IEEE/ACM Transactions on Networking, Volume 10, No. 5, October 2002, Pages 589-603

Kurose, J.F., Ross, K.W. (2003). Computer Networking: A Top-Down Approach Featuring the Internet, Addison-Wesley, 2003

Liston, R., Srinivasan, S., Zegura, E., (2002). Diversity in DNS performance measures, Proceedings of the second ACM SIGCOMM Workshop on Internet measurement, November 2002, Pages 19-31

M2C Measurement Data Repository (2004). http://m2c-a.cs.utwente.nl/repository/, updated: unknown, available: September 22, 2004

M2C: Measuring, Modeling and Cost Allocation for Quality of Service, (2004). http://arch.cs.utwente.nl/projects/m2c/, updated: March 2, 2004, available: September 22, 2004

Mockapetris, P.V. (2004). Domain names - concepts and facilities, RFC 1034, available at: http://www.rfc-editor.org/rfc.html, November 18, 2004

Mockapetris, P.V. (2004). Domain names - implementation and specification, RFC 1035, available at: http://www.rfc-editor.org/rfc.html, November 18, 2004

Root-servers.org (2004). Root Server Technical Operations Assn, available at: http://www.root-servers.org, November 18, 2004

TCPDUMP public repository (2004). http://www.tcpdump.org/, updated: June 6, 2004

Van de Meent, R. (2003). M2C Measurement Data Repository, University of Twente, Enschede, The Netherlands, December 22, 2003

Van de Meent, R. (2004). University of Twente, email communication during October and November 2004

Wanrooij, W. van (2005). DNS zones revisited, Proceedings of the 11th Open European Summer School, July, 2005, Pages 84-92

AN API FOR IPV6 MULTIHOMING

Isaías Martínez-Yelmo
Alberto García-Martínez
Marcelo Bagnulo Braun
{ lmyelmo,alberto,marcelo } @it.uc3m.es
Departamento de Telemática
Universidad Carlos III de Madrid
Av. Universidad 30. 28911 Leganés
Madrid (Spain)

Abstract   This paper proposes an API for Multihoming in IPv6. This API is based on the *Hash Based Addresses* and *Cryptographically Generated Addresses* approaches, which are being developed by the IETF multi6 Working Group. The support of Multihoming implies several actions such as failure detection procedures, reachability tests, re-homing procedures and exchange of locators. Applications can benefit from transparent access to Multihoming services only if per host Multihoming parameters are defined. However, more benefits could be obtained by applications if they will be able to configure these parameters. The proposed Multihoming API provides different functions to applications which can modify some parameters and invoke some functions related with the Multihoming Layer.

Keywords: API, Multihoming, IPv6

1.   Introduction

Networked applications are fundamental tools in our daily lives. So, high available connections and resiliency [Yin and Twist, 2003] are usually required by enterprises and small-users. Providing this high availability is a difficult task because of the fact that network failures can always happen; thus, redundancy techniques such as Multihoming are needed. In IPv4, Multihoming is based on announcing all the prefixes of a site through all the providers using the Border Gateway Protocol (BGP). Therefore, if a connection fails, a new path could be found with another provider. Small-users never use BGP in their equipments because of the scalability problems of the protocol [Huston, 2001] and its complexity. So, Multihoming cannot be supported for small-users unless NAT-based boxes are used [Guo et al., 2004], with all the problems that

NATs present such as need for Application Level Gateways, disruption of end-to-end security, etc.

Some goals for Multihoming in IPv6 have been defined in [Abley et al., 2003], these goals are fault tolerance, load sharing, transport layer survivability and enhanced scalability for small-users. One of the proposed solutions combines Hash Based Addresses (HBA) [Bagnulo, 2004] and Cryptographically Generated Addresses(CGA) [Aura, 2004].

This paper proposes a Multihoming API for the approach based on HBA and CGA. It is structured as follows. In section 2, the Multihoming solution which is being developed actually by the IETF multi6 Working Group is presented. In section 3 a Multihoming API is described; the proposed API allows an ordered access to the Multihoming functionalities shown in the previous section. Future work is considered in section 4. Finally, conclusions about the presented work are exposed.

2.   Multihoming in IPv6

Several roles are played by IPv4 addresses and IPv6 addresses:

- *Identifier:* IP addresses are passed to upper layers to be used as identifiers for the local and remote end points of a communication.

- *Locator:* IP addresses reflect the topological location of a host in the Internet

- *Forwarding Label:* Routers forward packets taking into account their destination IP address.

Due to this overload of roles, when a communication path suffers a failure, it is impossible to change the locator of the communication, even if this communication could be continued using another locator, because the identifier would also change and the Transport Level could not identify new packets as belonging to the same flow [Nordmark, 2004].

The proposal of the IETF multi6 Working Group is based on a new Multihoming Layer placed between the IP routing sub-layer and the IP end-point sublayer [Nordmark and Bagnulo, 2005]. This layer manages a set of locators corresponding to a given identifier.

A goal started by RFC 3582 [Abley et al., 2003] is to avoid introducing new vulnerabilities in the deployment of Multihoming. The requirement of mapping different locators for a single identifier enables new vulnerabilities like flooding and hijacking attacks [Nordmark and Li, 2005]. Therefore, it is necessary to prevent these attacks, so the solution should provide a secure mapping between identifiers and locators. The solution based on HBA and CGA provides this secure mapping; either there is a restriction in the locators to use (HBA approach), or there is a secure way of exchanging new locators based on signatures(CGA approach). Thus, it can be assured that the locators are associated with the identifier which is being used in the communication.

Other functionalities are needed for the Multihoming support; for instance, it is needed to change the actual locators of an ongoing communication, this is called re-homing procedure. Nevertheless, a re-homing procedure should only be needed when a failure has been happened; thus, it is necessary to check the communication through reachability tests. There are two options:

- *Bidirectionally operational address pair:* The locator pair used in the communications is the same in both directions.

- *Unidirectionally operational address pair:* The locator pair used in each direction of the communication is different.

For each case, a reachability test is proposed in [Arkko, 2004].

Finally, if reachability tests are not successful, working locators must be found; reachability tests with the new pairs of locators must be performed until a pair allows a new path to establish the communication. Once a pair of valid locators is found, a re-homing procedure can be executed for those locators.

After presenting the different functions required for Multihoming support, we will explain the CGA and HBA approaches.

2.1   CGA (Cryptographically Based Addresses)

The CGA approach provides the secure mapping between identifier and locators through asymmetric cryptography. A CGA is an IPv6 address which can be used as a predefined valid locator, and its interface ID [Hinden and Deering, 2003] is related to a public key. This relation is due to the fact that the interface ID is a hash (SHA-1 hash algorithm [SHA-1, 1995]) of the data structure showed in the Fig.1. The data structure is called *CGA Parameters Data Structure* and contains a modifier, a subnet prefix, a public key and an optional field; only the leftmost 64 bits of the hash of the structure forms the interface ID. Furthermore, there should be a CGA per each subnet prefix owned by the host if we want the information about the public key to be accessible from any subnet prefix.

The establishment of a communication could be done through the DNS service, since a CGA is a valid IPv6 address and it would be probably mapped with a name. If new locators are to be added for its later use, an exchange between the multihomed host and the other side of the communication must be performed. This exchange includes the new locators, the CGA Parameters Data Structure and a signature of the locators with the private key associated with the public key contained in the CGA Parameters Data Structure. The security of this process relies on the fact that the other side of the communication checks that the hash of the received CGA Parameters Data Structures matches with the interface ID of the other host; this means that the public key inside the received CGA Parameters Data Structure belongs to the other host and the signature of the locators can be checked. Thus, if the check of the signature is successful, it implies that the locators are valid.

Note that an attacker requires bruce force methods to obtain a new pair of private/public keys to obtain a hash of the CGA Parameters Data Structure equal to the interface ID of the host which is being attacked. If [Aura, 2004] is read carefully, we can see that the complexity of the attack is $O\left(2^{59}\right)$ and additional security can be added to the CGA by means of the Sec parameter. The *Sec* parameter is embedded in the interface ID (the 3 leftmost bits of the ID) and requires that an adjustable size part of the leftmost 112 bits of another hash (again a SHA-1 algorithm), named hash2, equals to zero. With this requirement, the complexity of a bruce-force attack is $O\left(2^{59+16*Sec}\right)$. It has to be taken into account the fact that this extra security is not without a cost, since hosts have to make $O\left(2^{16*Sec}\right)$ hash2 operations until a CGA Data Structure fits with the Sec parameter condition.

Nevertheless, CGA have a problem due to the fact that the computational cost of asymmetric public operations for signing the locators with the private key is very large.

2.2   HBA (Hash Based Addresses)

The idea of HBA [Bagnulo, 2004] is to avoid the computational cost of CGA. This is due to the fact that HBA does not need asymmetric key cryptography for the exchange of locators. The solution proposed in HBA is to include in a HBA Parameters Data Structure all the known subnet prefixes by a host. As in CGA, a hash operation is applied to the HBA Parameters Data Structure, but in this case information about the known prefixes by the host is included. The leftmost 64 bits are again the interface ID which will be added to the subnet prefix. This process must be applied to all subnet prefixes contained in the HBA Parameters Data Structure; thus, after a HBA set of addresses is obtained, only these addresses could be used as locators in a Multihoming environment.

The interface ID is now a container of information about the different subnet prefixes of the host and the verification process of the HBA is similar to the CGA case, but in this case the verified information is the subnet prefixes owned by the host and not a public key. Due to this last fact, only prefixes of the host are known. When a packet with an unknown source address is received, it must be checked that the prefix belongs to the set of prefixes contained in the HBA Parameters Data Structure, and that the locator address belongs to the HBA set generated from the same HBA Parameters Data Structure. This means making a hash of the HBA Parameters Data Structure with a subnet prefix equal to the

Modifier (16 octets)
Subnet Prefix (8 octets)
Collision Count (1 octet)
Public Key (Variable Length)
Extension Fields (Optional, Variable Length)

Figure 1. CGA Parameters Data Structure

Type	Length	P	Reserved
Prefix[1]			
Prefix[2]			
...			
Prefix[n]			

Figure 2. Multi-Prefix extension for CGA

received. If the leftmost 64 bits are equal to the interface ID, the new address belongs to the HBA set and it can be accepted as a valid locator.

The bruce-force attack complexity is the same as in CGA approach and a Sec parameter is also used to improve the security.

2.3 Solution based on HBA and CGA

The use of HBA has several advantages over CGA: public key cryptography is not needed, so a great amount of computational complexity is avoided and it is not needed to check any signature of the locators. However, the HBA approach has a drawback, recalculation of the HBA set is necessary if a new subnet prefix wants to be added. Usually, a host knows a priori the prefixes which must be managed by it, but in some environments, such as in mobility, prefixes are only known a posteriori.

Nevertheless, HBA and CGA can use a common format for compatibility reasons [Bagnulo, 2004]. This can be done including each assigned Prefix/64 as an extension of the CGA Parameters Data Structure; this is done using an extension for CGA and it is called Multi-Prefix extension (see Fig.2). The public key field of the CGA Parameters Data Structure can be a random number or a public key; so, if the HBA includes a public key, asymmetric cryptography can be used for the exchange of new locators as occurs for CGA.

3. API proposal for Multihoming in IPv6

Nowadays, there are hundreds of applications running on the Internet and it is not desirable to change them if a new network service is introduced. So, the Multihoming Layer should be transparent to legacy applications while providing extended functions to the IPv6 API. An approach to provide the needed transparency could be to rely on predetermined parameters for old applications

Applications		
IPv6 API	Multihoming API	
TCP Layer	UDP Layer	SCTP Layer
Multihoming Layer		
IP Layer		
MAC Layer		
PHY Layer		

Figure 3.   Proposed Multihoming API scheme

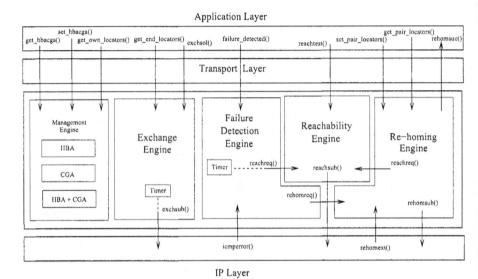

Figure 4.   Multihoming API Scheme

and allow new applications to use the Multihoming API to get enhanced features.

A scheme of the proposal is shown in Fig.3. This scheme allows new applications to make use of new features provided by the Multihoming Layer. This approach is inspired in [Komu, 2004].

3.1   API Scheme

The API scheme proposed can be seen in Fig.4. In the figure we can see the different HBAs, CGAs and HBAs+CGAs which are managed by the Multihoming Layer. The HBA can only manage subnet prefixes due to the fact that the authentication is always performed doing the hash test from the extended CGA Parameters Data Structure and comparing the result with the interface ID of the HBA. CGAs and CGAs+HBAs can manage locators, not only prefixes as consequence of the signature used for the exchange of locators. Also there are a Failure Detection Engine, a Reachability Engine, a Re-homing Engine and a Exchange Engine.

The socket interface is usually used in Operative Systems to manage ongoing connections; so, the Multihoming API should provide most of its features through this socket interface.

3.2 Address Generation

First of all, it is needed the generation of HBAs and CGAs. These functions are not related with any outgoing communication, so socket interface can not be used and an external library must be provided. The proposed functions are:

void *create_cga(uint64_t prefix, void *extfields, int extlength, uint8_t sec, void *pk, int pklength). This function creates a CGA and its input parameters are:

> *prefix:* The subnet prefix associated with the CGA which is introduced in the CGA Parameters Data Structure.
> *extfields:* Optional extension fields can be passed with this parameter.
> *extlength:* Length of the extension fields.
> *sec:* This parameter specifies the value of the Sec parameter in the CGA which sets the level of security against bruce force attacks for impersonating a given interface identifier.
> *pk:* With this parameter, public key of the CGA Parameters Data Structure is specified. If pk is equal to zero, an asymmetric key pair must be generated.
> *pklength:* Length in bytes of the public key.

This function selects a random number for the modifier, create the CGA Parameters Data Structure and finally generates the CGA according to the requirements of the Sec parameter. So, the output parameters will be the *CGA Parameters Data Structure*, the *CGA* itself and the *private key* if *pk* was equal to zero.

void *create_hba(void *multiprefix, int multilenght, void *extfields, int extlength, uint8_t sec, void *pk, int pklength). This function creates a set of HBAs which are generated with the same extended CGA Parameters Data Structure. Input parameters are:

> *multiprefix:* It is the Multi-Prefix extension for CGA. It contains the different subnet prefixes which will be used to generate the HBA set.
> *multilength:* Length in bytes of the Multi-prefix extension.
> *extfields:* Extensions fields can be included which are different from the Multi-Prefix extension.
> *extlength:* Length in bytes of the extension fields.
> *sec:* Again, the level of security is selected with this parameter.
> *pk:* The public key of the HBA if it wants to be used the functionality of CGA+HBA.

pklength: Length in bytes of the public key.

The function must select a random number for the modifier and another random number if the pk parameter is equal to zero. Finally, a set of HBAs must be generated according to the proposed generation process in [Bagnulo, 2004] which implies that the hash2 must apply with the Sec parameter. A subnet prefix is not needed because a subnet prefix from the Multi-prefix-extension is used for each HBA. The output parameters will be the *set of CGAs* and the *extended CGA Parameters Data Structure.*

3.3   Management Engine

Applications can benefit from the identifiers and locators could be needed for applications. The selection of an addressing model, if several are available in a host, implies how the alternative locators are communicated to other hosts. There are four possibilities:

- **CGA:** Exchange of locators protected by asymmetric key. A large computational complexity is needed to perform this approach. The authenticity of the public key is checked with two Hash operations. Locators can be notified to other hosts at any time.

- **HBA:** Exchange of locators is based on Hash operations. Only the generated set of HBA allows re-homing procedures.

- **HBA+CGA:** HBAs Data structure is an extension of the CGA data structure, so both functionalities can be provided at the same time.

- **None:** The host is upgraded with Multihoming support but HBAs or CGAs are not available. Only Multihoming functions will be performed if the other host of the communication can manage HBAs and/or CGAs.

A mobile node should select CGA or HBA+CGA, or a web server should select HBA because it needs to perform a lot of tasks per minute and the use of CGA with asymmetric cryptography operations to sign the locators would reduce its performance.

Actual IPv6 API allows to obtain the different IPv6 addresses which have been assigned to the different interfaces in a host. Nevertheless, it is impossible to know if an IPv6 address is a HBA or a CGA by simple inspection. The Multihoming Layer knows this information, so the Multihoming API could provide selection mechanisms and ways to access to the type of addresses that is being used by a given communication. The functions which provide these features will be:

void *get_hbacga(int typeaddr). This function allows applications to retrieve the addresses managed by the Multihoming Layer. The *typeaddr* parameter indicates the type of wanted addresses (HBA, CGA or HBA + CGA). The output will be a list of different addresses with the selected type if they exists.

It could be thought that an address selection mechanism is needed, but this is not necessary because the IPv6 API already supports this feature with the function bind [Stevens and Thomas, 1998].

Furthermore, it is needed to inform at the Mutlihoming Layer about the different available HBAs and CGAs in the host which must be managed by it:

int set_hbacga(void *hbacga, int typeaddr). This function should be used by a superuser program to configure the HBAs and CGAs at the Multihoming Layer. This function could be executed in the starting sequence of a host. Input parameters are:

> **hbacga:* A pointer to a list with the HBAs, CGAs or HBAs+CGAs.
> *typeaddr:* Type of addresses in the list.

The output value will be an integer and if it equals to zero, the function will have finished successfully.

Locators are managed by the Multihoming Layer and they are not all known a priori; nevertheless, it could be useful to know the available locators for a connection in some situations such as debugging, administration and management or getting traces:

void *get_own_locators(int fdsocket). This function obtains the locators that the host can manage with the socket fdsocket. This is necessary because locators can change if the host is in a mobile environment. The input parameter is *fdsocket* which is the file descriptor of the socket used for the communication. The output parameter will be the list of locators.

3.4 Exchange Engine

Short connections could not benefit from re-homing capabilities; for instance, a request-reply communication in HTTP 1.0. Thus, a timer is defined and when this timer expires, locators are exchanged. This exchange is necessary before a failure interrupts the communication, because if locators are not exchanged, re-homing can not be done. Nevertheless, the application could know in advance the time which will be employed in the communication; so, it will be interesting to force a exchange of locators if a large connection is going to be used, or to prevent the exchange if the communication is going to be short:

int exchsol(int fdsocket, int time) This function of the proposed Multihoming API allows to force a exchange of locator. It has the *time* parameter and there are three possibilities:

minus than zero: The exchange is prevented.
equals to zero: The exchange of locators is done immediately.
minor than internal timer: The internal timer is set to the value of time.

Due to the fact that this engine manages the exchange of locators with the other side of the communication, it should provide this information to upper layers:
   void *get_end_locators(int fdsocket) This function shows the locators of the other host in the communication and its parameters are the same as that the *getownlocators* function.

3.5   Failure Detection Engine

   A Failure Detection Engine is necessary for detecting failures in communications. Three mechanisms are under study in the IETF multi6 Working Group: a failure may exists if an ICMP Destination Unreachable message is received, packets are not received in the interval of an inactivity TCP timer or applications notify about problems in their communications. So, it is necessary that the Multihoming API provides a function to inform the Multihoming layer about problems in upper layers:
   int failure_detected(int fdsocket). This function allows upper layers to notify about problems in the communication and a reachability test must be requested (*reachreq()*). The output parameter will be an integer and if it equals to zero, the function will have finished successfully.
   If a failure is detected, the Failure Detection Engine has to send a notification to the Re-homing Engine (*rehomreq()*).

3.6   Reachability Engine

   The Reachability Engine performs reachability tests. If a notification is received, it verifies the communication with a reachability test that consists of sending a probe packet with a particular locator pair to confirm that a path is valid if a response is received.
   int reachtest(int fdsocket, struct sockaddr my_addr, struct sockaddr end_addr, socklen_t addrlen). This function performs a reachability test and its parameters are:

   fdsocket: File descriptor of the socket used for the communication.
   my_loc: Source locator.
   end_loc: Destination locator.
   loclen: Length of locator.

The locators used for the reachability test are *my_loc* and *end_loc*. The output parameter will be an integer and if it equals to zero, the function will have finished successfully.

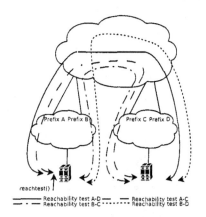

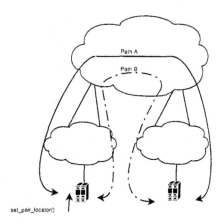

Figure 5. Reachability tests that can be performed

Figure 6. Rehoming of the communication between path A and B

Fig.5 shows the different paths which can be tested taking into account the pair of locators that can be formed. Only it is needed that one path provides connectivity.

3.7 Re-homing Engine

The Re-homing Engine manages re-homing procedures. It could be interesting for applications to obtain information about the occurrence of re-homing procedures. For instance, if an UDP application implements a slow-start algorithm as TCP, it could be interesting for the application to perform a slow-start algorithm after a re-homing procedure and try to obtain a fast adaptation to the new bandwidth.

rehomsuc() A signal is sent to applications to inform that a re-homing procedure has been performed by the other side of the communication.

int get_pairlocators(int fdsocket, struct sockaddr *my_loc, struct sockaddr *end_loc, socklen_t *loclen). This function obtains the pair of locators used in the ongoing communication. This request is solved by the Re-homing because last pair of locators used in a communication are always known after a re-homing procedure. Input parameters are:

fdsocket: File descriptor of the socket used for the communication.
my_loc: Pointer where the source locator will be saved.
end_loc: Pointer where the destination will be saved.
loclen: Pointer with space reserved to the locators. The function modifies its value to the length of locators.

The output parameter will be an integer and if it equals to zero, the function will have finished successfully.

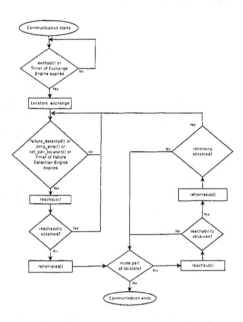

Figure 7.   Basic organizational chart of Multihoming Layer

int set_pair_locator(int fdsocket, struct sockaddr my_addr, struct sockaddr end_addr, socklen_t addrlen). This function sets the locators for the ongoing communication; so, it is like a re-homing solicitation. Its structure is the same as the *reachtest* function. If my_loc and end_loc are equal to zero the locators will be selected by the Re-homing Engine. It must be noted that a reachability test should be performed before a re-homing procedure; thus, the Re-homing Engine has to submit a solicitation for a reachability test to the Reachability Engine (*reachreq()*). This function can be used to force a re-homing if, for example, the QoS obtained by an application is not enough; an example could be a videoconference where many frames are dropped.

Fig.6 illustrates a rehoming procedure. After the locators have been exchanged and a new pair of locators has been selected after performing a reachability test. Then, the communication path A can be changed to path B without breaking the established connection.

3.8   Organizational chart of Multihoming Layer

In Fig.7 a basic organizational chart of the Multihoming Layer is shown. The figure shows the basic functions that must be performed to obtain Multihoming support. First of all, it is necessary the exchange of locators. If other locators are not known, it is impossible to find an alternative path. A rehoming procedure can be performed if the ongoing communication has some type of problem (lost of connectivity, low quality, ...). At this point a new path must be found, so a reachability test is used to allow us to test the connectivity between locators of different hosts. Finally, if an alternative pair of locators is found, a rehoming procedure can be tried.

All the proposed functions in this section are necessary to provide a enhanced Multihoming Service to the applications and the needed tools for administration and management.

4. Future Work

Different tasks can be performed in the future taking into account the proposal of this paper. It is necessary a deep study of the default parameters which must be configured in the Multihoming Layer to provide reliable Multihoming support to legacy applications. Also, it should be interesting a comparation of the performance between legacy applications, legacy applications making use of Multihoming in transparent mode and applications using the Multihoming API. Furthermore, a large work in close relation with the multi6 Working Group should be done until an Multihoming API can be provided in the future.

5. Conclusions

HBA and CGA provide a secure mapping between identifiers and locators. In this way, stable identifiers are shown to the Transport Layers while the locators used in the IP datagrams can be changed without disrupting the communication. CGA has a much bigger computational complexity due to the fact that asymmetric key operations are needed. Conversely, HBAs have a low computational cost due to the fact that they only use hash operations. Nevertheless, in HBA the different prefixes which would be used by a host must be known in advance because this information is included in the interface ID of IPv6 addresses through a hash operation. CGA has not this limitation because the locator is authenticated through an asymmetric cryptographic scheme. New locators which are not known a priori can be sent because they are signed with the private key of the Host.

HBA and CGA have different features which can be used at the same time by different applications. The API proposed in this paper manages the mapping method between identifiers and locators. Because of this feature, applications can select HBA, CGA or CGA + HBA depending on their needs.

Furthermore, other functions are added to improve the failure detection and the re-homing procedure. With these functions, applications can inform about failures in the communications or a re-homing procedure can be requested by the application (for example, if the received QoS is not enough). These mechanisms can provide faster response if applications detect failures sooner than lower layers. Other functionalities are also added, such as the solicitation of an exchange of locators or the possibility for applications to be informed about changes of the locators related with the ongoing communication. Legacy applications can obtain Multihoming support if there exists a default configuration which configures the minimal needed parameters.

Acknowledgement

The authors would like to thank to Carlos J. Bernardos for the ideas provided. This work has been partly supported by the E-Next Project FP6506869 and OPTINET6 project TIC-2003-09042-C03-01.

References

Abley, J., Black, B., and Gill, V. (2003). *RFC 3582: Goals for IPv6 Site-Multihoming Architectures*.

Arkko, J. (2004). *Failure Detection and Locator Selection in Multi6*. Internet Draft draft-arkko-multi6dt-failure detection-00.txt (work in progress).

Aura, T. (2004). *Cryptographically Generated Addresses (CGA)*. Internet Draft draft-ietf-send-cga-06.txt (work in progress).

Bagnulo, M. (2004). *Hash Based Addresses (HBA)*. Internet Draft draft-ietf-multi6-hba-00.txt (work in progress).

Guo, Fanglu, Chen, Jiawu, Li, Wei, and Chiueh, Tzicker (2004). Experiences in building a multihoming load balancing system. In *IEEE INFOCOM '04, Hong Kong, China. Volume: 2*, pages 1241–1251.

Hinden, R. and Deering, S. (2003). *RFC 3513: Internet Protocol Version 6 (IPv6) Addressing Architecture*.

Huston, G. (2001). *RFC 3221: Commentary on Inter-Domain Routing in the Internet*.

Komu, M. (2004). Application programming interfaces for the host identity protocol. Master's thesis, Helsinky Universitiy of Technology.

Nordmark, E. (2004). *Multi6 Application Referral Issues*. Internet Draft draft-nordmark-multi6dt-refer-00.txt (work in progress).

Nordmark, E. and Bagnulo, M. (2005). *Multihoming L3 Shim Approach*. Internet Draft draft-ietf-multi6-l3shim-00.txt (work in progress).

Nordmark, E. and Li, T. (2005). *Threats relating to IPv6 multihoming solutions*. Internet Draft draft-ietf-multi6-multihoming-threats-03.txt (work in progress).

SHA-1 (1995). *Secure Hash Standard*. Federal Information Processing Standards. Publication 180-1.

Stevens, W. and Thomas, M. (1998). *RFC 2292: Advanced Sockets API for IPv6*.

Yin, S. and Twist, K. (2003). The coming era of absolute availability.

SAMSON: SMART ADDRESS MANAGEMENT IN SELF-ORGANIZING NETWORKS

Kristóf Fodor, Dániel Krupp, Gergely Biczók, János L. Gerevich,
Krisztián Sugár
Department of Telecommunications and Media Informatics
Budapest University of Technology and Economics
Magyar Tudósok krt. 2., 1117 Budapest, Hungary
{fodork,dkrupp,biczok}@tmit.bme.hu, {gj198,sk335}@hszk.bme.hu

Abstract   In this paper we present the SAMSON (Smart Address Management in Self-Organizing Networks) protocol, which is a simple and effective solution for assigning unique addresses to nodes of a MANET. Our protocol reduces the configuration time of arriving nodes by optimizing the number of configuration messages and the number of hops the configuration messages have to pass through. Furthermore, SAMSON handles the merger and partitioning of networks efficiently.

Keywords: ad hoc network, auto address configuration, distributed algorithm

1.   Introduction

Nodes in a mobile ad hoc network (MANET) usually use short range wireless connections for connecting to each other, thus a data packet may have to travel through several hops to reach the destination party. Topology in these so-called multihop networks is rapidly changing due to the movement of the nodes, moreover, the set of devices participating in the communication is not permanent. These MANETs are independent from any pre-installed network infrastructure and may be formed by a group of mobile nodes spontaneously. Any node can leave the network at will, sometimes without informing the other participants about its departure. The multihop packet delivery between two parties can be based on any routing protocol specially designed for networks with dynamically changing topology (e.g., DSDV [Perkins and Bhagwat, 1994], AODV [Perkins and Royer, 1999], DSR [Johnson and Maltz, 1996]).

Although routing protocols are able to find the multihop route between any pair of nodes, they all assume that every device taking part in the communication owns a unique address. Thus, neither of these solutions deals with the question how the parties should obtain the unique identifiers. In managed IP-based fix networks a widespread solution is to set up a Dynamic Host Configuration Protocol (DHCP) [Droms, 1997] server, which returns unique and unused network identifiers on request. This and similar centrally managed approaches are not applicable in MANETs due to the fact that spontaneous networks lack any pre-installed and always available infrastructure.

Several address distribution solutions for MANETs exist, however they are either not scalable enough, or rather communication resource consuming. This paper describes a distributed protocol, which is able to configure a unique address for a newly joining node by optimizing the needed resources, and above that, it is capable of handling the partitioning and merger of separate MANETs. Our solution accomplishes these tasks without overloading the network burstfully, which makes the solution very well scalable over large MANETs. An often neglected but rather important issue is the fault tolerance of the address distribution system. It is expected that the system should continue working properly in case of any kind of failure on behalf of any node. The protocol presented in this paper successfully deals with these situations and manages the available address space in a way that no (permanent) address loss may occur in case of any participant's failure.

The remainder of the paper is organized as follows. Section 2 outlines the different concepts of address distribution mechanisms for MANETs by categorizing them, moreover presents the most important existing solutions. Section 3 describes our address distribution protocol, and Section 4 analyzes the optimization of the configuration time elapsed when assigning a unique address to a newly arrived node. Finally, Section 5 concludes the paper.

2.   Related Work

Considering the address space, the existing address distribution mechanisms can be grouped into two categories based on the length of the addresses. The first category consists of distribution mechanisms that use fixed length addresses, while the mechanisms in the second category deal with variable length addresses. By using a mechanism belonging to the former category, the length of the addresses should be chosen carefully, so that all nodes in the network can obtain a unique address. If the address space turns out to be too small, there is hardly any way to extend it in the future. However, fixed length addresses have the advantage that they can be handled easier than those of variable length.

The largely different way of treating the address space leads to different optimization goals and difficulties. In both cases the address space can be represented as a binary tree, where the leaves of the tree identify the assigned addresses. Algorithms operating on *non-fixed length* addresses (e.g., [Boleng,

2002]) try to keep the number of levels in the address tree as low as possible, thus providing the shortest possible address length supposing a given number of participants in the network. However, in the *fixed-length* case, the size of the tree (and the address space) is predefined and the goal of the algorithms is to assign a free leaf to each newly arriving node. At a first glance the latter goal seems to be easily achievable, but consider that in MANETs any node can leave the network at will without informing the others about its departure. These so-called *non-graceful departures* can lead to the *address leakage* phenomenon, when the network is unable to detect that some addresses are not engaged anymore. Of course, this may lead to significant shrinkage of the address space after a certain amount of time. In the rest of the paper we will focus on the fixed-address length approaches.

An other basis of categorizing the existing solutions is the manner they treat the state of the address space. Those approaches where none of the participants in the network maintain information about the reserved addresses are *stateless* solutions, while the ones which make an effort to store a quasi up-to-date version of the address space are called *stateful* solutions. It can be generally claimed about the stateless solutions that there is no centrally or distributedly stored knowledge of the address space. When a node is willing to join the network, it has to agree on its candidate address with all the other—already configured—parties. This is often done by flooding the network, which causes burstful load on the network each time a node joins.

Other approaches, which are called stateful address distribution mechanisms, store an up-to date state of the currently available addresses. These solutions have to take care of address space maintenance continuously, which generates a slight, but permanent traffic load. When designing such an algorithm, special care has to be taken maintaining the address space, because inconsistent states may lead to address leakage or, even worse, to *duplicate addresses* in the network.

Stateful address distribution mechanisms usually provide faster address allocation process than stateless ones, since the joining node does not have to agree on its candidate address with all the nodes in the network, instead it gets an address from a dedicated node. Very often a neighboring node—called *proxy*—carries out the address allocation on behalf of the requesters, since this neighboring node already has a valid address and adequate knowledge on the network structure.

The task of address distribution mechanisms does not end at the configuration of a newly joining node. Often a common demand is to handle the merger and the separation of different MANETs, called *network partitions*. In the former case it should be prohibited that nodes with the same address participate in the same partition, while in the latter case departed nodes should be identified and based on this information the partition should be reorganized. In order to detect nodes with the same address, several *Duplication Address Detection* (DAD) mechanisms were invented.

Many algorithms detect address collisions based on monitoring the packets containing routing information. If collision detection used by the algorithm is performed without sending extra messages, i.e., it is only based on observation, the method is called *passive duplicate address detection* mechanism. Such solutions were presented in [Weniger, 2003] and [Weniger, 2004]. There may be a stronger requirement toward the DAD mechanisms, which allow the partition merging processes to terminate only when there are no more nodes in the merged partition with the same address. This requirement is called *strong DAD* [Vaidya, 2002]. Solutions fulfilling this requirement usually perform global collision revealing mechanisms by flooding the detection packets through the whole network.

One of the first decentralized address assigning protocols was presented in [Cheshire et al., 2004] by the IETF (Internet Engineering Task Force) Zeroconf Working Group. The solution is based on the IP addressing scheme and assumes link-local connections between all parties, which means that all link-level broadcasts have to reach all nodes in the network. Thus, this restriction makes the solution directly unapplicable in MANETs where the communicating nodes may be in multihop distance from each other. Despite of this fact, the solution became the basis of several *stateless* approaches developed in the past few years.

Among others, the solution presented in [Nesargi and Prakash, 2002] is also based on the idea of the Zeroconf Working Group. It introduces a so-called *soft state maintenance* mechanism, which makes it possible to serve multiple join requests at the same time. Each node in the network maintains an array for the allocated addresses and an other one for addresses under allocation (pending addresses). Each device wishing to join the network, randomly chooses a candidate identifier and sends it to a neighboring proxy node, which already possesses a valid address. The proxy then floods the network with the address request including the chosen random address and waits for the replies. A node in the partition can only send back a positive acknowledgement for the request if it does not consider the requested address as allocated or as being under allocation. If the proxy node has received positive acknowledgements from all parties, then it assigns the candidate address to the joining node. The solution applies message flooding each time a node joins, which causes bursts in the network load. The protocol is simple and applicable in small MANETs, though the mentioned undesirable property makes it non-scalable over larger networks.

Although, the solutions described in [Cheshire et al., 2004] and [Nesargi and Prakash, 2002] differ in terms of the amount of information the nodes have to store about the address space, both methods use only premature techniques and explicit messages to avoid address collisions. In addition, configuration of a node takes a lot of time in both cases. The Weak Duplicate Address Detection [Vaidya, 2002] mechanism solves this latter weakness. It allows duplicate addresses in a network as long as every packet is routed to the right party. The joining nodes simply choose themselves an identifier (e.g., based on their MAC addresses) and they start using it, without checking whether the chosen address is already used by another node. As soon as an address conflict arises, the duplication of the concerned address has to be resolved immediately.

There is a group of address distribution mechanisms, where the state of the assigned addresses is registered in some way. For example, in the Self-Organising Node Address Management (SONAM) solution [Toner and O'Mahony, 2003], a special node is responsible for assigning addresses to newly arriving nodes. Whenever a node requests an address, the newly arriving node receives—in addition to the address—a list of assigned addresses and the version number of the returned list, moreover it becomes the new special node. If the actual special node disconnects from the network, the new special node will be the node with the highest list version number.

Another possible way for obtaining an address is presented in [Zhou et al., 2003]. Each already configured node in the Prophet system possesses an *f(n)* function with a seed and a state. New addresses are generated based on these. If a node knows the default seed and the default state used in the network, then it can foretell which addresses will conflict when merging its network with another one.

3. SAMSON

3.1 Basic structure

The highest priority design goals of the *Smart Address Management in Self Organizing Networks* (SAMSON) protocol are the balanced control traffic load and the short address configuration time. Thus, it is a *stateful* protocol, able to handle the joining of nodes quickly and efficiently by adapting to the high amount of address requests concentrated to certain parts of the network.

The SAMSON protocol divides the available address space of the network partition into equal disjoint ranges. Each of these ranges is assigned to a so-called *pool*. Thus, each pool represents an address range and is responsible for managing the addresses of the given address range. The pools are scattered throughout the whole partition and are usually located at those nodes where unique addresses can be assigned to newly joining nodes in the shortest time in average. The nodes where the pools are located at are called *carrier nodes*. A pool is not bound to a certain carrier node: it can move from a carrier node to another if it detects that the address requests could be served more efficiently (in terms of *total expectable address configuration time*) by being located at another node. Thus, every node in the partition can turn into a carrier node anytime. There is also no restriction on the number of pools that can be carried by a single carrier node at the same time.

Each pool can be uniquely identified by its managed address range, however, since the address ranges are equal, it is enough to identify a pool with the first address of the address range assigned to it. Sometimes it is desirable to treat a pool like a node (e.g., in case of sending an address request to it), therefore the first address of the address range is reserved for the pool itself. This way pools become *virtual nodes* and can be addressed by any node of the partition.

The network partition is initialized by a so-called *initiator node*. This node has to define the NETID, which is the unique identifier of the network partition. This identifier may be chosen by considering the lately observed network identifiers. A new pool is to be created at partition initialization time, or upon detecting that the address space of a pool will be exhausted soon due to the large number of configuration requests. This prediction is always to be made by the pools. In addition, a new pool must be generated when a network partition has been divided into two partitions in a way that no free addresses have remained in one of the partitions.

The pools are free to move in the network. Each pool chooses its next carrier node based on the frequency of address requests coming from different parts of the network. In order to measure the frequency of address requests we a defined a metric, which is used by the pool movement algorithm.

3.2   Joining process of a new node

A newly joining node can obtain a unique address by asking one of its neighbors for help in the address claiming process. This neighbor will be the *proxy node* of the joining node. The selection of such a proxy node is necessary, since during the address request process the joining node does not own any legal address that can be used in the MANET, only a link-layer address (MAC address), which can only be used to communicate with nodes in one-hop distance.

At first, the joining node a broadcasts a $HELLO\_REQ$ to discover its neighbors among its link-layer neighbors (Figure 1). After the reception of the replies sent in answer to the request, node a chooses one of its replying neighbors to be its proxy node during the address allocation. Then node a asks its chosen proxy node p to request a valid address from a pool in the network. If node a has a desired address it wants to get (for instance it used this address last time it joined the network), then node a includes the demanded address in the message sent to the proxy node. The proxy then sends an address request to the closest pool (O). If the request includes a desired address, pool O checks the engagement of this address at pool C, which is the responsible pool for the required address. Otherwise, if there is no address desire included in the request, pool O allocates its first free address for the joining node and returns it to the proxy node. The proxy node forwards the ready-to-use address to node a using node a's MAC address.

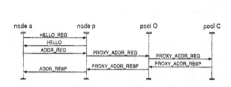

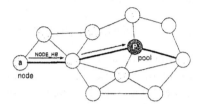

Figure 1.   A new node joins the network   *Figure 2.*   Keeping in touch with the pool

The closest pool can always be found at the special address 0. Thus, in addition to the first address of the address range assigned to a pool, each pool allocates itself a second address as well: a special address we named 0. This of course leads to address collisions, however, in the case of SAMSON it is allowed to have more of this special address in the network at the same time. These address conflicts do not have to be resolved. This way every address request packet sent to the address 0 is automatically delivered to the closest pool, irrespectively of the underlying routing protocol.

3.3   Wandering process of pools

Finding a good motion algorithm for pools is extremely important. If the pools are capable of moving to the areas where new addresses are requested more frequently then they can minimize in average the total time necessary for configuring addresses to arriving nodes. Finding these so-called *hotspots* is far not an easy issue, because the place of the hotspots may change from time to time with the changing of the arrival interval of new nodes at certain parts of the network. Moreover, the pools cannot have an up-to-date global knowledge about the topology of the network, except in case of certain kinds of underlying routing protocols (link-state routing protocols [Clausen and Jacquet, 2003]). Since one of our design goals was to create a protocol which may operate over any kind of ad hoc routing protocol, we designed an algorithm that doesn't assume any knowledge of the network topology.

Let us imagine a node a which carries a pool P. Pool P has to decide if it stays at node a or moves to the neighboring node b. In order to make a decision, P continuously monitors the address requests coming from different link-local neighbors of the carrier node or from the carrier node itself. Pool P increases its corresponding counter when it receives an address request message from one of the carrier node's neighbors or from the carrier node directly. Based on these counters, pool P periodically makes a movement decision. If pool P

finds that it received more address requests through the neighboring node b than through its other neighbors and the carrier node in total, then pool P initiates a *pool transfer*. In frame of this process the entire pool is transferred from node a to node b. Following this rule the total expected address configuration time always decreases. The proof of the statement will be presented in Section 4.

3.4 Maintaining the states of the addresses

Since the address management is operating in an ad hoc environment, the protocol has to be fit for handling the sudden, *non-graceful* departures of the nodes. If a node disappears from the network, its address should be assignable again after a certain amount of time. The SAMSON protocol supports the detection of node losses at two levels. First, every pool continuously checks whether the nodes whose addresses are from the address space of the given pool are still present. Second, the pools continuously check the availability of the other pools.

After getting an address from a pool, every node has to send so-called heartbeat messages (NODE_HB) periodically to the pool from which it has obtained the address from. This procedure can be seen on Figure 2. If a pool has not received a NODE_HB message from a corresponding node for a long time, then it requests a presence signal from the node. If the addressed node fails to answer this warning, then the node is regarded as detached from the partition, so the address of this node is set as free and ready to be redistributed.

It may also happen that a carrier node leaves the network without informing the other nodes. In this case not only the address of the departed carrier node, but also the carried pools should be retrieved. As described previously, the pools continuously check the presence of others. Each pool—except the first one—sends a so-called keepalive message (POOL_HB) to the pool which is just inferior in the order of the represented address space. The first node in the order sends the keepalive message to the last pool, thus the pools form a ring to check their availability. This way the departure of a pool can be detected by its successor pool, i.e. by the pool whose address range is the continuation of the address range of the disappeared pool.

If a pool realizes that a predecessor pool has left the network, then it has to regenerate the lost pool. First, the successor pool reallocates the given pool by reserving the concerned address space. Then, it immediately freezes the address space (no address can be assigned from this address space) and waits for NODE_HB messages. Since the regenerated pool has the same address as the lost one, furthermore the new location of the pool is propagated by the routing mechanism, the nodes that have an address from the concerned address space can send their heartbeat messages to the pool without noticing the regeneration. Thus, after a while the regenerated pool will be aware of the assigned addresses and therefore it can lift the blocking of the address space. From that time on the unused addresses of the pool can be assigned to newly joining nodes again. In this way the recovery period is directly proportional to the frequency of sending NODE_HB messages.

If two or more successive pools leave the network at the same time without informing the others, then they are recovered step-by-step: first the one which is the highest in the pool order, and finally the one which is the last in that order. Considering the fact, that neither the address reclaiming, nor the pool recovery processes are time critical, then the ratio of the period of the *POOL_HB* messages to the period of the NODE_HB messages may be chosen relatively big.

In case of losing all pools, the nodes must start to form a new partition.

3.5   Pool generation and deletion

As described previously, a pool can be generated in the partition initialization phase, moreover when a pool determines that its address space will be soon exhausted, or when there is no pool left in a partition after splitting up the original partition. In the first and third case the creator of the new pool is an arbitrary node, which noticed the absence of the pools by not reaching any virtual node at the special address 0. The node can simply generate the first pool in the order, i.e. the pool with the lowest addresses of the whole address space. In the second case, when there are already some pools in the network, the pool which detects the depletion of the free addresses has to send a pool request to the highest pool in the order. This so-called *chief pool* is responsible to generate a new pool and pass it to the requester. Moreover, if the new pool has addresses in a higher range than the current chief pool, then the new pool takes the role of the chief pool, and all the pools have to be informed about this. This way, two or more identical pools cannot be created at the same time.

Pools can be deleted if all the belonging addresses become free. If a pool detects that this is the case, the pool starts to delete itself. First, it sends a message to the chief pool indicating that the pool will be deleted and can be assigned to another nodes. Then, it sends an indication message to the first existing successor pool (it may happen that one or more successor pools are already deleted). After that, the pool destroys itself and the successor pool periodically informs the chief pool about the free pools it knows (at least this one). From now on, the successor pool sends the *POOL_HB* messages to the predecessor pool of the deleted pool. This way, the actual chief pool is always aware of the deleted pools, so it can reuse them, moreover the pool ring is kept alive.

3.6   Merging two partitions

When a node detects the presence of an other network partition (e.g., it receives a HELLO message containing a different NetID than its own partition), then it has to report this event to its pool. The pool that receives this notification has to forward the message to the chief pool, which then decides whether to merge the two partitions or not. If the decision is to merge the networks, then the chief pool sets up a tunnel to one of the nodes that noticed the presence of the other network. This node is called *bridge node*. Moreover, the chief pool instructs the bridge node to establish a bridge to a randomly selected neighboring node from the other partition. After that, the concerned bridge node in the other network will inform the chief pool in it's network (via a pool) about the established bridge and a tunnel will be set up between the chief pool and the bridge node in this network as well. From now on the two chief pools can communicate with each other through the tunnel–bridge–tunnel connection. Of course, it may happen that two tunnel–bridge–tunnel connections are established in parallel. In this case the chief pools have to agree which one to use.

After establishing the connection between the two chief pools, the chief pools have to agree on a new network identifier, furthermore they have to resolve the address conflicts. This latter task is done in one or two steps. First, they try to shift the address ranges of the pools to eliminate the duplicate addresses. Then, if the former step was not successful, i.e., in total there are more pools than the length of the address space divided by the length of one address block, then the corresponding pools have to harmonize the addresses they assigned to the nodes.

As it can be seen on Figure 3 the proximity of Partition *2* was detected by node *48*, which informed the chief pool *45* through pool *9*. Therefore chief pool *45* built up a tunnel to node *48*, node *48* set up a bridge to node *76*, and then another tunnel was built up between bridge node *76* and the chief pool *80* in Partition *1* by the aid of the pool located at node *40* (for locating the chief pool).

3.7   Dividing a partition

Partitions may be divided at any time without any prior indication. Thus, we designed the SAMSON protocol to be capable of reorganizing a partition in case it splits up into several disjoint partitions. The reorganization function is based on the pool recovery mechanism. Whenever a pool has to be regenerated, the presence of the chief pool has to be checked. If it is not available any more, then the network may be divided into two or more partitions. Therefore the new chief pool (which is automatically restored) in each new partition generates a new network identifier and floods it in the network partition. If there is no pool

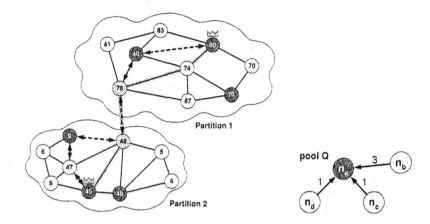

Figure 3.   Merging of two partitions

Figure 4.   A sample situation of pool motion

remaining in a group of disconnected nodes, then the first node (a) that realizes the loss of the pools starts to form a new partition by creating a pool (the first one in the partition). The other nodes can then connect to this partition directly by requesting a new address or by forming a new partition and merging it to the partition set up by node a.

4.   Analyzing the pool motion

Finding a good motion algorithm for pools is a relevant issue, since pools located at proper places (close to the *hotspots*) can keep the communication of the address claiming processes local, thus avoiding high traffic loads in the network. Furthermore, a good motion algorithm can reduce the average configuration time of newly arriving nodes.

To be able to examine the problem formally, let us assume the following. Let us take an N set of nodes and associate an R_i variate to its every $n_i \in N$ element. Among the $|N| = n$ element node set there is one Q pool, which handles every address claims. R_i variate indicates the number of address requests sent by node n_i (which is a proxy node in such a case) to the pool in one time slot. If we make the simplification, that during a time slot none of the newly configured nodes can configure another node, we can state the following about the *expected configuration time for node n_i (T_i)* in one time slot when the pool is located at node n_p:

$$T_i(n_p) = (2 \cdot T_{fw} \cdot d(n_i, n_p) + T_{serv}) \cdot \sum_{l=0}^{\infty} l \cdot P(R_i = l) \tag{1}$$

where constant T_{fw} is the average forwarding time of a message from one neighbor to the other, $d(n_i, n_p)$ is the distance in hops between the proxy node

n_i and pool Q that is located at n_p. Constant T_{serv} stands for the average service time of a request, and $P(R_i = l)$ indicates the probability that l address requests arrived during the time slot. According to equation 1, the expected configuration time for node n_i can be smaller only if the $d(n_i, n_p)$ distance is smaller.

The *total expected configuration time* (T) is the sum of T_is over the whole network. Thus, the total expected configuration time is

$$T(n_p) = \sum_{i=1}^{n} T_i = \sum_{i=1}^{n} ((2 \cdot T_{fw} \cdot d(n_i, n_p) + T_{serv}) \cdot \sum_{l=0}^{\infty} P(R_i = l) \cdot l) \qquad (2)$$

supposed that Q is located at node n_p. So, the goal is to find the node n_p (or one of them, if two or more nodes exist) that is the best carrier node for the pool Q in order to minimize the total expected configuration time in the network. The total expected configuration time is the following if the pool is at an optimal location:

$$T_{min} = \min_{n_s \in N}(T(n_s)) = \min_{n_s \in N}(\sum_{i=1}^{n} \sum_{l=0}^{\infty} (2 \cdot T_{fw} \cdot d(n_i, n_s) + T_{serv}) \cdot P(R_i = l) \cdot l) \qquad (3)$$

Let us call n_{opt} the node where $T(n_{opt}) = T_{min}$, i.e. which is at the optimal position. Finding this n_{opt} node is possible if the whole connectivity graph of the network is known. In this case, the optimal position can be calculated with an $O(n^3)$ algorithm, since the problem can be transformed to a similar problem, which is about finding the centrum of a graph. However, knowing the total connectivity graph of a network without sending explicit messages is possible only if the routing mechanism is a link-state protocol. Since it was among the design goals of the SAMSON protocol that the mechanism should work over any routing protocol, we supposed that pool Q has only local knowledge of the connectivity graph (e.g., it knows its neighbors).

In order to examine how the pool motion rule presented in Section 3.3 can decrease the total expected address configuration time, let us take a look at Figure 4. Pool Q is located at node n_a and it has to decide whether it should move to an other neighboring node. It can be seen that two address requests have arrived in total from nodes n_c and n_d, and three requests from node n_b during the examined time period. In this case pool Q can be placed at a more optimal position by moving it from node n_a to node n_b. This movement is done according to the motion rule of the SAMSON protocol.

We can draw a general conclusion from the observation presented in the previous paragraph.

Theorem 1 (The SAMSON moving rule is optimal). Let us name with $N(n_a)$ the set of the neighboring nodes of node n_a. Furthermore let us depict with $K(n_i, n_a)$ the expected number of arriving requests to node n_a through the link between nodes n_i and n_a, and with $E(n_a) = \sum_{l=0}^{\infty} l \cdot P(R_a = l)$ the expected number of requests directly arriving to node n_a. In addition, let us suppose that node n_a is the carrier node of pool Q. If there is a node $n_b \in N(n_a)$ for which the

$$K(n_b, n_a) > E(n_a) + \sum_{n_i \in N(n_a), n_i \neq n_b} K(n_i, n_a) \tag{4}$$

inequality stands, then the

$$T(n_a) > T(n_b) \tag{5}$$

inequality stands as well. This means that in this case the total *expected configuration time* of the joining nodes over the whole network can be minimized by moving the pool Q from node n_a to node n_b. By replacing its location to node n_b, the total expected address configuration time of the joining nodes over the whole network will be decreased.

Proof. Let us depict with B the set of nodes which are sending their requests to n_a through node n_b (including node n_b). Then:

$$
\begin{aligned}
T(n_a) = & \sum_{n_j \in N \backslash (B \cup \{n_a\})} (2 \cdot T_{fw} \cdot d(n_j, n_a) + T_{serv}) \cdot E(n_j) \\
& + \sum_{n_j \in B} 2 \cdot T_{fw} \cdot (d(n_j, n_b) + 1) \cdot E(n_j) + \sum_{n_j \in B} T_{serv} \cdot E(n_j) + E(n_a) \cdot T_{serv}
\end{aligned} \tag{6}
$$

$$
\begin{aligned}
T(n_b) \leq & \sum_{n_j \in N \backslash (B \cup \{n_a\})} 2 \cdot T_{fw} \cdot (d(n_j, n_a) + 1) \cdot E(n_j) + \sum_{n_j \in N \backslash (B \cup \{n_a\})} T_{serv} \cdot E(n_j) \\
& + \sum_{n_j \in B} (2 \cdot T_{fw} \cdot d(n_j, n_b) + T_{serv}) \cdot E(n_j) + E(n_a) \cdot (2 T_{fw} + T_{serv})
\end{aligned} \tag{7}
$$

The inequality 7 is true since there may be some nodes that are connected directly to nodes n_a and n_b as well. Thus, it is enough to see the following:

$$
\begin{aligned}
T(n_b) \leq & \sum_{n_j \in N \backslash (B \cup \{n_a\})} 2 \cdot T_{fw} \cdot (d(n_j, n_a) + 1) \cdot E(n_j) + \sum_{n_j \in N \backslash (B \cup \{n_a\})} T_{serv} \cdot E(n_j) \\
& + \sum_{n_j \in B} (2 \cdot T_{fw} \cdot d(n_j, n_b) + T_{serv}) \cdot E(n_j) + E(n_a) \cdot (2 \cdot T_{fw} + T_{serv}) \\
< & \sum_{n_j \in N \backslash (B \cup \{n_a\})} (2 \cdot T_{fw} \cdot d(n_j, n_a) + T_{serv}) \cdot E(n_j) \\
& + \sum_{n_j \in B} (2 \cdot T_{fw} \cdot (d(n_j, n_b) + 1) + T_{serv}) \cdot E(n_j) + E(n_a) \cdot T_{serv} = T(n_a).
\end{aligned} \tag{8}
$$

From which, after simplifications we can get

$$\sum_{n_j \in N \backslash (B \cup \{n_a\})} E(n_j) + E(n_a) < \sum_{n_j \in B} E(n_j). \tag{9}$$

And this is just another form of inequality 4, since the left side of the inequality expresses the expected number of configuration requests that are sent to n_a but not through n_b, while the right side is the number of requests arriving at n_a through node n_b including the address requests addressed directly to n_b. So, taking into account that

$$\sum_{n_j \in B} E(n_j) = K(n_b, n_a), \text{ and } \sum_{n_j \in N \backslash (B \cup \{n_a\})} E(n_j) = \sum_{n_i \in N(n_a), n_i \neq n_b} K(n_i, n_a) \tag{10}$$

we get the inequality 4, which was the starting point. Thus, the theorem is proven, i.e., the total expected address configuration time always decreases when the pool moves based on the proposed moving algorithm.   □

5.   Conclusion

In this paper we have presented the SAMSON address distribution protocol which is able to assign unique identifiers to nodes in a self-organizing network. We have highlighted some limitations of existing address distribution approaches, and we incorporated the lessons learnt to our novel mechanism. The proposed solution is highly distributed and is able to handle network partitioning and merger. The presented protocol can cope with multiple joins at the same time and tolerates message losses and link failures. Furthermore, the described method comes up with a unique feature among ad hoc address distribution protocols: it can adapt to the node arrival intensity distributed in space. Thus, it is able to provide low configuration time for newly arriving nodes, even in case of a large number of participants in the network.

References

Boleng, Jeff (2002). Efficient Network Layer Addressing for Mobile Ad Hoc Networks. In *Proc. of International Conference on Wireless Networks (ICWN02)*.

Cheshire, Stuart, Aboba, Bernard, and Guttman, Erik (2004). Dynamic Configuration of IPv4 Link-Local Addresses. IETF Internet Draft.

Clausen, Thomas and Jacquet, Philippe (2003). Optimized link state routing protocol. IETF Internet Draft.

Droms, Ralph (1997). Dynamic Host Configuration Protocol. RFC 2131.

Johnson, David B and Maltz, David A (1996). Dynamic source routing in ad hoc wireless networks. In *Mobile Computing*, volume 353. Kluwer Academic Publishers.

Nesargi, Sanket and Prakash, Ravi (2002). MANETconf: Configuration of Hosts in a Mobile Ad Hoc Network. In *Proc. of INFOCOM 2002*.

Perkins, Charles and Bhagwat, P. (1994). Routing over Multihop Wireless Network of Mobile Computers. In *SIGCOMM '94: Computer Communications Review,*, pages 234–244.

Perkins, Charles and Royer, Elizabeth (1999). Ad Hoc On-Demand Distance Vector Routing. In *Proc. of the 2nd IEEE Workshop on Mobile Computing Systems and Applications*, pages 90–100.

Toner, Stephen and O'Mahony, Donal (2003). Self-Organising Node Address Management in Ad Hoc Networks. In *Personal Wireless Communications, IFIP-TC6 8th International Conference*, volume 2775, pages 476–483.

Vaidya, Nitin H. (2002). Weak Duplicate Address Detection in Mobile Ad hoc Networks. In *Proc. of the 3rd ACM international symposium on Mobile ad hoc networking and computing (MobiHoc '02)*, pages 206–216. ACM Press.

Weniger, Kilian (2003). Passive Duplicate Address Detection in Mobile Ad hoc Networks. In *Proc. of IEEE Wireless Communications and Networking Conference (WCNC) 2003*.

Weniger, Kilian (2004). Passive Autoconfiguration of Mobile Ad hoc Networks. Technical report.

Zhou, H., Ni, L., and Mutka, M. (2003). Prophet Address Allocation for Large Scale MANETs. In *Proc. of INFOCOM 2003*.

Keyword Index